CASE STUDIES IN
ENVIRONMENTAL ETHICS

CASE STUDIES IN ENVIRONMENTAL ETHICS

PATRICK G. DERR AND EDWARD M. McNAMARA

ROWMAN & LITTLEFIELD PUBLISHERS, INC.
Lanham • Boulder • New York • Oxford

ROWMAN & LITTLEFIELD PUBLISHERS, INC.

Published in the United States of America
by Rowman & Littlefield Publishers, Inc.
A wholly owned subsidiary of the Rowman & Littlefield Publishing Group, Inc.
4501 Forbes Boulevard, Suite 200, Lanham, Maryland 20706
www.rowmanlittlefield.com

PO Box 317
Oxford
OX2 9RU, UK

British Library Cataloguing in Publication Information Available

Library of Congress Cataloging-in-Publication Data

Derr, Patrick George, 1949–
     Case studies in environmental ethics / by Patrick G. Derr and Edward M. McNamara.
        p. cm.
     Includes bibliographical references and indexes.
     ISBN 0-7425-3136-8 (alk. paper)—ISBN 0-7425-3137-6 (pbk. : alk. paper)
     1. Environmental ethics—Case studies. I. McNamara, Edward M., 1971– II. Title.
     GE42.D47 2003
     179'.1—dc21   2003009170

♾™ The paper used in this publication meets the minimum requirements of
American National Standard for Information Sciences—Permanence of Paper
for Printed Library Materials, ANSI/NISO Z39.48-1992.
Manufactured in the United States of America.

CONTENTS

CONTENTS

PREFACE

Few individuals who work, teach, or consult in any of the fields called "applied ethics" will need to be persuaded that "casework" is useful. In medical ethics, business ethics, legal ethics, and environmental ethics, case studies are central to both teaching and research.

Cases help us tease out the meaning of different ethical theories by providing a range of contexts in which their consequences can be explored and clarified. They help us sort out our own theoretical commitments by making it possible to compare their implications with the implications of our own most deeply held moral beliefs. And, of course, they help us develop the intellectual skills once subsumed under the old term "casuistry"—they help us learn just how to connect theory and practice. These issues are discussed later in the introduction.

Precisely because they serve so many different and important purposes, good case studies are difficult to write. They must be sufficiently detailed ("thick" is the term some scholars prefer) to bring theoretical nuances into play. They must be sufficiently succinct to fit their role as adjuncts. Perhaps most crucially, they must be fair and accurate.

In preparing the case studies included in this volume, we have been acutely aware that *truth* is one thing and *fairness* another. Consider the following synopsis of Case 26: Tasmanian Tigers:

> They work for their government. When they began their project, they had nothing but tissue fragments, state-of-the-art laboratories, and a very determined boss. But gene by gene, chromosome by chromosome, the molecular

geneticists and their assistants have pressed on. Their goal: to bring back from extinction *Thylacinus cynocephalus*—the most fearsome predator ever to walk their continent. Their probable completion date: 2005. Thylacine's tentative release-to-the-wild date: 2010.

Although this synopsis is *true*, it is grotesquely *unfair*. No one who read only this account of the Australian National Museum's interesting and ambitious tiger restoration project could ever hope to form a well-considered opinion on the issue of whether the project should go forward. (The synopsis suggests *Jurassic Park*. In reality, the thylacine is a marsupial that has been extinct for only seventy years.)

We are reasonably hopeful that those who read this volume will find little in it that is untrue. We are much less hopeful that readers, and especially readers who are also teachers, will find nothing in it that they regard as unfair. Indeed, it seems inevitable that anyone who brings to these cases a rich set of opinions on questions of environmental ethics and policy, especially on questions of environmental theory, will find more than one case that seems unfair. We hope, however, that readers with different theoretical perspectives will find that their own perspective is neither particularly slighted nor particularly privileged. We hope, in other words, that every reader will find his or her perspective on environmental ethics and policy seriously tested by at least some of the cases presented here.

We have not presumed to label the following cases as "animal rights" cases, "wilderness preservation" cases, "developing country" cases, and so forth. Labels are powerful; at least to the extent that they reflect prior theoretical commitments, they are often also prejudicial. Almost all the cases that follow raise a variety of issues, and to subsume an entire case under just one label would almost always privilege one particular ethical theory at the expense of others. So in lieu of such labels, we provide an index of cases that indicates which cases might be most useful for exploring which issues. The reader will notice that most cases can be found under three or more topical headings.

Except to the extent to which some cases share so many themes that the reader's convenience is likely to be served by their proximity, the order in which the cases appear in this volume has no obvious or hidden significance. Teachers assigning these cases to students will no doubt order and group them in the ways that best fit the topical progression of their courses.

We hope that you will find this volume a useful teaching and learning tool. We welcome suggestions regarding ways in which it could be made even more useful. We can be reached at casebook@clarku.edu.

ACKNOWLEDGMENTS

We would like to thank our wives, Christine Derr and Lynn McNamara, for their support and encouragement. We would also like to thank the students who have studied environmental ethics and environmental policy in our courses at Clark University and Holy Cross College. Their enthusiasm and curiosity have been a constant source of inspiration. In particular, for valuable ideas about some of the case studies presented here, we would like to thank Jamie Salo, Yasuyo Maruyama, Jeremy Child, David Carter, Michelle Feld, Alex Toth, and Peter Wright. For their gracious assistance with some of the sources, we thank Ryan Colker at the Renewable Natural Resources Foundation; Rachel Shea at the Goddard Library of Clark University; Annette Vadnais at the W. E. B. DuBois Library of the University of Massachusetts, Amherst; and Arvind Suslara at the Jeanne X. Kasperson Research Library of the Marsh Institute.

INTRODUCTION

Why Cases? Which Theories?

Every day, each of us makes choices about the kind of impact that we will have on the natural world. Sometimes the choices are small and personal: Will we buy another string of holiday lights? Sometimes they are large but still personal: Will we risk prison by participating in an illegal raid to scuttle whaling ships? Often they are public and collective: Will we urge our elected officials to open the Arctic National Wildlife Refuge to oil extraction?

One reason to take courses in environmental ethics or environmental policy is simply because these questions are so important and so interesting. They are fun—even if sometimes infuriating or depressing—to study. Another reason to study environmental ethics or policy is to develop new skills and acquire new knowledge that will enable us to choose more wisely.

This book is full of choices. Every case is followed by a set of questions, and few of the questions are easy. Should the John Day Dam be taken down? Should wolves have been restored to Yellowstone National Park? Is it moral to drive ceramic spikes into old-growth trees in order to deter loggers from cutting them down? What should corporations do to prevent another Bhopal? All these questions are controversial, and good reasons can be adduced for many different answers.

When scholars adduce reasons to defend their own answers to questions like these, they invariably appeal to high-level theories. In environmental ethics, these theories have names like anthropocentrism, biocentrism, ecocentrism, deep ecology, the land ethic, ecofeminism, social ecology, and animal rights theory. In ethics, as in economics or natural science, theories are extremely important and useful tools. A good theory helps us solve problems and make choices wisely and consistently.

One of the purposes that the cases in this volume will serve is to help you explore what each ethical theory really means. To learn what the mathematical theory of the calculus really means, it is necessary to *use* it to solve progressively more diverse and difficult problems. Similarly, to learn what an ethical theory (for example, the land ethic or deep ecology) really means, it is necessary to use it—to apply it to progressively more diverse and difficult ethical problems.

For most readers, however, it will not be enough to ask what different environmental theories *mean*. They will also want to decide which theory is *right* or at least closest to being right. Is it ecofeminism? Is it animal rights theory? Is it social ecology? And how can one decide?

The second purpose of the cases in this volume is precisely to *help* you decide. Physicists and economists try to settle arguments about which theory is best by applying the rival theories to real problems and asking which theory has done a better job of solving it. Scholars who want to settle arguments about which ethical theory is best do something similar: They apply rival theories to real moral problems and then ask which theory has done a better job of solving the problem.

To oversimplify, in science the theory that does the better job is the one that "fits the facts"—the one that "correctly predicts" something we are able to measure or observe. In ethics, it is a bit more complicated, but the process is the same. Each of us has a large stock of what might be called "deeply held moral beliefs." You might believe, for example, that it is wrong to torture sentient animals for mere sport, to act in ways that gravely imperil future generations, or to cause the extinction of endangered species. If you do, then these deeply held beliefs enable you to test different ethical theories in the same way that physicists test their theories: If a given ethical theory *conflicts* with your deeply held belief, you will conclude that the theory has made a false prediction, and you may reject the theory.

But that is only one of the ways that cases help us test theories. In any discipline—ethics or economics or philosophy—the best theories usually have more *scope*, more *accuracy*, and more *power*. In the preceding paragraph, we were concerned with testing a theory's *accuracy*—the extent to which, when applied to specific problems, the theory predicted the right result. In the natural sciences, those results are normally checked by empirical tests or experiments; in ethics, those results are usually checked against our most deeply held moral beliefs or intuitions. So in ethics, a theory that, when applied to specific cases, generates conclusions consistent with those deeply held intuitions can be said to have more accuracy.

But accuracy is only one of the things we seek from a good theory. One of the deepest purposes of a good theory is not just to *fit* the facts but also, at least now and then, to *challenge* them. And this is especially important in ethics since it is likely that many of our inherited or intuitive beliefs may not even be consistent with each other. When a scientific theory successfully confronts and overthrows an accepted "fact," we say that theory is *powerful*. When the theory of plate tectonics helped to overthrow once-accepted "facts" about the age of the earth, for example, scientists knew it was a powerful theory.

Similarly, in ethics we should not expect that the best theory will simply *fit* all our deeply held moral intuitions. Rather, we should expect that it will have the power, at least now and then (and perhaps quite often), to *challenge* and even overthrow them. And when an ethical theory does successfully confront and overthrow one of our beliefs in this way, we should conclude that the theory is powerful. Animal rights theorists, for example, argue that a strength of their theory is that it can capitalize on many people's beliefs about race and gender in ways that show that those same people have false beliefs about the moral status of animals.

Finally, in every discipline, including ethics, we want theories with *scope*— theories that can be used to solve a very broad range of problems. A theory's scope is determined by the range of problems to which it can be usefully applied. Maxwell's electromagnetic theory was a triumph in part because it was the first theory with enough scope to solve problems about both electricity and magnetism. An ethical theory that can shed light on problems about natural resources *and* problems about animal experimentation *and* problems about human population growth has more scope than a theory that provides insights into only one of those issues.

We have tried to write these cases in a way that will enable you to use them to test different theories for their accuracy, their power, and their scope.

A WORD ABOUT ETHICAL THEORIES

For a thorough discussion of all the leading theories of environmental ethics, the reader is urged to consult any of the dozens of excellent textbooks now in print in the areas of environmental ethics and environmental policy. For readers who would like a quick introduction to the theories, we provide this brief discussion.[1]

About Value

Some things are valuable because of the ways in which they can be used or the benefits that they provide. Computers, sprocket wrenches, and dictionaries would be examples. These things are said to have "instrumental," or "extrinsic," value. Other things are valuable independently of any way that they can be used or any benefit that they provide. According to Thomas Jefferson, human beings would be an example. These things are said to have "inherent," or "intrinsic," value.

What *kind* of value a thing has affects the way we consider our behavior toward it. If a thing has only instrumental value, it can be harmed, but it cannot be wronged. How I treat it will depend only on my consideration of its value *to me* and *to others*. But if a thing has inherent value, like a human person, then it can be wronged. How I treat it should depend not only (if at all) on my consideration of its value to me and to others but above all on a consideration of how my behavior will affect *it*: whether, for example, my behavior is fair, decent, respectful, and so forth.

Perhaps the most important question that different theories of environmental ethics attempt to answer is this: Which things in the world around us have inherent value? That is, which things deserve moral consideration not only because of their value to us or to others but also for their own sake? If we prefer to discuss moral questions in the popular language of "rights," this question becomes, Which things have rights?

About Valuation

Some ethical theories hold that only individual things—whether human persons, animals, or plants—can have inherent value. These are *individualistic* theories. Anthropocentrism and strong animal rights theory are two examples. Other theories contend that it is only the system or community of individuals—for example, the entire ecosystem or the "land community"—that can have inherent value. These are *holistic* theories. Aldo Leopold's land ethic is an example.

Finally, some ethical theories, such as egalitarian biocentrism, assert that inherent value can be had in only one degree or quantity—that whatever has inherent value has it equally. Other ethical theories, such as weak animal rights theory, hold that things can possess inherent value in different degrees—that even among things with inherent value, some can be more valuable or deserve more consideration than others.

Anthropocentric Ethics

According to anthropocentric ethics, only human beings possess inherent value. Other things can and do have value, but it is only instrumental value: They are valuable because of their usefulness or importance to humans. According to anthropocentrism, our only direct ethical duties are toward other human beings. But anthropocentrism can incorporate duties toward the environment as indirect duties to other humans: If we fail to protect the environment, we fail in our duty to protect human health and welfare. An example of an appeal to anthropocentric ethics would be the argument that we should reduce air pollution in order to reduce the number of premature deaths, asthma attacks, and cases of emphysema caused by pollution. Claims that we should conserve resources for "future generations" are also anthropocentric.

The specific content of our duties toward the environment, on this approach, will always depend on our understanding of the ways in which the environment affects human interests. Anthropocentric arguments may thus need to incorporate information from such disciplines as ecology, biology, sociology, and psychology.

Social Ecology

Although most versions of social ecology are anthropocentric in the sense just discussed, social ecology is better approached as a methodological perspective than as a substantive moral theory. The central claim of all versions of social ecology is that environmental problems can be understood and hence solved only when they have been carefully traced back to their social origins. Confronted with the rapid loss of rain forests, for example, social ecologists will want to investigate the social factors driving deforestation: local patterns of landownership, national debt issues, international trade, and so forth.

There are as many varieties of social ecology as there are approaches to social analysis. One can do social ecology while viewing economic issues from either a free-market or a socialist perspective, for example, or with special attention to questions of race or class or gender. In every case, however, the presumption will be that human behaviors that degrade the environment are rooted in the social and economic and political structures that surround the behavior.

Strong Animal Rights Theory

There are two quite different versions of strong animal rights theory: One invokes utilitarian theory, and the other invokes the concept of an "experiencing subject." Each is an individualistic theory that concludes that, in principle, human beings (or their interests or concerns) are no more valuable or important than any (or many) other animals or their interests or concerns.

Utilitarian Animal Rights Theory

In general, utilitarians hold that the only ultimately important values and disvalues are pleasure and pain. Whatever produces the greatest balance of pleasure over pain is, for that reason, morally best. Some utilitarians, such as Peter Singer, argue that it should not matter who experiences the pain: Whether felt by a man or a woman, a boy or a girl, or a horse or a rat, pleasure is good, and pain is bad. Species membership has no moral importance provided that an animal is sentient (that is, can feel pleasure and pain). Thus, according to utilitarian animal rights theory, all sentient animals deserve equal moral consideration, and the proper solution to environmental questions will be the solution that maximizes the balance of pleasure over pain for all sentient animals, not just for human beings.

Interests-Based Animal Rights Theory

The alternate approach to strong animal rights theory rejects utilitarianism and instead appeals to the notion of "being an experiencing subject." According to this approach, any animal that experiences its own life has inherent value. The most common versions of the theory assert, in brief, that if the life of an animal is a value to that animal, then that animal has inherent value and has it equally with all other such animals, including human beings. Tom Regan is one well-known proponent of this theory.

Weak Animal Rights Theory

Like both versions of strong animal rights theory, weak animal rights theory rejects anthropocentrism and asserts that nonhuman animals have inherent value and deserve moral consideration for their own sake. But unlike those theories, weak animal rights theory rejects the view that whatever has inherent value must have it equally. Instead, on this approach, animals can have different degrees of inherent value, depending, for example, on their different levels of sentience, awareness, and so forth. Advocates of weak animal rights theory regard it as a great virtue of their theory that they do not have to figure out where to "draw the line" between those animals that have inherent value equal to humans and those animals that have none at all. Mary Anne Warren is an advocate of weak animal rights theory.

(It is worth noting that, of the several philosophical theories surveyed here, weak animal rights theory is perhaps the view that most nearly approximates the traditional positions of the three Western monotheisms. Like Judaism, Christianity, and Islam, weak animal rights theory can assert that although humans have the *highest* value, *every* animal has at least *some* value and so deserves moral consideration.)

Biocentric Ethics

The theories discussed above all confer inherent value or moral considerability on a wider or narrower set of animals. But animals are only one part of the Earth's living community. Biocentrism extends inherent value to all living things, including plants as well as animals. Paul Taylor, for example, defines biocentrism as "an attitude of respect for nature," which involves a moral commitment to live one's life in a way that respects the welfare and inherent worth of all other organisms.

Ecocentric Ethics and the Land Ethic

With ecocentric ethics, we move from individualistic to holistic approaches to environmental ethics. Ecocentrism asserts that our ethical duties are not to individuals but to the ecosystem as a whole. Whether a particular organism has value and, if so, its degree of value will depend on its role in the larger system. Aldo Leopold is widely credited with having presented the first important holistic theory of environmental ethics in his *Sand County Almanac*. In the final chapter of the book, subtitled "The Land Ethic,"

Leopold asserts that the ethical community includes all members of the land—animate and inanimate, human and nonhuman. As summed up in Leopold's book, the land ethic holds that "a thing is right when it tends to preserve the integrity, stability, and beauty of the biotic community. It is wrong when it tends otherwise."

Modern writers commonly interpret the land ethic as strictly holistic—that is, as assigning rights only to ecosystems and never to the individual entities included in the system. Although this accords well with contemporary ecocentric theories, Leopold's own writings suggest that he may have intended a hybrid approach that attributed value to both the system and its individual members.

Deep Ecology

Deep ecology is perhaps best understood as biocentrism with a strong social emphasis. As articulated by Arne Naess, it rejects "mainstream" environmentalism (represented by such groups as the Sierra Club, the Natural Resources Defense Council, the Audubon Society, and so forth) as "shallow." Deep ecology embraces biocentric egalitarianism (as defined previously) but focuses much of its attention on social issues. It asserts, for example, that the lifestyle of persons in affluent nations must be dramatically changed and that the human population of the Earth should be greatly reduced. Deep ecologists are critical of globalization as well, arguing for decentralization in the political and economic spheres and for increased respect for cultural diversity.

Ecofeminism

There are almost as many versions of ecofeminism as there are of social ecology. Indeed, one common variety of ecofeminism just *is* social ecology done with a special concern for and sensitivity to issues of gender. In this version, ecofeminism might be understood as nonandrocentric anthropocentrism—that is, as an approach to environmental ethics that is human centered but that endeavors to construe "human" in a feminist (or at least gender-neutral) rather than a patriarchal sense.

Another important version of ecofeminism rejects anthropocentrism and argues that the oppression of women is systematically linked—in our social structures and our ways of thinking—to the oppression of nature. According to this approach, sexism and naturism are so tightly connected that women will not be able to achieve genuine equality until nature itself is recognized as an equal. Karen Warren is a well-known exponent of this view.

NOTE

1. Recommended readings for each of the theories discussed here can be found (along with many other outstanding materials) on the website of the Center for Environmental Philosophy at the University of North Texas at www.cep.unt.edu.

1

GORILLA RANGERS

He had driven from the provincial capital of Goma as soon as military conditions permitted it. It was late November 1996, and now Norbert Mushenzi, director of national parks in the Congo's North Kivu province, surveyed the buildings of the Virunga National Park headquarters compound at Djomba. It had been home to several hundred park employees and their families. Now it was shattered and abandoned, its walls pockmarked by bullets.

Civil war had again swept through the region, and the eastern part of the Congo (then called Zaire) was awash with refugees and armed members of different factions. Thousands had been killed, most of them civilians. But even as his nation disintegrated, Mushenzi was determined to save Africa's oldest national park. He had come to look for his rangers. To the east, he could see the beginning of the park: a lush forest rising in misty waves to the summits of the Virunga volcanoes, home to some of the world's last mountain gorillas.

"Is anyone here?" he shouted. "It's Mushenzi! Answer me!"

Amazingly, his shout was answered. Several of his park rangers, looking like refugees, emerged from the trees. Knowing that their connection to the government made them targets for the rebels, they had buried their weapons and uniforms and fled into the forest with their families. They were hungry but alive.

"And the gorillas?" Mushenzi asked.

Incredibly, as far as the men knew, the gorillas were safe. Unfortunately, many of the rangers were not. One ranger's entire family, including his brothers and all their wives and children, had been slaughtered in an ambush. Three had lost their fathers. In all, since the start of the civil war, forty-four Virunga rangers had lost their lives, along with an uncounted number of their children and wives.

And somehow, through it all, despite the fact that they had not been paid in more than two years, despite the fact that their houses were in ruins and their lives in constant jeopardy, the rangers kept patrolling, kept trying to protect their gorillas. "I am living on hope," one explained, "This is my life."[1]

DISCUSSION

This case, unlike all the others in this volume, begins with a human drama. There is a reason. Many international organizations have done magnificent work to help save the mountain gorilla, including the Dian Fossey Gorilla Fund International (DFGFI),[2] the Morris Animal Foundation's Mountain Gorilla Veterinary Project (MGVP),[3] and the International Gorilla Conservation Programme (IGCP).[4] But even with the critical support and assistance provided by these groups, the fate of the mountain gorilla, at least for some foreseeable decades, will likely depend on the brave Congolese, Rwandan, and Ugandan park rangers who daily battle poachers and other human threats. Simply put, if the rangers fail in their job, it seems unlikely that any other effort will save the mountain gorilla.

Mountain gorillas are a subspecies of eastern gorilla. They are rare—far rarer than the species of gorillas still seen in captivity. There are about 100,000 western gorillas (of which there are two subspecies) living in many parts of central and western Africa. There are only about 12,000 eastern gorillas (of which there are three subspecies), and they are found only in Rwanda, Uganda, and the Democratic Republic of the Congo. Of these, more than 11,000 belong to the eastern lowland subspecies. The majority of the remainder belong to the Bwindi subspecies. Only about 355 are mountain gorillas, and nearly all these are found in the three national parks that straddle the Congo–Rwanda–Uganda border: Virunga Park on the Congolese side, Parc des Volcans on the Rwandan side, and Bwindi Impenetrable Forest National Park in Uganda. None live in captivity. Yet despite its rarity, thanks to the work of Dian Fossey and the scientists who have followed her, this rarest of the gorillas is probably also the best known of all the great apes.

The biggest threats to the survival of the mountain gorilla are all human: deliberate poaching, accidental killing in the snares and traps left (illegally) for other kinds of bush meat, death at the hands of frightened troops or armed rebels, and even infection (such as with measles) resulting from contact with humans. Few of these threats show any sign of disappearing. Six mountain gorillas (four females and two infants) are known to have been killed in two poaching incidents in the summer of 2002. In the words of Netzin Steklis, director of DFGFI's Scientific Information Resources Center, "For a small population like this, the death of these four females is a catastrophe."[5] Against all these threats, the gorilla's principal defense is the constant vigilant patrolling of the rangers.

The tribal and political violence in and around the gorillas' last sanctuaries goes back decades, but the 1990s were particularly bloody. In Rwanda, Hutu extremists murdered hundreds of thousands of their countrymen and drove millions more into refugee camps in the Congo and other neighboring countries. A million refugees settled on the edges of Virunga National Park, and to survive, they cut firewood and hunted bush meat. The refugee camps also housed insurgents bent on restoring Hutu rule in Rwanda. In 1996, the Rwandan army invaded the Congo to eliminate the threat. In May 1997, an entire band of ten gorillas was slaughtered by a Congolese army patrol. By 1998, the Congo was again fractured by civil war. Sadly, for both the gorillas and the rangers, it had all happened before: In the civil war of the 1960s, more than twenty park rangers lost their lives, and as many as a quarter of its gorillas may have been killed.

The mountain gorilla is threatened in other ways as well. With a total population of only 355 animals—up from a low of about 250 in 1981—genetic diversity is a serious issue. Indeed, according to Dr. Steklis, the loss or saving "of even one female could have a significant impact on the survival of the species."[6] But if they can be protected from human dangers, the gorillas may recover and even flourish. They have no natural predators. Females begin breeding at about age ten and thereafter breed every three or four years on average. More than two-thirds of the infants, if not killed by humans, will live to adulthood. A typical female will see three of her daughters survive and reproduce; within the dynamics of gorilla family groups, this means that just four young females can have a total of 427 descendants in fifty years— provided that the gorillas are protected.

QUESTIONS

1. Local authorities and park employees in Rwanda, Uganda, and the Congo have received a great deal of assistance from Western governments

and international organizations in their efforts to save the mountain gorilla. Obviously, the Delhi Sands Fly (see Case 10: The Delhi Sands Fly), though perhaps closer to extinction, is not receiving such assistance. Some would say this is an example of a systematic prejudice in favor of "charismatic megafauna." Is it? If so, is it ecologically irresponsible or morally unjust?

2. Except for orangutans, which live in the forests of Borneo and Sumatra, nearly all the world's great apes (see Case 2: The Great Ape Declaration) live in sub-Saharan Africa and typically in developing countries ravaged by HIV/AIDS and wracked by poverty, civil war, ethnic and religious violence, and chronic food shortages. It is precisely these human conditions that engender the most serious threats to the great apes: poaching, habitat destruction, bush-meat taking, and so on. To desperately poor Rwandan refugees struggling to recover from genocidal chaos, the enormous efforts being made to save the mountain gorilla might seem peculiarly Western, perhaps even neocolonial. Is it? If so, is there anything wrong with that?

3. Clearly, the principal threats to the mountain gorilla are rooted in the social and political problems of poverty, political instability, and so forth. To what extent, if any, should conservation groups involve themselves in national social and political issues in order to preserve a particular species or habitat?

NOTES

1. Based on Jeremy Schmidt, "Soldiers in the Gorilla War," *International Wildlife*, January/February 1999. The full text of the original article is available at www.nwf.org/internationalwildlife/1998/gorilla.html.

2. Information about DFGFI can be found at www.gorillafund.org.

3. Information about MGVP can be found at www.morrisanimalfoundation.org.

4. Information about IGCP can be found at www.fauna-flora.org/around_the_world/africa/gorilla.htm.

5. DFGFI, "Fossey Fund Sets Up Crisis Action Plan to Fight Major Loss of Mountain Gorillas," October 30, 2002, available at www.gorillafund.org/000_core_frmset.html.

6. DFGFI, "First Attempt Made at Mountain Gorilla Reintroduction," December 13, 2002, available at www.gorillafund.org/cont_frm/pressreleases/pr_20021213.html. In October 2002, Rwandan authorities rescued a two-year-old female from

poachers. The article describes some of the difficulties involved in attempting to release a young gorilla that has been removed from its original social group.

SOURCES

Dian Fossey Gorilla Fund International. "Newly Discovered Populations of Eastern Lowland Gorillas." November 21, 2002. Available at www.gorillafund.org/cont_frm/pressreleases/pr_20021121.html. See also www.nwf.org/internationalwildlife/1998/gorilla.html and www.gorillafund.org/000_core_frmset.html.

"Frequently Asked Questions about the Life of Mountain Gorillas." Available at www.gorillafund.org/cont_frm/05_gorilla_faq.html.

Schmidt, Jeremy. "Soldiers in the Gorilla War." *International Wildlife* 29, no. 1 (January/February 1999): 12–21.

2

THE GREAT APE
DECLARATION

The Great Ape Project is dedicated to securing legal and moral rights for certain species of primates. The core principles of the Great Apes Declaration Group are set out in its declaration:

DECLARATION ON GREAT APES[1]

We demand the extension of the community of equals to include all great apes: human beings, chimpanzees, gorillas and orangutans. The "community of equals" is the moral community within which we accept certain basic moral principles or rights as governing our relations with each other and enforceable at law. Among these principles or rights are the following:

1. The Right to Life
   The lives of members of the community of equals are to be protected. Members of the community of equals may not be killed except in very strictly defined circumstances, for example, self-defence.

2. The Protection of Individual Liberty
   Members of the community of equals are not to be arbitrarily deprived of their liberty; if they should be imprisoned without due legal process, they have the right to immediate release. The detention of those who have not been convicted of

any crime, or of those who are not criminally liable, should be allowed only where it can be shown to be for their own good, or necessary to protect the public from a member of the community who would clearly be a danger to others if at liberty. In such cases, members of the community of equals must have the right to appeal, either directly or, if they lack the relevant capacity, through an advocate, to a judicial tribunal.

3. The Prohibition of Torture

The deliberate infliction of severe pain on a member of the community of equals, either wantonly or for an alleged benefit to others, is regarded as torture, and is wrong.

ABOUT THE GREAT APE PROJECT

Anyone who indicates their endorsement of the Declaration on Great Apes can become a supporter of the organization, which takes the Anti-Slavery Society as its political model. We already have supporters in more than twenty nations. We will start operating at a national level in as many countries as possible. Activities range from public education, to campaigning, to the adoption of individual imprisoned non-human great apes. From small-scale, local interventions, we will work up towards an international level, so as to bring about a momentous but well-grounded change in the status of chimpanzees, gorillas and orangutans.

Our long-term goal is a United Nations Declaration of the Rights of Great Apes. When this historic result has been achieved, we will advocate the setting up of guarded territories so that chimpanzees, gorillas and orangutans can continue to live as free beings in their own ways.

DISCUSSION

The Great Ape Project does not seek to obtain protection for all primates but only for the four "great apes": gorillas, orangutans, chimpanzees, and bonobos. The project defends this focus and explains its strategic importance as follows:

The Great Ape Project is not seeking to move the species barrier simply to re-erect it in another place, but to demolish it altogether. . . . The Great Ape Project is arguing for the inclusion of our fellow great apes in the "community of equals" . . . because they possess a variety of characteristics which are morally relevant . . . such as complex emotional life, strong social and family bonds, and self-awareness. . . .

But why just the great apes? Because we need to start somewhere. . . . The Great Ape Project focuses on great apes not because they are the only morally considerable animals, but rather because their rich individuality, combined with their dire predicament, makes them one of the most obvious cases for challenging the claim that membership of the human species is the only basis for moral standing. . . . [The Great Ape Project] cannot ignore the specific structures and mechanisms of the real world if it wants to make practical moral progress. . . . [We] are demanding the three most basic rights that all humans possess—but, for this very reason, we have to limit the range of those for whom we are demanding so much. This has led us away from the traditional attitude of asking for a little for all towards one of asking everything for some. This goal, being revolutionary rather than reformist in nature, will establish a precedent for many other animals.[2]

New Zealand has recently incorporated some of the precepts of the Great Ape Project into an animal welfare law. Section 85 of the Animal Welfare Act of 1999 allows research or testing on a primate only if the following can be shown:

(a) That the use of the non-human hominid in the research, testing, or teaching is in the best interests of the non-human hominid; or
(b) That the use of the non-human hominid in the research, testing, or teaching is in the interests of the species to which the non-human hominid belongs and that the benefits to be derived from the use of the non-human hominid in the research, testing, or teaching are not outweighed by the likely harm to the non-human hominid.[3]

Opponents of the law argued that primates, and particularly chimpanzees, are important to medical researchers and that the law would retard necessary medical research. To this objection, the Great Ape Project replies that the same *similarity to humans*, which makes the great apes such useful research subjects, should entitle them to the same ethical and legal protection that we give to members of our own species.

QUESTIONS

1. Is the "species line" that the Great Ape Project has drawn morally justifiable? Where *should* we draw the line demarcating those entities

entitled to legal and moral rights from those not so entitled? Whether or not the line is based on species membership, should it be based on genetic, psychological, or cognitive criteria? If so, on what criteria? Should it, as many animal rights theorists argue, be based simply on an ability to feel pain?

2. Even if the Great Ape Project's focus on four species is not theoretically justified—as, indeed, the project comes close to conceding in its FAQs (frequently asked questions)—is it morally justified by tactical and political considerations?

3. Is it morally correct, as the Great Ape Project asserts, that it is better to demand full moral rights for members of a few species than to seek more modest gains for members of many species?

4. Is being morally considerable (or "having moral standing" or "being intrinsically valuable") an all-or-nothing kind of property? Much of the philosophical literature on the question assumes that it is.[4] But at least in the West, much of the theological literature assumes that it is not. Muslims, Jews, and Christians would all argue that everything God has created is good and deserves respect and moral consideration but not that it is *equally* good and deserving of *equal* respect and consideration (see Case 39: Peace with All of Creation). Assuming that humans have "full" moral standing, can a snail or a dog or a gorilla have only *no* standing or *full* standing? Or could each have its own unique degree of standing? To oversimplify the question, who is right: the philosophers or the theologians?

5. Reread question 2 from Case 1: Gorilla Rangers. If you were one of the impoverished human refugees struggling to survive along the Congo–Uganda–Rwanda border, would the Great Ape Project's focus on legal and moral rights for animals seem important to you?

NOTES

1. The Great Ape Declaration and other information on the Great Ape Project are available at www.greatapeproject.org/gapintroduction.html.

2. The Great Ape Project, "Frequently Asked Questions," section 4.1, available at www.greatapeproject.org/gapfaq.html.

3. *Animal Welfare Act*, 1999 (N.Z.).

4. Mary Anne Warren is one of many notable exceptions and has offered a sharp critique of the view that whatever possess inherent value must possess it equally. See

her "Difficulties with the Strong Animal Rights Position," *Between the Species* 2, no. 4 (fall 1978): 433–41.

SOURCES

Animal Welfare Act, 1999 (N.Z).

The Great Ape Project. www.greatapeproject.org.

Warren, Mary Anne. "Difficulties with the Strong Animal Rights Position." *Between the Species* 2, no. 4 (fall 1978): 433–41.

RATS, RABBITS, AND THE EPA

M ost readers are well aware that nonhuman animals are used in a variety of biomedical research programs. Courses in environmental ethics often devote some attention to such research because its moral justifiability clearly depends, at least in part, on the moral status of the animal subjects. What is not as widely known, however, is that very many of the animals used as research subjects are used not to find a cure for cancer or an AIDS vaccine but rather to satisfy the regulatory requirements of the U.S. Environmental Protection Agency (EPA). We excerpt a small section of such a research protocol here:

4.3.3.1 Repeated-Dose Toxicity Test Methodology
   Repeated-dose toxicity studies evaluate the systemic effects of repeated exposure to a chemical over a significant period of the life span of an animal (rats, rabbits, or mice). Chronic repeated-dose toxicity studies are concerned with potential adverse effects upon exposure of the greater part of an organism's life span (e.g., one to two years in rodents). Subchronic repeated-dose studies are concerned with the effects caused by exposure for an extended period, but not one that constitutes a significant portion of the expected life span. Subchronic studies are useful in identifying target organ(s), and they can be used is selecting dose levels for longer-term studies. Typically, the exposure regimen in a subchronic study involves daily exposure (at least 5 consecutive days per week) for a period of at least 28 days or up to 90 days (i.e.,

about 4 to 13 weeks). A recovery period of two to four weeks (generally included in most study designs) following completion of the dosing or exposure period provides information on whether or not the effects seen during the exposure period are reversible upon cessation of treatment. The dose levels evaluated in repeated-dose toxicity studies are notably lower than the relatively high limit doses used in acute toxicity studies. The NOAEL (no observed adverse effect level), usually expressed in mg/kg/day, defines the dose of test material that produces no significant toxicological effects. If the test material produces toxicity at the lowest dose tested (i.e., there is no defined NOAEL), the lowest dose that produced an adverse effect is defined as the LOAEL (lowest observed adverse effect level). While these studies are designed to assess systemic toxicity, the study protocol can be modified to incorporate evaluation of potential adverse reproductive and/or developmental effects.[1]

DISCUSSION

It is important to both human and nonhuman members of ecosystems that materials released into those ecosystems by human activity do not cause adverse effects. Hence, in setting use and exposure and discharge standards for such materials, the EPA requires and uses the results of repeated-dose toxicity tests, among other kinds of data. Whatever the long-term benefits of such standards, they certainly do not benefit the animal subjects of the tests: The animals are euthanized in the course of the research.

Consider a single material. Zinc dialkyldithiophosphate is a chemical that can be added, in very small amounts, to lubricating oils. In engine oil, along with other additives, it prolongs the oil's useful life (thereby reducing the volume of new oil needed and the volume of dirty oil to be disposed of) and improves its performance (thereby increasing vehicle mileage, thus reducing gasoline consumption). It is also relatively persistent: When zinc dialkyldithiophosphate finds its way into the soil or into surface or groundwater systems, it remains there for a long time. This raises a number of important regulatory issues: Should the EPA permit petroleum companies to use the material as an oil additive? Will organisms subjected to repeated-dose exposure to the material be adversely affected? In part, an ecologically responsible answer to the first question would seem to require a scientifically robust answer to the second.

QUESTIONS

1. Much of the animal experimentation performed for medical purposes is designed and intended solely to benefit human beings. But the repeated-dose toxicity evaluation of zinc dialkyldithiophosphate is intended to protect not only humans (such as automobile mechanics) but also the ecosystems into which the material may be released. Does the fact that other animals and even whole ecosystems may benefit from such research change any of the moral issues posed by the (lethal) use of animals in the research studies? If so, how?

2. Is it easier or more difficult to justify the use of rabbits in repeated-dose toxicity studies of zinc dialkyldithiophosphate than it is to justify their use in equally lethal tests of, for example, a potential asthma medication or a new ingredient for a cosmetic?

3. In general, the larger the number of animals used in a particular test, the more reliable the results of the study. For example, we can better evaluate the carcinogenic potential of a substance if it is tested on 1,000 rats than if it is tested on 100. How should the EPA strike a balance between the value of better data and the number of test animals used to obtain it?

4. The rats used in experiments such as the one described in this case are bred specifically for such testing. They would not exist if they had not been bred specifically for use as test animals. Is this fact relevant to the question of whether using the animals as research subjects is moral?

NOTE

1. American Chemical Council, Petroleum Additives Panel, Health, Environmental, and Regulatory Task Group, "High Production Volume (HPV) Challenge Program: Test Plan for Zinc Dialkyldithiophosphate Category," September 24, 2002, available at www.epa.gov/chemrtk/zincdial/c14066tp.pdf. Recent testing protocols for a wide range of chemicals are available from the EPA at www.epa.gov/chemrtk/whatsnew.htm.

SOURCE

American Chemical Council, Petroleum Additives Panel, Health, Environmental, and Regulatory Task Group. "High Production Volume (HPV) Challenge Program: Test Plan for Zinc Dialkyldithiophosphate Category." September 24, 2002. Available at www.epa.gov/chemrtk/zincdial/c14066tp.pdf.

4

TIGERS AND TOURISTS

Advertisements offering well-to-do travelers a chance to see the Indian tiger are common in environmental magazines, travel websites, and the travel sections of major newspapers. Here is an excerpt of an advertisement from Tiger Package Tours:

> Earlier the hunting preserve of the Maharajas of Jaipur, the Park at Ranthambore was once the scene of royal hunting parties. Today, it is famous for its tigers and is one of the best places in the country to see these majestic predators in the wild. Tigers can be spotted quite often even during the day, at their normal pursuits—hunting and taking care of their young. With the strict measures that have been taken, [they are] accustomed to human activity and are not disturbed by it.[1]

Tourism is thriving in Ranthambore Park to such an extent that the normally elusive tiger is no longer bothered by the foreign tourists who flock to its home.

DISCUSSION

What visitors to Ranthambore and other tiger preserves will not see are the human costs associated with the creation and operation—the "strict measures"—of such preserves.

The 400-square-kilometer Ranthambore Park was created in 1973, largely as the result of an international effort to preserve the Indian tiger. The park consists of both core and buffer areas. The core areas are strictly off-limits to local villagers. In the buffer areas, the taking of forest products, fuelwood, and livestock fodder is severely restricted. In 1979, twelve entire villages in buffer areas were abolished and their thousands of residents displaced in order better to protect the tigers' forest habitat. Such dislocation is associated with all the Indian preserves. Sometimes, as at Ranthambore, it is done by government fiat in order to enlarge the preserve; at other times, it happens as a result of the economic collapse that results from new restrictions on the local population's use of forest resources; sometimes, locals are simply displaced by new businesses moving in to tap the tourist industry.

Only rarely are villagers—expelled from lands on which their families have depended for generations—compensated. Almost never are they given comparable new land in exchange. As a result, tension between those who manage the preserves and those who were displaced to create them is high: In some places, tigers have been killed or fires set to damage their habitat, and surreptitious entry, in order to take fuelwood or other resources, is a continual problem. The Indian scholar Ramachandra Guha asserts that Project Tiger and its sponsors (such as the World Wildlife Fund) have caused "a direct transfer of resources from the poor to the rich." "In no case," Guha claims, "have the needs of the local population been taken into account."[2]

Tiger preserves have brought some economic benefits to the communities they affect. Money generated by tourism has funded improvements to local infrastructure, such as roads. The preserves—especially the luxury lodges and hotels associated with them—do create new jobs. But there is no evidence that the preserves have helped reduce the enormous income disparities that predate their creation. If anything, the majority of the poor who were displaced are worse off, and the few who manage the reserves are better off. Many of the tourism dollars never reach Ranthambore at all: Only travel agents who promote the system and who usually are thousands of miles away benefit.

QUESTIONS

1. Should families who lived in a village for generations (perhaps centuries) be forced to move in order to provide protected habitat for tigers?
2. To what extent should efforts to protect the tiger restrict local residents' access to the basic means of subsistence, such as fuelwood?

3. Those who benefit most from the tiger preserves are the tour opera-
tors who bear none of the social impacts associated with the creation
of the preserves. Should local people who are adversely impacted by
the preserves be compensated by those who profit from the parks? If
so, what sort of system should be established to ensure that this takes
place? Do tourists visiting the parks have any obligation to support or
encourage such a system?

4. Compare this case to Case 8: Matinicus Island and Case 15: Oil and
ANWR. Should the fact that certain families have been living in a particular ecosystem for generations or even centuries give them any special voice in decisions about how that ecosystem is used?

NOTES

1. "All India Travel Guide: Ranthambore National Park," available at www.all-in-
dia-travel-guide.com/jungle-wildlife-lodges/ranthambhor-jungle-lodges.html.

2. Ramachandra Guha, "Radical Environmentalism and Wilderness Preservation: A Third World Critique," *Environmental Ethics* 11, no. 1 (spring 1989):
71–83.

SOURCES

"All India Travel Guide: Ranthambore National Park." Available at www.
all-india-travel-guide.com/jungle-wildlife-lodges/ranthambhor-jungle-lodges.html.
Guha, Ramachandra. "Radical Environmentalism and Wilderness Preservation: A
Third World Critique." *Environmental Ethics* 11, no. 1 (spring 1989): 71–83.
Wildlife Chronicle. "Project Tiger." Available at http://66.96.219.61/Project_Tiger.
htm.

5

YELLOWSTONE WOLVES

Prior to the arrival of European settlers, the gray wolf ranged over all of North America, from Mexico City to the Arctic Circle, except parts of the southeastern United States, where a related species, the red wolf (*Canis rufus*), lived. In 1930, the last known gray wolf (*Canis lupus*) in the conterminous United States was killed. It was the end of a century-long campaign to eradicate the species from the lower forty-eight states and thereby eliminate its impact on game and livestock.[1]

The wolf still thrived in Canada and Alaska, however, and over time parts of the northern United States were recolonized by wolves migrating down across the border. When the gray wolf was listed as an endangered species in 1978, the listing exempted both Alaska (where the wolf was neither endangered nor threatened) and Minnesota (where the wolf population, already numbering in the thousands, was considered robust enough to be listed only as "threatened"). By 1986, a population of about sixty-five wolves had reestablished itself in the northwestern corner of Montana, principally inside Glacier National Park.

The Endangered Species Act not only requires the U.S. Fish and Wildlife Service (FWS) to endeavor to protect endangered or threatened species; where the condition of its former ranges makes it possible, the act also requires FWS to attempt to restore such species to those former ranges. To this end, FWS undertook a program to reintroduce the gray wolf to two areas with relatively intact ecosystems: a section of central Idaho consisting of 20,000 square miles of contiguous national forest, with 6,000 square miles of protected wilderness at its core, and, much more controversially, the greater Yellowstone region, which includes Yellowstone National Park.[2]

FWS plans to reintroduce the gray wolf to Yellowstone were met by disbelief and resistance from livestock ranchers in Wyoming, Montana, and Idaho who feared the economic losses that could be caused by wolf predation. Wildlife biologists argued that such predation was unlikely because of the abundance of natural prey (wild ungulates such as elk) in the proposed restoration area, but ranchers were not reassured. Finally, in order to reduce resistance to the plan, two modifications were made.

First, in order to address the issue of economic losses from livestock predation, a private environmental group, Defenders of Wildlife, agreed to establish a fund to compensate any rancher who could document livestock loss due to wolf predation. Second, and perhaps more important, FWS agreed to classify the reintroduced animals as "experimental." This designation increased FWS's flexibility because it permits the reintroduced animals to be treated as members of a threatened rather than an endangered species. FWS explained the consequences of this change as follows:

> There would be no violation of the Act [ESA] for unintentional, nonnegligent, and accidental taking of wolves by the public, provided the take was incidental to otherwise lawful activities. . . . The Service may designate certain Federal, State, and/or tribal employees to take wolves that . . . pose a threat to livestock or property. Private land owners or their designates would be permitted to harass wolves in an opportunistic noninjurious manner on their leases or private property . . . [and] would be permitted to take (injure or kill) a wolf in the act of wounding or killing livestock on private land. . . . Once six or more breeding pairs are established in the Park or experimental area, livestock owners or their designates could receive a permit from a Service-designated agency to take (injure or kill) gray wolves that are attacking livestock on permitted public livestock grazing allotments. . . .
>
> Wolves that repeatedly (two times in a calendar year) attack domestic animals other than livestock (fowl, swine, goats, etc.) or pets (dogs or cats) on private land would be designated as problem wolves and relocated from the area by the Service or a designated agency. After the relocation, wolves that continued to depredate on domestic animals would be considered chronic problem wolves and would be removed from the wild.

Although FWS officials and other policymakers believed that the compromise "experimental" designation was necessary in order to gain public acceptance of the restoration program, some environmental groups objected bitterly. In a press release announcing the Sierra Club Legal Defense Fund's intention to sue FWS to have the designation declared illegal, the organization asserted, "It's not a wolf-saving plan, it's a wolf-killing plan."[3]

The suit failed to stop the reintroduction program. FWS immediately went to work to implement the reintroduction plan. It was this:

> The Park's wolf reintroduction plan requires transferring 45 to 75 wolves from southwestern Canada, representing various sex and age classes, over a 3- to 5-year period. The capture of about 15 wild wolves from several different packs using standard capture techniques[4] will be done annually over 3 to 5 years. Captured wolves will be transported to the Park. Wolves from the same pack will be placed in individual holding pens of about 0.4 hectare (1 acre) for up to 2 months for acclimation to the new environment. The acclimation pens will be isolated to protect the wolves from other animals and to prevent habituation to humans. . . . After release, each wolf will be monitored by radiotelemetry to ensure quick retrieval, if necessary. . . . Food (ungulate carcasses) will be provided until the wolves no longer use it.

DISCUSSION

There have been no wolves in Yellowstone since 1930. In the more than seven decades since, Yellowstone's original ecosystem has found a new ecological composition without the wolves. Their successful reintroduction will have a significant, perhaps even dramatic, impact on that composition. In this respect, it is an exciting experiment in restoration ecology.

As a part of its planning process, the National Park Service had hired scientists to study the ecological effects of restoring the wolves to Yellowstone.[5] It was particularly concerned about grizzly bears (an endangered species) and game species. With regard to grizzly bears, the scientists predicted that "although some predation of wolves on bear cubs and adults (females with cubs) would occur, the level would be insignificant." With regard to game species such as elk and mule deer (the two species expected to be the wolves' primary prey), scientists predicted that there would be "some decline in population over a 10-year period after reintroduction." The scientists noted that more research would be needed to determine whether sport hunting would have to be restricted to compensate for big-game losses to wolf predation.

The species that would be most impacted by the successful reintroduction of the wolf would be the coyote (*Canis latrans*). Although the coyote and the wolf have different ecological niches, the niches overlap. Where the two species compete directly for food, the top predator, the wolf, would win. The scientists predicted that coyote populations would be displaced from wolf areas into more peripheral areas but that the coyote would survive because it can subsist on a wide variety of prey, including small mammals, that the wolves would not hunt.

So far, the reintroduction program seems to be a stunning success. Yellowstone is now home to nineteen functioning wolf packs composed of a total of 164 wolves.[6] Packs are established in all parts of the park and in twelve areas outside the park. Since the reintroduction program began, a total of forty-four wolves have died in the park. The leading causes of death were twelve shot or killed while or after attacking livestock, eight killed by other wolves, eight having died from other natural causes, five hit by motor vehicles, and five shot illegally. The last wolf of the original group of fourteen Canadian wolves reintroduced in 1995 died in January 2003. Known as "No. 2," he is credited with establishing the first new pack in the park (named the Leopold pack) and is believed to have fathered eight litters.[7]

QUESTIONS

1. Should gray wolves be reintroduced to ranges that, like Yellowstone, still have ecosystems in which they can be expected to prosper?
2. The program to restore the Yellowstone and central Idaho ecosystems to their "natural" states involves intensive human intervention and management. Does this undermine the naturalness of the ecosystems that will result?
3. Whether or not political considerations require that ranchers grazing their stock on public lands be compensated for animals lost to wolves, does justice require such compensation? Are losses due to predation from reintroduced wolves different from losses due to other natural events, such as drought and disease?
4. Designating the reintroduced animals as "experimental" permits property owners to do things that would otherwise be forbidden, such as killing endangered animals that attack their pets or livestock. Does

this aspect of the reintroduction plan turn it into a "wolf-killing plan" as the Sierra Club Legal Defense Fund charged?

5. Attempts to reintroduce the red wolf to some of its former ranges have failed miserably, with the death of thirty-eight of forty-four of the animals. How should FWS officials decide when and where to attempt reintroduction programs? Should they be attempted when the prospects that the reintroduced animals will survive is thought to be less than fifty-fifty?

6. There were no coyotes in Yellowstone before the wolf was eradicated. There, as in all parts of the lower forty-eight states, the coyote expanded its range dramatically when wolves were eradicated. In order to truly restore Yellowstone to its pre-1930 ecological composition, the coyote would have to be eradicated. Should park managers make coyote eradication a goal?

NOTES

1. For a history of wolf eradication in the United States, see Barry Holstun Lopez, *Of Wolves and Men* (New York: Scribner, 1978).

2. All material attributed to FWS here is taken from the *Federal Register* 59, no. 224, November 22, 1994, 60252.

3. For a brief description of this controversy, see Hank Fischer, *Wolf Wars* (Helena, Mont.: Falcon Press, 1995), 151–55.

4. Standard capture technique: Buzz a parcel of woods containing wolves with a helicopter until the wolves bolt into open country, then shoot them from the helicopter with a tranquilizer gun.

5. The result of this work was Robert Cook, ed., *Ecological Issues on Reintroducing Wolves into Yellowstone National Park*, Scientific Monographs, NPS/NRYELL/NRSM-93/22, U.S. Department of the Interior, National Park Service, 1993. The main chapter used for this section is "Effects of Restoring Wolves on Yellowstone Area Big Game and Grizzly Bears: Opinions of Scientists," by David Lime, Barbara Koth, and Jonathan Vlaming.

6. The latest information on the population and distribution of Yellowstone wolves is available at www.yellowstone-natl-park.com/wolf.htm. [Hint: Turn your computer speaker volume down a bit before you log on.]

7. "Last of Original Wolves Moved to Park Dies," *Salt Lake City Tribune*, January 9, 2003, available at www.sltrib.com/2003/Jan/01092003/nation_w/18601.asp.

SOURCES

Cook, Robert, ed. *Ecological Issues on Reintroducing Wolves into Yellowstone National Park.* Scientific Monographs, NPS/NRYELL/NRSM-93/22. Washington, D.C.: U.S. Department of the Interior, National Park Service, 1993.

Fischer, Hank. *Wolf Wars.* Helena, Mont.: Falcon Press, 1995.

"Last of Original Wolves Moved to Park Dies." *Salt Lake City Tribune,* January 9, 2003. Available at www.sltrib.com/2003/Jan/01092003/nation_w/18601.asp.

Lopez, Barry Holstun. *Of Wolves and Men.* New York: Scribner, 1978.

6

REYKJAVÍC RAIDERS

A minke whale typically dies 3.3 minutes after being hit with a penthrite grenade, which is designed especially for whaling. Half the whales die instantly, and 9 percent live for more than ten minutes.[1]

In 1986, the International Whaling Commission (IWC) issued a four-year moratorium on all commercial whaling. The stated purpose of the moratorium was to allow time to assess the condition of whale populations and investigate the ecological feasibility of sustained harvesting of various whale populations. Several nations objected strongly to this moratorium, citing both economic and cultural reasons. Some of the objecting nations asserted that they had been whaling for generations and that whaling was an integral part of the economic and cultural identity of their coastal communities. The Japanese Ministry for Agriculture, Forests, and Fisheries also opposed the moratorium on the grounds that whales, rather than aggressive fishing fleets, were responsible for globally declining fish catches. Nevertheless, all nations agreed to cease commercial whaling by 1988.

Although the moratorium was a major step in the protection of whales, environmental groups were worried about an important exception in the moratorium. Nations were allowed to harvest whales of some species for "research" purposes, provided that the majority of the harvest products (whale meat, oil, bone, and so on) were consumed locally. Such research could be conducted to determine approximate population counts for whale species and to investigate the effects that the whales have on fish populations. Several nations, including Iceland, Japan, and Norway, immediately announced that they would continue to take whales under the "research exemption" despite the outcries of environmental groups.

On November 9, 1986, Iceland learned just how far some environmentalists were willing to go to protect the whales. In Reykjavík harbor, the prows of the *Hvalur 6* and *Hvalur 7*, half of Iceland's entire whaling fleet, could be seen poking up out of the water. Both ships had been scuttled by having their sea valves opened and smashed, flooding the ships with water. That same day, workers arriving at Iceland's only whale-processing plant (in Hvalfjord, fifty miles north of Reykjavík) discovered that the facility had been wrecked with sledgehammers and cyanic acid. Damage to the plant was estimated at two million dollars.

Icelandic authorities did not have a difficult time ascertaining who was responsible for the sabotage. The Sea Shepherd Conservation Society, an environmental group founded in reaction to the allegedly too-moderate position of Greenpeace, claimed full responsibility for both the sunken vessels and the damage at the processing plant. In defending the actions, Paul Watson, head of the Sea Shepherds, stated, "Our organization has full right to sink the whalers because Iceland is violating the moratorium." As to the destruction of property, Watson said, "Respect for life takes precedence over respect for property which is used to take life."

Two members of the group, Rod Coronado of the United States and David Howitt of Great Britain, had taken jobs at a fish factory in Reykjavík and spent several weeks reconnoitering their targets. On November 8, the two spent eight hours dismantling and destroying the refrigeration systems, laboratory equipment, and computer files of the Hvalfjord facility with sledgehammers and cyanic acid. After disabling the Hvalfjord facility, the two drove to Reykjavík harbor, where the whaling company's four ships were docked. Coronado and Howitt boarded two of the ships and opened their sea valves, sinking the ships. They were unable to sink the other two ships because of the presence of watchmen. Shortly after the attack, Coronado and Howitt left Iceland on a flight to Luxembourg.

As details of the raid came to light, the Sea Shepherds came under intense criticism from all sides. Greenpeace International likened the act to a terrorist attack and predicted that it would set back international environmental efforts. A newspaper in British Columbia (the home ground of Watson and the Sea Shepherds) also made the comparison with terrorism, asking, "Is Vancouver to become a sanctuary for international terrorists?" Several other environmental leaders criticized the actions by claiming that sabotage was not an effective way to achieve a long-term halt to whaling.

The Reykjavík raid was, of course, illegal. But it seems to have been carried out in a way fully compliant with the internal guidelines of the Sea Shepherds. Those guidelines state,

> Sea Shepherd crew members cannot use weapons; they cannot use explosives; they cannot undertake any action that could result in a physical injury to humans; they must take responsibility for their actions; and they must accept moral and legal consequences for their actions.

In accordance with the last two principles, Watson flew back to Iceland in 1988 to turn himself in to the authorities. Iceland held Watson for twenty-four hours without charge and then expelled him without cause. Watson never saw the inside of a courtroom in Iceland.

Five years later, in 1993, Norway unilaterally renounced the IWC moratorium and began issuing permits for minke-whale hunting. At the time, IWC scientific advisers estimated the minke population at 87,000 in the northeastern Atlantic and 900,000 worldwide. Norway issued permits to thirty-one whaling boats, most in the Lofoten Islands. The boats took a total of 226 minke whales. By 1999, Norway had expanded the quota to 753 minke whales and issued permits to thirty-six vessels, nearly all of them operated by families in small coastal villages, the inhabitants of which had hunted whales for generations.

National Public Radio interviewed some of the whalers in the small village of Rena.[2] Jans Swenson's comments were typical:

> Norway has obliged itself to use this quota calculation model that is developed by the International Whaling Commission scientific committee. It's a very precautious model. So quotas, if they increase, they will increase very, very slowly.

Bjorn Blikfeld was less polite, calling antiwhaling activists "terrorists" and accusing them of cynically misleading their supporters:

> Patrick Moore, the former director of Greenpeace Canada, said, "People don't understand ecology. Therefore, we have to make them save the whales. We have to tell them that whales are good. Good whales, kind whales, faithful whales"—it sells better than the truth: that whales are quite stupid, like a cow, for example. And that they are, except for their size, not very different from other animals.

But as far as the Sea Shepherds are concerned, it is Swensen and Blikfeld who are criminals. Asked about his involvement in the sinking of two Norwegian whaling ships, Watson replied,

> Well, I don't look on them as acts of violence. . . . We're dealing with criminal, pirate whaling operations here. How can they justify what they're doing, which is ignoring international regulations and continuing to kill whales? And having a very serious impact on the survival of many whale species. The killing's being done by these criminal whaling operations. Last year they killed 300 minke whales. That is a crime.

DISCUSSION

Individuals, organizations, and nation-states that support some version of the IWC moratorium generally cite some combination of recognizable versions of the following five goals: 1) preserving whale populations as an economic resource, 2) preserving whale populations as an ecological resource (either in themselves or as a component of oceanic and coastal ecosystems), 3) preserving whale populations as a social or cultural resource, 4) preserving whale populations as an aesthetic resource, and 5) preventing the morally wrongful killing of individual animals.

Presumably, all interested parties share at least the second of these goals: No organization or nation-state has advanced the notion that the extinction of any whale species would be a positively good thing. But there is plainly very serious disagreement about the other goals: whether whales should be exploited as an economic resource, whether it is morally wrong to kill a whale—these are hotly debated questions. For individuals pondering their own attitudes toward the IWC moratorium, it is useful and important to ask, Which of these goals are really compelling? For nation-states, the moratorium raises an additional problem: Although whales spend much of their lives in coastal waters, they are migratory species and cannot be protected by merely national actions. Whatever our reasons for *wanting* to protect whale populations, our *ability* to protect them is completely dependent on the voluntary cooperation of other sovereign states whose governments and citizens may have quite different reasons.

Despite the criticism that the IWC has received from both environmentalists and whaling nations, few would argue that whales (or even whalers) would be better off today without the IWC. Indeed, all seem to agree that without the IWC's intervention in the middle of the twentieth century, at least several species of whales might have been hunted into extinction.

For many individuals, one especially controversial aspect of the whaling moratorium is whether and how it should be applied to indigenous peoples who wish to continue or resume whaling, often for both cultural and economic reasons. In 1998, for the first time in almost seventy years, eight members of the Makah tribe paddled a canoe out from the coast of Washington to hunt gray whales. The hunt was approved by the IWC and the National Marine Fisheries Service, which had pressed the Makah's case before the international body.

The Makah believe that resuming their whale hunting will instill pride in their people and help the younger generation learn their culture. The 1,800 members of Makah will share the whale meat; its sale would be illegal under tribal and federal law. The only income that the Makah might earn will be from the sale of artifacts carved out of whalebone, which is legal under both federal and tribal law. The Makah have updated their traditional techniques, however. Sitting in the canoe next to the harpooner is a man with a .50-caliber rifle; he will shoot the whale in the brain as soon as the harpoon strikes. Nearby are two powerful speedboats that will help finish off any whale that is merely wounded by those in the canoe and then tow the carcass to shore.

While it is true that some indigenous peoples want to whale for deep cultural reasons, it is also true that some nations opposed to the moratorium see whaling by indigenous peoples as a potential opening toward much broader commercial whaling. When the World Council of Whalers elected Tom Happynook, chief of the Huuayaht Nation, as its chair, the council perhaps was more concerned with its public image than with Mr. Happynook's whaling expertise.

Although many people seem to believe that some kinds of whaling, such as ritual whaling by indigenous peoples, are morally more acceptable than others, it is not clear how such a view follows from either a human- or a life- or a nature-centered ethical system. After all, if the whales have a right not to be killed, it should be wrong for *anyone* to kill them.

Finally, notice that this is the first of many of the cases in this volume that involve some kind of illegal activity. Others are Case 7: High-Seas Fish Wars, Case 8: Matinicus Island, Case 20: Leopold and Traps, Case 21: Monkey-Wrenching, and Case 22: Saving Mink, Killing Voles. Every serious moral theory and every world religion acknowledges that it is sometimes right and perhaps even obligatory to violate an unjust law. American history is replete with morally admirable lawbreaking: From the Boston Tea

Party to the Underground Railroad to the civil rights movement, every century presents numerous examples of heroic individuals putting their lives and their freedom at legal and physical risk to resist immoral (albeit then-legal) social structures and practices. But, of course, it is one thing to *invoke* the moral legacy of John Adams and Martin Luther King Jr.; it is another to *deserve* it.

QUESTIONS

1. Of the five previously listed goals serving as possible reasons to support some version of a whaling moratorium, which are the most important?
2. Of the same five goals, which are easiest to justify from the perspective of a human-centered system of values? Which might require an eco-centric or biocentric system of values for a compelling vindication?
3. In international negotiations about the moratorium, what kinds of persuasive tactics are fair? The United States, for example, has been accused of threatening some IWC member states with trade sanctions if they did not accept the moratorium. The government of Japan has admitted offering development aid to other member states as an inducement to weaken the moratorium. Are such tactics an inevitable component of transnational environmental regulation? Are they fair?
4. Were the Reykjavík raiders morally justified in violating Icelandic law?
5. Compare the different instances of lawbreaking presented in this volume. Which, if any, are morally justified? Which, if any, are not? What are the important differences between the instances that you believe *are* justified and the instances that you believe are *not* justified?
6. The feeling that whaling by indigenous people is morally *different* than other kinds of whaling is apparently widespread. Can the feeling be justified? Is there any rational basis for refusing to allow the people of Iceland, Norway, and Japan to continue a thousand-year tradition of whaling while permitting indigenous peoples to continue or resume theirs? Indeed, are the Japanese or Norwegians less indigenous to their islands than the Makah are to Oregon? What exactly does *indigenous* mean in this context?
7. Review Case 1: Gorilla Rangers. It raises many of the same moral, social, and ecological issues as this case. But no one in the West and almost no one in Africa has suggested that indigenous African peoples

should be permitted to hunt gorillas. What accounts for the gorilla's more favored status? Is it their rarity? Their social and cognitive abilities? Their ecological role?

NOTES

1. High North Alliance, *Living Off the Sea: Minke Whaling in the North East Atlantic* (Reine i Lofoten, Norway: Norwegian Fisherman's Association, 1994), 12.
2. *Living on Earth*, National Public Radio, February 11, 1994, Steve Curwood, host, transcript available at www.loe.org/archives/940211.htm.

SOURCES

Blichfeldt, Georg, ed. *11 Essays on Whales and Man.* Reine i Lofoten, Norway: High North Alliance, 1994.

Dobra, Peter M. "Cetaceans: A Litany of Cain." *Boston College Environmental Affairs Law Review* 7, no. 1 (1978): 165–83.

Fenyves, Charles. "A Militant Turn for Conservationists." *U.S. News and World Report*, November 24, 1986, 72–73.

Manes, Christopher. *Green Rage: Radical Environmentalism and the Unmaking of Civilization.* Boston: Little, Brown, 1990.

"Militants Sink 2 of Iceland's Whaling Vessels." *New York Times*, November 10, 1986, A1, A9.

"Saboteurs Wreck Whale-Oil Plant in Iceland." *New York Times*, November 11, 1986, A10.

Scarf, James E. "Ethical Issues in Whale and Small Cetacean Management." *Environmental Ethics* 3 (1980): 241–79.

"Sinking Feeling." *Time*, November 24, 1986, 45.

Skare, Mari. "Whaling: A Sustainable Use of Natural Resources or a Violation of Animal Rights?" *Environment* 36, no. 7 (1994): 12–20.

Walsh, John. "Can Fish Quota Save the Whales?" *Science* 224 (1984): 850.

——. "Saving the Whales Faces New Hazard—Research Whaling." *Science* 233 (1986): 718–19.

——. "Whaling Tensions Rise as Moratorium Approaches." *Science* 225 (1984): 488–89.

Watson, Paul. "Raid on Reykjavík." *Earth First!*, December 21, 1986, 1, 6.

7

HIGH-SEAS FISH WARS

On March 9, 1995, in international waters more than 200 miles from the coast of Newfoundland, an Ottawa Department of Fisheries and Oceans patrol ship chased the Spanish fishing vessel *Estai* for four hours. The chase ended when the patrol ship fired its machine gun across the bow of the trawler. The *Estai* was brought into port in Newfoundland and impounded. Its captain was jailed for fishing violations.

Spain and its partners in the European Union condemned the action as high-seas piracy. Canada's fisheries minister, Brian Tobin defended the action, stating, "Any government worth its salt must act to prevent the disappearance of another fish stock from the planet."[1]

The fish stock in question is the Atlantic turbot, also known as the Greenland halibut, an unappetizing fish that the Spanish export to Japan to be used in manufacturing fish meal and fish fingers. In 1995, the Northwest Atlantic Fisheries Organization had set the annual quota for the Grand Banks turbot catch at 27,000 tons total, a dramatic reduction from recent catches of 60,000 tons. The European Union was allotted 3,400 tons, Canada 16,300 tons, and other fishing nations the remaining 7,300 tons. When the Canadian government estimated that EU ships had taken 7,000 tons of turbot—more than twice their quota—in just the first two weeks of the 1995 season, it called, on March 3, for a sixty-day moratorium on turbot catches until the quota could be sorted out.

When the *Estai* was taken into custody four days later, its turbot catch was ten times that of any nearby Canadian boat. Worse, 80 percent of the turbot found aboard were less than half the length of a mature fish, suggesting that the mesh of its abandoned nets had been only half the required size. Canada also charged that the *Estai* was carrying two sets of books and systematically underreporting its catch.

Fishing rights are a sensitive issue for both Spain and Canada. Spain has the largest fishing fleet in Europe and the third largest in the world, with 18,890 vessels with 85,000 crew members. Spain also has historical ties to the Grand Banks, having fished there since the fifteenth century. Canada knows the political and economic costs of fish conservation efforts. A Canadian moratorium on Grand Banks cod fishing, instituted in 1992, resulted in the unemployment of 50,000 Canadian fisherman and plant workers, mostly in Newfoundland.

The *Economist* described some of the problems this way:

> Over-fishing has two principal causes, both of which are the responsibility of governments within their 200-mile zones. First, without regulations constraining their behaviour, fishermen have little incentive to conserve fish stocks. If all fishermen restrained themselves, each would benefit from enlarged fish stocks in the future. But no fisherman sees any gain in doing so individually unless he knows that competitors will do the same. Second, this problem is exacerbated by subsidies. As fish stocks have dwindled, governments have pumped out huge sums to keep fishing communities going. According to the UN, the world's fishing fleets make an annual loss totalling around $54 billion, much of that met by public subsidies. Such money, while preserving some remote coastal communities, also perpetuates over-fishing.[2]

DISCUSSION

This case can be usefully compared to Case 8: Matinicus Island. In the present case, we see a national government intervening—perhaps illegally—to enforce an international agreement. In the Matinicus Island case, we see private individuals intervening—again perhaps illegally—to enforce a community agreement.

The high seas seem to present a perfect example of what Garrett Hardin has called a *commons*. Although it is in everyone's long-term interests not to overexploit the commons, it is also in each fisherman's short-term interests to take as much as they can get right now. Given these realities, it is much easier to get *agreement* than *compliance* with the international fishing regulations.

QUESTIONS

1. Was the Canadian action against the *Estai* justified? If some national governments fail to police the compliance of their own fleets with international fishing agreements, are the governments of other nations entitled to ignore normal 200-mile jurisdictional limits?
2. Do the fishing stocks on the Grand Banks meet the criteria for what Garrett Hardin would call a *commons*? If so, would the absence of effectively enforced catch limits necessarily lead to "the tragedy of the commons"?
3. According to the *Economist*, government subsidies to fishing communities impacted by catch quotas have exacerbated the problem of depleted fish stocks. Is this analysis plausible? Should governments discontinue the subsidies regardless of the social consequences?
4. In what ways are the issues raised by this case similar to the issues raised by the Matinicus Island case? What, if anything, do these cases suggest about the interaction and efficacy of national, international, and community efforts to conserve biotic resources?

NOTES

1. Colin Nickerson, "Fish Spawning Ill Will at Sea, Dwindling Stocks Are Straining International Relations," *Boston Globe*, March 26, 1995, A2.
2. *Economist*, April 22, 1995, 17–18.

SOURCES

Nickerson, Colin. "Canada Brings Home Trawler, Tensions with Europe Rise." *Boston Globe*, March 13, 1995, A2.
———. "Canada Frees Vessel, Easing Tension with EU, Bond Is Posted; Step May Bring Talks." *Boston Globe*, March 16, 1995, A2.
———. "Canada and Spain Approach Truce in Fishing Dispute." *Boston Globe*, April 14, 1995, A5.
———. "Canada Stuck to Its Gunboats in Turbot War." *Boston Globe*, April 17, 1995, A1, A6.
———. "Canadians Lash Out in Fishing War, Cut One Trawler's Lines, Send 18 Spanish Vessels Fleeing." *Boston Globe*, March 27, 1995, A1, A8.
———. "Europeans Halt Talks on Fishing, Spanish Trawlers Appear Set to Contest Canadian Ban." *Boston Globe*, March 28, 1995, A1, A12.

———. "Europe-Canada Ties Deteriorate, EU Curbs Relations over Seized Ship." *Boston Globe*, March 14, 1995, A2.

———. "Fish Spawning Ill Will at Sea, Dwindling Stocks Are Straining International Relations." *Boston Globe*, March 26, 1995, A2.

———. "Spanish Boats, Awaiting Protection, Defy Canada and Resume Fishing." *Boston Globe*, March 15, 1995, A2.

———. "Spanish Boats Defy Canada, Resume Fishing." *Boston Globe*, March 29, 1995, A2.

———. "Canada's Gunboat Diplomacy." *Boston Globe*, March 12, 1995, A5.

8

MATINICUS ISLAND

The fact that such [self-]regulatory systems exist goes against the basic assumption . . . that fishermen are fiercely competitive and unable to work together for their mutual benefit. . . . It also weakens the assumption that a fishery which is not regulated by central authorities is not regulated at all.

—Svein Jentoft and Trond Kristoffersen[1]

Along the coastal waters of eastern Canada and the United States—in the Grand Banks off Newfoundland, for example, and in Georges Bank off New England—severe overfishing is leading to economic and ecological ruin (see Case 7: High-Seas Fish Wars). Despite government restrictions on gear, catch, and seasons, fishers are overexploiting the once productive biotic resources on which their livelihoods depend. Closer to shore, however, some fishing communities have avoided self-destructive overexploitation for decades with little, if any, government involvement. Anthropologists Francis P. and Margaret C. Bowles have studied the lobster and herring fisheries off Matinicus Island, Maine. The island's fishermen and lobstermen (hereafter "fishers") claim a well-defined area of approximately seventy-seven square miles around the island.

The island's lobster fishery has operated successfully for over a century without official state recognition despite many changes, including expansion into regional markets and dramatic improvements in boat design, fishing technology, and navigational equipment. And while the number of fishers has deviated little from the original number of thirty-six, fishers move in and out of the fishery. Over the 1970–1982 period, Bowles and Bowles (1989, 239) observed that twenty-one men entered or left the fishery.

Island fishers strictly control who will be accepted into their fishery. One must live on the island and either have island kinship ties or purchase property from a local fisher who then becomes an informal sponsor. The latter approach is akin to an apprenticeship program. In addition, one must demonstrate a willingness to cooperate with other fishers and respect their fishing rights and equipment. An individual must also make the necessary investments: Wharf access, a boat, and traps cost a minimum of about $125,000 in the 1980s (Bowles and Bowles 1989, 236). The system clearly pays off, however: Anthropologist James Acheson found that local incomes are almost 40 percent higher than incomes of lobster fishers in the more open areas off Maine's coast.

Local fishers actively defend the territory from outsiders through extralegal means. The Bowleses write,

> They customarily signal a territory violation by opening the door and tying a half-hitch around the buoy of an outsider's trap. If this signal is ignored, an island lobsterman may haul up the outsider's traps and dump them together so that the buoys and warps become tangled. Actual trap cutting ensues only if these measures fail to convey the wisdom of removing the offending gear from the disputed area. (Bowles and Bowles 1989, 243)

Although Matinicus Island's self-imposed lobstering restrictions have existed for over a century, Acheson (1993, 80) points out that the state government of Maine could "annihilate the entire territorial system if it so chose" simply by enforcing the laws concerning trap cutting. The island's communal management system is able to exist, says Acheson, "only because of the benign neglect of the state."

Some other efforts at self-regulation have not enjoyed such benign neglect. From the 1930s to the 1960s, Gulf coast shrimpers negotiated price agreements with local wholesalers through their fishers' unions and trade associations. Because the wholesalers would agree to a premium price only if the shrimp were big enough to justify the higher prices, the agreements reduced the numbers of small shrimp taken from Mississippi waters (Johnson and Libecap 1982, 1007–8.) In the early 1960s, however, the agreements were dismantled by the federal government as a violation of the Sherman Antitrust Act, a government decision that was based on an older case, *Manaka v. Monterey Sardine Industries*, which held that a cooperative association of boat owners is not freed from the restrictive provisions of the Sherman Antitrust Act . . . because it professes, in the interest of the conservation of important food fish, to regulate the price and the manner of taking fish unauthorized by legislation and uncontrolled by proper authority.[2]

Ironically, the strategy of raising prices to conserve shrimp stocks and raise incomes has since been adopted by state governments: All Gulf coast states have imposed minimum-size rules for harvesting shrimp.

DISCUSSION

Scholarly attention to self-regulated "commons" has grown in recent years. Ostrom (1990, 90–101) has attempted to identify characteristics that enable a group to manage a commons over a long period without overexploitation. She suggests that boundaries must be well-defined, rules must be linked to local conditions, and sanctions must be imposed when rules are violated. In most cases, she suggests, a strong community tradition and noninterference by governments are also essential.

Because offshore fish stocks are often highly mobile, self-regulation on the basis of territorial segregation does not seem feasible. Current regulatory approaches (see Case 7: High-Seas Fish Wars) to these stocks therefore rely on quota systems. But in his discussion of Matinicus Island and other community-run fisheries, Leal (1996) concludes,

> [These cases] challenge the notion that fishers will always be locked into the tragedy of the commons unless there is state control. . . . Communities can avoid the tragedy of the commons. They offer hope for many coastal fishing areas around the world. They offer some lessons that can be applied to the more complicated question of curtailing overexploitation of offshore fisheries. Given the failure of government to regulate fishing successfully, a self-regulated fishery is an idea whose time has come.

QUESTIONS

1. Clearly, the Matinicus Island lobster fisheries meet the conditions that Ostrom suggests are essential for effective local management of a shared commons. Are there other kinds of commons that meet them as well?

2. Given the tragic depletion of fishing stocks in the North Atlantic, Leal seems to be at least partially correct when he concludes that government regulatory efforts failed. Does it follow from this that self-regulation should be tested in international commons?

3. Informal arrangements such as those on Matinicus Island require that regulatory officials leave local communities free to design their own arrangements. But cutting traps is not only *informal* but also *illegal* (compare Case 20: Leopold and Traps). Is it fair for government regulators to allow profitable community management arrangements such as those on Matinicus Island to continue by failing to enforce relevant statutes? If so, on what basis should they decide which arrangement to tolerate and which to dismantle?

4. Like Case 16: The Grand Staircase, this case raises questions about the proper role of different levels of government in managing ecological resources. In Case 16, national authorities refused to defer to local preferences; in the present case, state and national authorities clearly have deferred to local preferences. Did authorities do the right thing in both cases? If so, what contextual differences in the cases justify the authorities' different decisions?

NOTES

1. The narrative and discussions sections of this case are excerpted, with permission, from Donald R. Leal, *Community-Run Fisheries: Avoiding the "Tragedy of the Commons,"* PERC Policy Series, ed. Jane S. Shaw, no. PS-7 (Bozeman, Mont.: Political Economy Research Center, September 1996). Donald R. Leal is a senior associate of PERC (Political Economy Research Center, 502 South 19th Avenue, Bozeman, Montana 59718. E-mail: perc@perc.org).

2. *Manaka v. Monterey Sardine Industries*, 41 F. Supp. 531 (D.C. Cal. 1941). Compare annotations to 15 U.S.C.A. § 521.

SOURCES

Acheson, James. "Capturing the Commons: Legal and Illegal Strategies." In *The Political Economy of Customs and Culture: Informal Solutions to the Commons Problem.* Edited by Terry L. Anderson and Randy T. Simmons. Lanham, Md.: Rowman & Littlefield, 1993, 69–83.

Bowles, Francis P., and Margaret C. Bowles. "Holding the Line: Property Rights in the Lobster and Herring Fisheries of Matinicus Island, Maine." In *A Sea of Small Boats*. Edited by John Cordell. Cambridge, Mass.: Cultural Survival, 1989, 228–57.

Jentoft, Svein. 1989. "Fisheries Co-Management: Delegating Responsibility to Fishermen's Organizations." *Marine Policy*, April 1989, 137–54.

Jentoft, Svein, and Trond Kristoffersen. "Fishermen's Co-Management: The Case of the Lofoten Fishery." *Human Organization* 48, no. 4 (1989): 355–65.

Johnson, Ronald, and Gary Libecap. "Contracting Problems and Regulation, the Case of the Fishery." *American Economic Review* 12 (December 1982): 1007–8.

Leal, Donald R. *Community-Run Fisheries: Avoiding the "Tragedy of the Commons."* PERC Policy Series, ed. Jane S. Shaw, no. PS-7. Bozeman, Mont.: Political Economy Research Center, September 1996. Available at www.perc.org/publications/policyseries/community_full.html.

Ostrom, Elinor. *Governing the Commons: The Evolution of Institutions for Collective Action*. Cambridge: Cambridge University Press, 1990.

9

TAKING LAKE TAHOE

The Tahoe basin is a spectacular 500-square-mile area straddling the Nevada–California border. It is ringed by 10,000-foot snow-capped peaks whose slopes descend to Lake Tahoe itself. The lake is at an elevation of 6,000 feet. Because most of the terrain in the basin is very steep and hence vulnerable to erosion, almost all the development in the region has taken place along the shore.

Sixty-three streams drain into Lake Tahoe from the surrounding mountains, and collectively they provide about 90 percent of the lake's inflow. With a depth of 1,646 feet, Tahoe is the second-deepest lake in the United States and tenth deepest in the world. Twenty-two miles long and twelve miles wide, the lake covers almost 200 square miles, or about 38 percent, of the entire basin. The lake's single outlet, the Truckee River, was dammed in 1874, raising the level of the lake by six feet but adding only 0.6 percent to its volume. Because the volume of the lake is so large and the outflow so small, the average residence (or retention) time for any drop of water entering the lake is exceptionally long: 700 years. As a result, whatever nutrients or pollutants manage to find their way into the lake are effectively trapped for most of a millennium.[1]

The lake was first "discovered" by white settlers in 1844. Heavy logging in the area began shortly thereafter, primarily to support the mining and railroad industries. Today, logging no longer plays a significant role in the basin's economy; tourism is Tahoe's principal industry. Only 54,000 people live in the region year-round, but over two million visit the basin each year for skiing, gambling, and outdoor recreation. Eight million people live within 150 miles of Lake Tahoe, primarily within the San Francisco and Sacramento areas.

The beauty of the area inspired calls for the establishment of a national park in the early twentieth century, but the idea was never adopted, partly because of all the development that had already occurred in the basin. The U.S. Forest Service did, however, begin to buy up land in the area in 1899 and now owns 65 percent of the entire basin. California and Nevada have acquired an additional 6 percent for state parks.

Around the middle of the twentieth century, residents and scientists began to notice that the clarity of Lake Tahoe's water was declining dramatically. Erosion caused by development was quickly identified as the cause. Development had increased erosion in two ways: first by disturbing the ground during construction work but also, and more important, by permanently increasing the fraction of the land with impervious coverage. Because water cannot be absorbed by packed dirt, asphalt, concrete, or building roofs, rainwater runoff is concentrated on a smaller and smaller land surface, inevitably leading to increased erosion. In steep terrain like the basin, the runoff also moves faster, carrying a heavier load of nutrients into the lake.

Since the clarity and quality of the water are crucial to the region's tourism-based economy, efforts were quickly launched to protect Lake Tahoe. In 1969, President Nixon signed the bill that created the Tahoe Regional Planning Agency (TRPA). This body was charged with coordinating local, state, and federal activity to develop land use and environmental regulations to preserve the ecological characteristics of the basin. Over the years, it has developed and managed an impressive variety of initiatives on issues as wide-ranging as bicycle corridor development, woodstove retrofitting, and urban redevelopment.[2]

As TRPA began its work in the early 1970s, it was faced with two competing economic and ecological attitudes in the basin. Since the late 1800s, two factions have vied for control over Lake Tahoe. The first sees the beauty of the lake as an argument for development: More hotels and casinos will draw more people to visit and enjoy the lake's beauty. The other sees the need to preserve the lake and the surrounding area as an argument against too rapid or too extensive development.

The most controversial of TRPA's actions have been its attempts to bring land use practices in line with its long-term vision for the basin. TRPA's regional plan states plainly that the "primary function of the region shall be as a mountain recreation area with outstanding scenic and natural values." Acting on this vision, TRPA has implemented strict land use controls. One of these controls is the Individual Parcel Evaluation System (IPES), which evaluates every proposed development's impact on erosion hazards and runoff potentials before deciding whether the development will be allowed on a particular parcel.[3] Projects on steep slopes or near streams—precisely the most scenic and highly desired parcels—are the least likely to be approved. TRPA intends that the IPES process will redirect residential development toward those areas that are already primarily urban and that are served by existing infrastructure.

To those citizens who would like future generations to see Lake Tahoe and the surrounding basin in at least relatively pristine condition, TRPA's actions seem reasonable. Indeed, given the lake's 700-year residence time, simple caution would seem to support TRPA. Other things being equal, for example, it would take Tahoe 270 times as long to clear itself as Lake Erie.

But there is more to the issue than hydrology. The Fifth Amendment to the U.S. Constitution erects a barrier against government usurpation of its citizens' property. This amendment's "takings clause" states, "nor shall private property be taken for public use, without just compensation." The takings clause—written by founders who had seen British troops seize the property of American colonists at will and without recompense—ensured that individual property owners could not be unfairly burdened by projects intended to enhance the public good. Over the years, in its interpretation of the clause, the U.S. Supreme Court created a distinction between "physical takings" and "regulatory takings." A physical taking occurs when the landowner is dispossessed of his or her property (such as to make way for a road) or when there is a physical invasion of property (such as by an electrical cable or natural gas pipeline). A regulatory taking neither dispossess the landowner nor physically invades the property; rather, it involves a government regulation that limits the owner's *use* of the property and so lowers its economic value.

The law regarding physical takings is simple: Without exception, the landowner must be fairly compensated. The law on regulatory takings is not so simple. In determining whether a landowner is entitled to compensation (and, if so, how much compensation), the courts are required to use a complex multistage test. First, the court must decide whether the regulation has destroyed *all* the property's economic value. If so, the analysis ends, and the landowner must be compensated; if not, the court proceeds to the second step. Here, the court must decide whether the regulation in question "advances a legitimate government interest." If not, the regulation itself may be declared void, and the "taking" issue becomes moot; if so, the court proceeds to the third step. Here, the court must decide whether the "government's interest" is sufficiently important to outweigh the landowner's interest in developing the property. If so, then the landowner is *not* entitled to compensation; if not, then a taking has occurred, and the landowner is entitled to compensation.

Several landowners in the Tahoe basin have sued the TRPA, claiming that the regulations it has imposed to restrict development on steep slopes and within stream environment zones constitute an illegal taking (or, in the alternative, that they constitute a taking for which compensation must be paid). Courts have thus far held both that "TRPA regulations substantially advanced a legitimate government interest: the protection of Lake Tahoe Basin—a national treasure"[4] and that the TRPA regulations do not deprive property owners of their property interests "in a manner requiring compensation."

The Supreme Court, in deciding on a development moratorium imposed by TRPA, offered this analysis in support of the lower court's decision against the property owners: "Land-use regulations are ubiquitous and most of them impact property values in some tangential way. . . . Treating them all as *per se* [requiring compensation] takings would transform government regulation into a luxury few governments could afford."[5]

DISCUSSION

This is not the only case in this volume that raises or is alleged to raise issues about "takings" (see also Case 10: The Delhi Sands Fly, Case 11: Mr. Cone's Woodpeckers, and Case 31: The Dark Skies Ordinance).

The Tahoe case raises several interesting issues. Perhaps first, in terms of public controversy, is a question about fairness. One commentator on the decision quoted in the previous paragraph offered the sardonic analysis that the only winners under the Supreme Court's decision were "those homeowners fortunate enough to have built their homes before the moratorium was in place."[6] Not only are existing home owners exempted from the TRPA regulations, they actually benefit from them: "[The decision] conferred a huge windfall on current homeowners. Land densities and housing stock were both reduced. The two forces together drove up the price of built homes, which current owners can capture either by use or by sale."[7] To the extent that this critique offers an analysis of economic realities, it is undoubtedly true. But the commentator's insinuation that just because the Court's decision has winners and losers it is ipso facto unjust is patently unsound: If that inference were legitimate, every court decision would be unjust. The question of whether land use regulations are fair or just is rarely simple. Indeed, as Case 11: Mr. Cone's Woodpeckers shows, even the question of whether the regulations will achieve their ecological purposes is sometimes complicated.

The Tahoe case also presents an issue about what some authors call "door locking"—a heated theme in many debates about immigration policy but also a theme in local and regional zoning and land use issues. Many rural communities, confronted with a sudden influx of people moving away from urban areas, have implemented restrictive land use policies to slow or even stop the influx of new residents. The policies take many shapes, including very large minimum lot size requirements or prohibitive water and sewage connection fees. From the perspective of city dwellers wanting to move into such communities, the residents of rural communities adopting such policies are often accused of wanting to "lock the door behind them." From the perspective of those who moved first, such policies are usually defended as necessary measures to protect important environmental values. The truth may be that humans often act for multiple motives and that such regulations may reflect both a desire to "lock the door" and a genuine concern for environmental values. This can make the moral evaluation of such regulations difficult: Should one condemn them for their less admirable motive(s) or praise them for their more admirable motive(s)? Indeed, how can one really claim even to know the motives?

One way to guess at the relative importance of these two motives might be to look at the extent to which the (already resident) policymakers are willing to restrict their own behavior in deference to environmental values. In the Tahoe case, for example, it seems clear that new home construction within stream zones or on steep slopes would adversely affect water quality in the Tahoe basin. But it is also clear that the behavior of those who live in existing homes can and does adversely affect Lake Tahoe. For example, the use of chemical lawn fertilizers is not prohibited within the basin despite the fact that it is one of the major sources of excess nutrients that may eventually overload the lake. Before jumping to the conclusion that this is evidence of TRPA hypocrisy, however, remember this: The TRPA has no authority to control fertilizer use, and one must ask whether the motives of those who write land use regulations really matter. Even if restrictions on new development were intended to benefit existing home owners, perhaps ecologically they are still the right thing to do. Arguing that the Tahoe property owners affected by the new regulations were entitled to compensation, Chief Justice Rehnquist nevertheless conceded the propriety of the regulations:

> Lake Tahoe is a national treasure and I do not doubt that respondent's efforts at preventing further degradation were made in good faith in furtherance of the public interest. But, as is the case with most governmental action that furthers the public interest, the Constitution requires that the costs and burdens be borne by the public at large, not by a few targeted citizens. Justice Holmes's admonition of 80 years ago again rings true: "We are in danger of forgetting that a strong public desire to improve the public condition is not enough to warrant achieving the desire by a shorter cut than the constitutional way of paying for the change" (*Mahon* 260 U.S. at 416).[8]

QUESTIONS

For most of these questions, it may be useful to compare this case to Case 10: The Delhi Sands Fly and Case 11: Mr. Cone's Woodpeckers. For some, it may also be useful to review Case 8: Matinicus Island, Case 16: The Grand Staircase, or Case 31: The Dark Skies Ordinance.

1. Should the government be required to pay for *all* the economic impacts of regulation—even if, as the Supreme Court has pointed out, this would make regulation so expensive that a government could rarely afford it?
2. Review the three-stage test currently used by U.S. courts to decide whether a regulatory "taking" merits compensation. Is it socially and morally fair? If not, formulate your own test.
3. What factors, if any, should determine whether and the extent to which the government should compensate a private landowner when environmental or other regulation impacts the economic value of their property? Does it matter, for example, whether the particular use prohibited by the regulation was generally understood at the time of purchase to be environmentally benign?
4. In a purely economic sense, the Supreme Court's decision to uphold TRPA development restrictions increased the value of developed res-

idential land parcels and decreased the value of undeveloped residential land parcels. Would it be fair to tax the owners who had already built their homes in order to compensate the owners who had not?
5. To what extent can private landowners be fairly required to bear the burden of protecting regional or global environmental values? Such protection is intended to benefit all, but the economic impact of any single regulation typically falls on just a few. Is this situation made "fair" if environmental regulations are sufficiently diverse that almost everyone is affected by at least some regulation—so that, in the total regulatory scheme, everyone bears some share of the burden? In other words, if at least some regulation affects everyone, is there less moral weight to any particular individual's claim that they deserve compensation?
6. There is also the "when" issue. Is it fair to penalize landowners who bought their property before the regulations were put in place but did not build before the regulations were put in place? Can they fairly complain that they are the victims of "door locking"?

NOTES

1. By comparison, the depth of the Great Lakes ranges from 1,332 feet (Lake Superior) to 210 feet (Lake Erie), and the average residence time ranges from 191 years (Lake Superior) to only 2.6 years (Lake Erie). Lake Erie's very short retention time was a key factor in the lake's ecological recovery. See *The Great Lakes Environmental Atlas and Resource Book*, 3rd ed., jointly published by the governments of Canada and the United States, available at www.epa.gov/glnpo/atlas/intro.html.
2. Visit TRPA's home page at www.trpa.org.
3. For information on this system as used by TRPA, see www.trpa.org/ipes.html.
4. *Kelly v. Tahoe Regional Planning Authority*, 855 P.2d 1027, 1034 (Nov. 1993).
5. U.S. Supreme Court, *Tahoe-Sierra Preservation Council v. Tahoe Regional Planning Agency*, 00-1167 (April 23, 2002), available at http://supct.law.cornell.edu/supct/html/00-1167.ZS.html.
6. Richard A. Epstein, "Taking by Slivers," *National Law Journal*, May 6, 2002, A21, available at www.nlj.com/oped/050602epstein.shtml.
7. Epstein, "Taking by Slivers," A21.
8. U.S. Supreme Court, *Tahoe-Sierra Preservation Council v. Tahoe Regional Planning Agency*.

SOURCES

Elliot-Fisk, Deborah L., et al. "Lake Tahoe Case Study." In *Status of the Sierra Nevada: Sierra Nevada Ecosystem Project Final Report to Congress*, addendum, chapter 7. Davis: University of California, Centers for Water and Wildland Resources, 1996, 217–76. The full report is available at http://ceres.ca.gov/snep/pubs/add.html.

Epstein, Richard A. "Taking by Slivers." *National Law Journal*, May 6, 2002, A21.

Hardin, Garret. "The Tragedy of the Commons." *Science* 162, no. 3858 (1968): 1243–48.

Kelly v. Tahoe Regional Planning Authority, 855 P.2d 1027 (Nov. 1993).

Pryor, Kim. "Tahoe Untangled: The Tahoe Regional Planning Agency's Bi-State Battle." *Planning*, August 1999, 14–18.

Public Law 91-148; 83 Stat. 360; 94 Stat. 3233; Pub. L. 96-551; Cal. Govt. Code § 66800; Nev. Rev. Stat. § 277.200.

Strong, Douglas H. *Tahoe: An Environmental History*. Lincoln: University of Nebraska Press, 1984.

———. *Tahoe: From Timber Barons to Ecologists*. Lincoln: University of Nebraska Press, 1999.

Tahoe Regional Planning Authority. www.trpa.org.

———. *Regional Plan for the Lake Tahoe Basin: Goals and Policies*. Adopted by the Governing Board, September 17, 1986, printed April 1999.

U.S. Supreme Court. *Tahoe-Sierra Preservation Council v. Tahoe Regional Planning Agency*, 00-1167 (April 23, 2002). Available at http://supct.law.cornell.edu/supct/html/00-1167.ZS.html.

10

THE DELHI SANDS FLY

*I consider myself an environmentalist, but this is offensive
to me. . . . This is not some sylvan glen. . . . This is not a lion,
tiger or a bear. Or even an owl. This is a fly.*

—Julie Biggs, city attorney, Colton, California[1]

On September 23, 1993, the Delhi sands flower-loving fly was listed in
the *Federal Register* as an endangered species, the first fly to be listed as
such. However, the fly's scarcity and size (at approximately one inch long, it
is one of the largest flies in North America) have failed to impress those in
California who see the fly as an impediment to growth and progress.

The U.S. Fish and Wildlife Service (FWS) has concluded that the fly is
endemic to Delhi sands, a fine-grained strata that once covered about forty
square miles. Most of this original habitat area was destroyed by agricultural
conversion in the 1800s. The remaining fragments of suitable habitat continue to be destroyed by the construction of homes, businesses, and associated roads and infrastructure. This extensive habitat loss and degradation
have reduced the fly's range by more than 97 percent. Only five populations
of the fly still exist. All are on privately owned land, and all are threatened by
urban development activities.

The fly's small colony sizes and fragmented habitat make it especially
vulnerable to random fluctuations in annual weather patterns, availability
of food, and other environmental stresses. Small colony size also leads to
loss of genetic variability, reducing the ability of the small populations to
respond successfully to environmental stresses. Finally, small populations

exhibit increased inbreeding, which can allow the expression of deleterious recessive genes ("inbreeding depression").

Only fifty-seven public comments were received on the FWS's proposal to list the fly. Of these, nine supported the listing, forty-six opposed the listing, and two were neutral. In addition, a petition containing forty-eight signatures opposed the listing.

The listing was opposed by the City of Rialto, the Board of Supervisors for the County of San Bernardino, the Riverside County Farm Bureau, the Riverside Habitat Conservation Agency, the Agua Mansa Industrial Growth Association, and four elected officials. One conservation organization and eight individuals supported the listing.

The opposition to the listing of the fly reflects the concern that this action will have serious negative impacts on the local economy. The concern is not unjustified: Federal authorities forced San Bernardino County to spend almost $4 million to move the "footprint" of a new hospital by 250 feet in order to preserve a few acres of fly habitat and create a corridor allowing the insect to move to nearby dunes. Neither the county nor neighboring private landowners have received any compensation for what they regard as a "taking" of their property. The Aqua Mansa Enterprise Zone, an industrial development project expected to create 20,000 jobs over fifteen years, remains stalled on the drawing board because it would destroy prime fly habitat.

DISCUSSION

Deep ecologists such as Arne Naess have argued that an adequate environmental ethic must include a commitment to local autonomy and decentralization. In this case, deep ecology's commitment to local autonomy seems to conflict with its commitment to biospherical egalitarianism since local opinion was overwhelmingly against the federal government's decision to list the fly as an endangered species. Such conflicts—which moral philosophers often call *dilemmas*—are hardly unique to deep ecology: Even hard-core anthropocentrists can find themselves confronted with conflicting duties. But dilemmas may be especially common in environmental ethics for the simple reason that most scholars in the field propose an expansion of the moral community, with the result that there are more duties and interests between which conflicts may arise.

Much of the opposition to listing the fly as an endangered species was based on the negative impact the listing will have on local and regional economic growth. The FWS responded to this criticism by explaining its legal mandate under the Endangered Species Act (ESA) as follows: "In accordance with 16 U.S.C. 1533 (b)(1)(A) and 50 CFR 424.11 (b), listing decisions are made solely on the basis of the best scientific and commercial data available. . . . [E]conomic considerations have no relevance to determinations regarding the status of species." In this regard, the ESA differs in an interesting way from the Occupational Safety and Health Act (OSHA). By statute and by U.S. Supreme Court ruling under the statutes, OSHA is required to consider economic impacts when formulating rules to protect human workers from occupational injury and disease. Under the ESA, as currently interpreted, the FWS is forbidden to consider such impacts.

Finally, the Delhi sands fly case raises an interesting constitutional issue. The U.S. Constitution reserves to the states and to the people all powers not explicitly granted to the federal government. In the case of the ESA, the constitutionality of the law is grounded in Congress's authority to regulate interstate commerce. In its legal challenge to the listing of the fly as an endangered species, the National Association of Home Builders asserted that since the fly exists only within the state of California and has never been traded across state lines, the federal government had no constitutional authority to protect it. The Supreme Court denied the builders' challenge and made the following argument in defense of FWS's listing:

> [When] a species becomes extinct, . . . [it] has a substantial effect on interstate commerce by diminishing a natural resource that could otherwise be used for present and future commercial purposes. . . . Plants and animals that are lost through extinction undoubtedly have . . . what economists call an "option value"—the value of the possibility that a future discovery will make useful a species that is currently thought of as useless. To allow even a single species whose value is not currently apparent to become extinct therefore deprives the economy of the option value of that species. . . . [I]t is impossible to calculate the exact impact that the loss of the option value of a single species might have on interstate commerce. In the aggregate, however, we can be certain that the extinction of species and the attendant decline in biodiversity will have a real and predictable effect on interstate commerce.[2]

QUESTIONS

1. Like Case 8: Matinicus Island, Case 9: Taking Lake Tahoe, and Case 16: The Grand Staircase, this case raises questions about the roles of

local and national authority. What role should local and regional opinion play in environmental policy decisions? Does effective environmental protection necessarily promote centralized regulatory decision making?

2. What role should economic considerations play in environmental decisions? Are economic considerations less important when protecting endangered species than when protecting human employees? Would RCBA (risk-cost-benefit analysis) be a useful analytic tool in this case? Opponents of the FWS listing can easily estimate the economic costs of protecting the fly: Lost jobs and stalled construction have relatively clear values. How could proponents of the listing calculate the value of the fly? And how could the Supreme Court ever calculate the future "option value" of the fly to interstate commerce?

3. Reread Julie Biggs's chapter-opening statement. Is her apparent preference for "charismatic megafauna" morally justified? Would the issues or proper resolution of this case be any different if the endangered species were a large mammal or an attractive bird? Does the Delhi sands fly deserve the same kind of concern as the mountain gorilla (see Case 1: Gorilla Rangers)?

4. The fly's small range and population make it particularly susceptible to extinction because of natural events, such as variation of weather patterns. According to the scientist quoted in Case 26: Tasmanian Tigers, humans have an especially strong duty toward those species that human activity has threatened. Since humans are responsible for reducing the Delhi fly's range and population, do humans now have a special obligation to attempt to save the species from such natural occurrences?

5. Have the landowners who have been unable to develop their property because of the Delhi fly's listing suffered a "taking" in the sense explained in Case 9: Taking Lake Tahoe? If so, are they entitled to compensation?

6. The argument of the Supreme Court seems to be this: Since at some point in the future the Delhi sands fly might be found to have a value that would make it an object of interstate commerce, Congress's authority to regulate interstate commerce applies to it right now, even though it is not an object of such commerce. Taking this argument at it face value, is there *any* part of the natural, social, or personal world to which it cannot be applied?

NOTES

1. *Washington Post*, April 4, 1997, A1.
2. *National Association of Home Builders v. Babbit*, 130 F.3d 1041, 1053–54 (D.C. Cir. 1997).

SOURCES

Federal Register 58, no. 183, September 23, 1993, 49881–87.
Naess, Arne. "The Shallow and the Deep, Long-Range Environmental Movement." *Inquiry* 16 (spring 1973): 95–100.

MR. CONE'S
WOODPECKERS

*The red-cockaded woodpecker is closer to extinction today
than it was a quarter century ago when the protection began.*

—Michael Bean, Environmental Defense Fund[1]

In 1982, Benjamin Cone Jr. inherited 7,200 acres of land in Pender
County, North Carolina. For the next decade, he managed the land in ways
intended to benefit local wildlife. For example, he planted chuffa and rye for
wild turkey, helping to restore wild turkey populations in Pender County. To
provide better habitat for quail and deer, he cleared sections of the land's understory by conducting frequent small, controlled burns.

Red-cockaded woodpeckers are listed as an endangered species. They
nest in the cavities of very old trees but prefer a clear understory. By cutting
only small amounts of his timber and conducting controlled burns to benefit quail and deer, Cone made his land more inviting to the woodpeckers.

In 1991, Cone decided to sell some timber from his land. The presence
of the red-cockaded woodpecker was formally recorded, and Cone hired a
wildlife biologist to determine the number of birds. (There were believed to
be twenty-nine birds in twelve colonies.) In accordance with the U.S. Fish
and Wildlife Service (FWS) management guidelines then in effect, a circle
one mile in diameter was drawn around each colony, and within these cir-
cles no timber could be harvested. If Cone harvested the timber, he would
be subject to a severe fine and/or imprisonment under the Endangered
Species Act (ESA).

Based on the wildlife biologist's survey, the FWS ruled that about 22 percent of Cone's land could not be harvested. But Cone was still required to pay
taxes on the land's full assessed value, which includes the value of the timber.

In response to these limitations, Cone has changed the way he manages his
land. In the past, he had clear-cut a fifty-acre block every five to ten years. That
created edge habitat for wildlife and roughly simulated the effect of a small, intense fire, the kind that would start the cycle of succession again every five to
ten years. His land was thus attractive to a variety of wildlife on a sustained basis. But since the woodpeckers were found and 1,560 acres of his land set aside
for them, Cone has clear-cut 300 to 500 acres every year. His explanation: "I
cannot afford to let those woodpeckers take over the rest of the property."[2]

Cone's new management plan will eliminate old trees on the areas he can
still harvest, thus preventing the woodpecker from moving into those areas by
denying it any old timber cavities in which to nest. Eventually, the acres already set aside for the woodpecker will rot or burn, and Cone's land will be
free of the woodpecker—and so will his neighbors' land: After Cone informed
the owner of some nearby property about possible liabilities in connection
with the red-cockaded woodpecker, the owner clear-cut the entire property.[3]

DISCUSSION

The details of Mr. Cone's particular story are quite controversial. The National Wildlife Federation (NWF), for example, has called his story is a "fairy
tale," and the Competitive Enterprise Institute has called the NWF criticisms
"outright lies." What seems less controversial, according to both property
owners and environmental leaders, is that the manner in which the FWS currently enforces the ESA has motivated many property owners to adopt management plans specifically designed to eliminate habitat suitable for endangered species.

Michael Bean, an Environmental Defense Fund attorney who helped write
the ESA, has described these management plans as "rational decisions, motivated by a desire to avoid potentially significant economic constraints . . . [in
the face of] the familiar perverse incentives that sometimes accompany regulatory programs."[4] An official of the Texas Parks and Wildlife Department has
written that the ESA has caused the loss of more habitat for the black-capped
vireo and the golden-checked warbler than it has prevented.[5]

The root problem, according to most observers, seems to be this: The
ESA requires FWS biologists to control how land is used if it is deemed im-

portant to an endangered species. Employees of the FWS determine whether farming, logging, building, or even walking on the land will be allowed. In practical effect, the FWS assumes management of the land on behalf of the listed species, and the owner of the land is required to comply with FWS decisions. But the FWS is neither required nor funded to compensate the owners of the land it controls: In the sense explained in Case 9: Taking Lake Tahoe, FWS restrictions do not count as a "taking" and hence do not require compensation. From some landowners' perspective, the ESA has had the unintended effect of making rare species an economic liability.

Several proposals have been put forward to mitigate this effect, and all are intended to avoid the issue of whether FWS actions constitute a taking. Some advocate property tax credits for landowners involved in long-range habitat protection. Some suggest that per-animal bounties be paid to landowners for endangered species found on their land. Others have proposed that the FWS pay a modest rental fee for land set aside for endangered species.

The issues may be even more complex when public land is involved. Many communities depend on economic activities related to the harvesting of renewable resources, such as timber, from public lands. At present, the ESA does not permit the FWS to consider the social or economic impact that actions taken under the ESA may have on such communities (see the discussion of Case 10: The Delhi Sands Fly). The controversy following the 1990 listing of the northern spotted owl as a threatened subspecies illustrates the problems. Logging was halted on millions of acres of federally owned national forests in Washington and Oregon, resulting in the loss of tens of thousands of jobs and economic depression in much of the region.

Curiously, federal laws do not permit environmental groups to bid for the lease of national forestlands in order to protect endangered species habitat. Only someone planning to harvest the timber can bid in a U.S. Forest Service timber sale. For example, it would be illegal for The Nature Conservancy to purchase timber rights in order to protect an ecosystem and then not cut down the trees.

QUESTIONS

1. Is it plausible to believe that the ESA has had the unintended consequence of influencing the management of privately held property in ways that have reduced the habitat available to endangered species?

If so, how might the ESA be amended to eliminate this unintended effect?

2. Did the FWS regulations imposed on Mr. Cone constitute a legal "taking" in the sense explained in Case 9: Taking Lake Tahoe? If so, was it a taking for which compensation ought to have been paid?

3. Should private landowners be compensated if their property use is limited by FWS regulations? If so, what kind of compensation would be fair? At a minimum, should tax laws be altered so that protected land is not taxed at its full, unregulated value?

4. In the case of public lands, should the FWS be required to consider the economic impact of its decisions on local communities? If so, how can such impacts be balanced against vital ecological values, such as biodiversity and species preservation? Should communities adversely impacted by FWS actions be compensated in some way?

5. Should individuals or groups concerned to protect particular public lands be permitted to purchase the right to harvest timber on those lands even if they do not intend to use the right?

6. Note that Mr. Cone was employing ecologically sound forestry practices to improve the habitat his land provided to wildlife. When deciding what restrictions to impose on a particular parcel of land, should the FWS take into consideration whether the owner has been a "good actor" on environmental issues? (On this issue, compare the WWOS's regulatory strategies as described in Case 37: DRUMET Poland—A Different Approach.)

NOTES

1. Transcript of a talk by Michael Bean at a U.S. Fish and Wildlife Service seminar, November 3, 1994, Marymount University, Arlington, Virginia.

2. Ike C. Sugg, "Ecosystem Babbitt-Babble," *Wall Street Journal*, April 2, 1993, A12.

3. Lee Ann Welch, "Property Rights Conflicts under the Endangered Species Act: Protection of the Red-Cockaded Woodpecker," PERC Working Paper no. 94-12 (Bozeman, Mont.: Political Economy Research Center, 1994), 47.

4. Transcript of a talk by Michael Bean.

5. Larry McKinney, "Reauthorizing the Endangered Species Act—Incentives for Rural Landowners," in *Building Economic Incentives into the Endangered Species Act*, ed. Wendy Hudson (Washington, D.C.: Defenders of Wildlife, May 1994), 74.

SOURCES

Bean, Michael. Transcript of a talk by Michael Bean at a U.S. Fish and Wildlife Service seminar, November 3, 1994, Marymount University, Arlington, Virginia.

Kostyak, John, and Suzanna Jones. "Statement of the National Wildlife Federation on Reauthorization of the Endangered Species Act," for the Subcommittee on Clean Water, Fisheries and Wildlife of the Senate Committee on Environment and Public Works, October 20, 1994.

16 U.S.C. § 1536(e)–(h); *Endangered Species Act* § 7(e)–(h).

12

THE GOD SQUAD

The Endangered Species Act (ESA) was adopted by Congress and signed by President Nixon in 1973. A little less than two years later, it became the center of a major controversy. In 1975, the snail darter was listed as an endangered species, and a population of the endangered fish was promptly discovered in the Little Tennessee River, smack dab in the middle of the site on which the Tellico Dam was being constructed by the Tennessee Valley Authority (TVA).

Environmental groups immediately sued the TVA, using the ESA as a lever to stop construction of the Tellico Dam. Eventually, the case went to the U.S. Supreme Court, and in June 1978, the Court upheld the injunction stopping the dam. In its finding that the ESA prohibited any federal action that would harm the fish, the Court looked to the plain meaning of the ESA. In unambiguous language, the law prohibited any federal action that would "jeopardize the continued existence . . . or result in the destruction or modification of habitat" of an endangered species. The Court's decision concluded that "Congress intended endangered species to be afforded the highest of priorities." To the delight of environmentalists and many local residents, the dam seemed dead. The $100 million that had already been spent on construction would be lost to protect a two-inch-long bottom-dwelling fish.

Their judicial options now exhausted, proponents of the dam turned to Congress, asking that it change the law. It did. Within months, Congress amended the ESA to create a special "Exemptions Committee" since known as the "God Squad." This committee was statutorily empowered to declare projects exempt from the strict requirements of the ESA. The God Squad has at least seven members: 1) the secretary of agriculture; 2) the secretary of the Army, on behalf of the Army Corps of Engineers, which is responsible for permitting dams; 3) the chairman of the Council of Economic Advisors; 4) the administrator of the Environmental Protection Agency; 5) the secretary of the interior; 6) the administrator of the National Oceanic and Atmospheric Administration; and 7) a representative, to be appointed by the president, from each state affected by the project in question.

The God Squad process was straightforward. The committee was charged with holding a hearing and determining whether a particular project should be exempted from the ESA. In order to grant the exemption, five of the seven committee members had to agree to each of the following four findings:

1. There are no reasonable and prudent alternatives to the proposed project or action.
2. The benefits of such action clearly outweigh the benefits of alternative courses of action consistent with conserving the species or its critical habitat, and such action is in the public interest.
3. The action is of regional or national significance.
4. Neither the federal agency concerned nor the exemption applicant made any irreversible or irretrievable commitment of resources prohibited by subsection (d) of this section.

In the end, again to the delight of environmentalists and many local residents, the God Squad determined that an exemption was not warranted for the Tellico Dam, largely because of the very unfavorable economics of the project. (The Army Corps of Engineers had ranked the site as one of the least favorable in the entire Tennessee valley system.) Not to be denied, dam proponents went back to Congress, which passed a special law specifically exempting the Tellico Dam project from federal environmental regulations.

DISCUSSION

The large majority of expert commentators who have examined the Tellico case have concluded that it was a case of political power triumphing over both good economics and good ecology. The Army Corps did not want to build the dam. Local residents and national environmental groups opposed it. Two very powerful senators promoted it—and got it. It is now known as well that the snail darter thrives in many other habitats: The dam did not threaten its continued existence.

The God Squad still exists but meets only infrequently. On average, it hears fewer than one appeal per year. In part, this is due to the way in which the amendments that created it were drafted, as only a major project can be brought before it. In part, it is a reflection of the infrequency with which officials who administer the ESA are willing to stop federal projects.

QUESTIONS

Other cases in this volume that raise questions about or under the ESA are Case 5: Yellowstone Wolves, Case 10: The Delhi Sands Fly, and Case 11: Mr. Cone's Woodpeckers.

1. Suppose that economic considerations actually had favored the dam—that it would generate electricity at favorable costs, create local jobs, and so on. Suppose also that building the damn really would have eliminated the snail darter's last habitat. Under these suppositions, the God Squad probably would have approved the project. Should it have? Should economic factors be allowed to override the continued existence of a species? Would it matter whether the species was an insect, a fish, or a primate?

2. Look carefully at the list of officials who make up the God Squad. Does it include all the most relevant decision makers? Does it seem biased either toward or against upholding the ESA? If you had drafted the amendments creating the committee, would you have defined its membership differently?

3. All seven committee members are presidential appointees, although only one is chosen by the president for the specific purpose of serving on the God Squad. Should one person have so much influence over this process?

4. The development projects discussed in Case 10: The Delhi Sands Fly involve municipal, county, and state government actions but no federal government action. Accordingly, the projects cannot be brought to the God Squad. Is it fair that only the federal government can appeal for an exemption from ESA requirements?

SOURCES

Deutsch, Stuart L., and A. Dan Tarlock, eds. *Land Use & Environment Law Review.* Vol. 19, 1988. Deerfield, Ill.: Clark, Boardman, Callaghan, 1990.

McKinney, Larry. "Reauthorizing the Endangered Species Act—Incentives for Rural Landowners." In *Building Economic Incentives into the Endangered Species Act.* Edited by Wendy Hudson. Washington, D.C.: Defenders of Wildlife, May 1994, 1–17.

National Wildlife Federation. *Fairy Tales and Facts about Environmental Protection.* Washington, D.C.: National Wildlife Federation, February 1994.

Stroup, Richard L. *Endangered Species Act: Making Innocent Species the Enemy.* PERC Policy Series, ed. Jane S. Shaw, no. PS-3, April 1995. Available at www.perc.org/publications/policyseries/endangered_full.html.

Sugg, Ike C. "Ecosystem Babbitt-Babble." *Wall Street Journal,* April 2, 1993, A12.

Tennessee Valley Authority v. Hill, 437 U.S. 153 (1978).

Welch, Lee Ann. "Property Rights Conflicts under the Endangered Species Act: Protection of the Red-Cockaded Woodpecker." PERC Working Paper no. 94-12. Bozeman, Mont.: Political Economy Research Center, 1994.

13

THE JOHN DAY DAM

Construction of the John Day Dam began in July 1958 and was completed in 1971 at a cost of $511 million. Above it, Lake Umatilla now extends seventy-six miles to the foot of McNary Dam; below it, Lake Celilo stretches twenty-five miles to the Dalles Dam. John Day was the last of the major Columbia/Snake River dams to be completed. Lake Umatilla drowned out the last navigational hazards on the lower Columbia, opening it and the Snake to barge and boat traffic from the Pacific Ocean all the way to Lewiston, Idaho.

Some of the environmental benefits of the John Day are obvious and easy to quantify. Its 2.2-million-kilowatt powerhouse produces enough electricity to meet the needs of two cities the size of Seattle. A modern coal-fired generating plant with the same capacity would burn more than 80,000 railway cars of coal per year, in the process releasing more than 40,000 tons of fly ash, 400,000 tons of sulfur dioxide, and about 80,000 tons of nitrogen oxides (all *after* antipollution scrubbing) into the atmosphere. It would also produce a small mountain of coal ash.

As part of the Columbia/Snake inland waterway system, the John Day also makes possible huge fossil fuel economies in transportation: A single four-barge tow carries 500,000 bushels of grain, 15,000 tons of freight, or 3.5 million gallons of liquid. Moving the same load over land would require 538 fully loaded tractor-trailer trucks or two trains, each pulling 71 fully loaded jumbo cars. Each year, barge traffic on the Columbia/Snake River system carries tens of millions of tons of grain, lumber, and other goods.

Nevertheless, the John Day is now at the center of a major environmental controversy involving energy policy, species preservation, restoration ecology, tribal treaty rights, and agricultural irrigation policy. In a nutshell, many experts are now asking: Is it time to take the John Day down?

The John Day, like the other Columbia and Snake dams, interferes with salmon runs in two distinct and synergistic ways. The first set of problems are mechanical. Despite fish ladders and other accommodations, the dams make it more difficult for salmon to migrate upriver to their spawning grounds. Powerhouse turbines also kill many young salmon migrating downriver to the ocean. The second set of problems are ecological: The large lakes behind the dams drown many of the sandbars on which the salmon spawn. The net result is that fewer fish are able to reach their spawning grounds and, on reaching them, find fewer places to spawn. On the ecological side, it is the John Day, with its seventy-six-mile impound lake, that has drowned the longest stretch of spawning grounds.

Before 1980, policy discussions concerning the operation and environmental impacts of the Columbia River dams were dominated by agricultural and industrial voices. However, increasing concern about the plight of the salmon led to the passage of the 1980 Northwest Power Act. The act's purposes were to open Columbia policy discussions to a broader range of constituencies, to promote resource conservation and alternative energy generation, and to rebuild the salmon runs on the Columbia. Following the act's passage, new policies were implemented to help curb the decline of the salmon runs without drastically altering dam operation. Hatcheries were built to replenish the fish stocks in the rivers, and efforts were made to "bus" migrating fish around the dams in barges. By 1997, it was clear that both efforts were expensive failures. In the terse summary of the Independent Science Advisory Board to the Northwest Power Planning Council, "The Columbia Basin's web of more than 90 fish hatcheries—at a cost to the region of more than $700 million—is not working. . . . [T]he practice of driving the fish around the dams in barges—at a cost of $4 million annually—is failing."[1] Biologists also worry that the hatchery programs, which now account for more than half the adult salmon returning to the Columbia, have reduced the fish's genetic diversity. By 2000, few could or did dissent from the experts' consensus: Despite all efforts to help the salmon coexist with the dams, the fish were losing—and badly.

Salmon-count data are complex, variable, and, in any individual year, often surprising.[2] Nevertheless, the general trend of salmon counts going through the fish ladders at the John Day and its sister dams seems clear. Coho counts, which averaged about 28,000 from 1968 through 1971, averaged only 4,830 from 1989 through 1998—an 83 percent drop. For the same periods, average chinook counts have dropped from 231,500 to 143, 701 (a 38 percent drop) and sockeye counts from 69,500 to 36,736 (a 47 percent drop). Average steelhead counts increased by 35 percent, from 101,500 to 137,363.

Tribal groups have long pressed their fishing rights in the context of discussions of the dams. The decline of the salmon is a disappointment to sport fisherman and an outrage to environmentalists. But to the region's Native American tribes, who were granted sovereign treaty rights to fish the river, it is also a cultural injury, an economic disaster, and a historical injustice. Under the provisions of the 1980 Northwest Power Act, combined with growing environmental concern and accumulating scientific data, the tribe's voices began to have an impact.

And so it is that today, in response to the question, Is it time to take the John Day down?, a growing coalition of experts, Native Americans, and ordinary citizens responds yes.

The proposed restoration project would involve drawing down Lake Umatilla and then completely breaching the central sections of the John Day. As a restoration ecology project, it would be as radical as anything ever undertaken in the United States. By eliminating a major dam from the Columbia/Snake system, it would make it easier for salmon to migrate upriver, and by restoring seventy-six miles of currently drowned spawning grounds, it would significantly assist the fish's ultimate survival and recovery—with many positive social and economic impacts. Tribal groups, who have long pressed their claims under treaty agreements, look forward to restored salmon runs.

But other impacts of the proposed restoration will be very broad indeed and difficult to predict with any confidence. The Columbia basin ecosystem will be altered in ways that affect many species beyond the salmon. Regional agriculture, which is almost completely dependent on irrigation water drawn from the Columbia, is certain to be significantly impacted. The transportation of millions of tons of lumber, grain, fuel, and other items will be shifted from efficient barge transport to less efficient and more polluting overland modalities.

The Columbia River dams produce 40 percent of all the hydropower generated in the United States and 12 percent of the total U.S. electrical energy supply. Nearly two-thirds (65 percent) of the electricity used in the Pacific Northwest is generated by the Columbia River dams. Taking down the John Day will undoubtedly exacerbate power shortages in the western states and accelerate the construction of new plants using fossil fuel. Some regional industries, such as aluminum smelting (which now employs 9,000 people and produces 42 percent of the nation's raw aluminum) depend so critically on the availability of inexpensive hydropower that they may simply disappear with the loss of the dam's generating capacity.

DISCUSSION

Most parties to the discussion seem to agree that something needs to be done to save the salmon. The question is, what? A number of alternative proposals, more or less far-reaching than the plan to breach the John Day, are also on the table.

Environmentalists and indigenous tribes with fishing rights along the Columbia support an ambitious plan that would involve constructing massive new channels around the sides of all the major Columbia dams, draining all the impound lakes, and re-creating 140 miles of free-flowing river. This plan would restore the salmon's spawning grounds and presumably the salmon runs and leave the dams standing (although dry and idle) for possible future use. But constructing the huge channels would cost more than $500 million and deprive the United States of more than a third of its total hydroelectrical generating capacity.[3]

Another option would involve drawing down Lake Umatilla by forty feet. This would restore thirty-five miles of free-flowing river, exposing many sandbars and inlets for migrating salmon and potentially restoring about half the ecosystem drowned by the lake. But even this plan would shut down barge traffic that currently carries an estimated $2.2 billion of potatoes, grain, lumber, wood chips, and other agricultural goods.[4] Biologists suggest that the benefits of this option would be significant but not dramatic: "Salmon runs, currently 10,000–20,000 for spring chinook and 1,000–2,000 for fall chinook, could double—maybe."[5]

A third proposal, favored by a consulting group in Oregon, calls for a surface collection and bypass system. The system would collect fish above the dams and divert them around the powerhouses. This plan would reduce the dams' generating capacity by only 5 percent and, at a cost of $100 million to $150 million, would be far more economical than some of the other proposals. Environmental biologists, however, point out that this plan does not address the problem of lost habitat: As long as much of the salmon's natural spawning ground remains drowned by reservoirs, it is not clear that the salmon runs can be restored.[6]

Industrial groups in the region have promoted fish lifts that would carry migrating fish past the dams. A prototype lift at the Conowingo Dam in the upper Chesapeake Bay was built at a cost of only $12 million and has dramatically increased the number of shad that have been able to enter the Susquehanna River. In 1972, it lifted 182 fish; in 1994, 32,330.[7] By 2001, with the lift system expanded to all the major dams on the Susquehanna, Conowingo lifted more than 200,000 shad.[8] With five dams, proponents argue, the Susquehanna is a good model for the Columbia and a fair test of the system. But critics argue that the shad's recovery may be due not to the lift system but to the impact of antipollution legislation on the quality of Susquehanna water.

Finally, like Case 14: Not on Cape Cod, Case 15: Oil and ANWR, and Case 16: The Grand Staircase, this case illustrates some of the complex ecological, social, and economic issues related to energy generation and energy policy. (For the consumption side of the energy problem, see Case 30: A Breath of Fresh Air and Case 32: The Answer Is Blowing in the Wind.)

QUESTIONS

1. In some respects, hydropower is obviously better for the environment than nuclear or fossil fuel generation: It generates no toxic wastes and emits no greenhouse gases. But it always disrupts, to some degree or other, natural river ecosystems. Suppose that it is ultimately determined that the Columbia salmon runs can be restored only by breaching or bypassing *all* the major dams. What policy would you recommend?

2. Government officials will ultimately make a "best guess" between the several restoration proposals outlined in this case. Suppose you were one of these officials. Assuming that you are determined to restore the salmon runs but want to do so with as little economic and social disruption as is necessary, which proposal would you recommend? How would you justify your choice?

3. In evaluating the fish-lift proposal, policymakers will need to determine whether the Susquehanna shad restoration program is an appropriate model for the Columbia salmon restoration program. What kind of information would be needed to settle this question? If we do not have that information now, how should policymakers proceed in its absence?

4. Columbia salmon were hard hit by energy shortages in California in 2000 and 2001. The federal salmon recovery plan normally requires that millions of gallons of water be diverted from the powerhouses and sent over dam spillways every spring and summer when salmon are migrating downstream so that the fish will not be killed by power-house turbines. However, from 2000 to 2002, the Bonneville Power Administration (BPA) sharply curtailed dam spills in order to maximize power production in response to severe energy shortages in California. Did the BPA make the proper decision, or should it have stuck to the recovery plan and denied California the power even if this meant regional blackouts?

5. Dams not only destroy habitat but also create it. Although salmon habitat was substantially impaired by the dam, new habitat for water-fowl (such as the great blue heron, which now thrives on Lake Umatilla) is created by the impoundment lakes. Should this new habitat and the species it serves be given any consideration when deciding whether to drain the reservoirs?

6. Is it morally important that the salmon's habitat has been damaged by human action? If aquatic species were threatened by dams built by beavers (see Case 19: Massachusetts Question One), would there be less reason or justification to intervene?

7. Suppose that all the Columbia dams are ultimately taken down. What would be the best way to replace their electrical generating capacity?

NOTES

1. Jonathan Brinkman, "Salmon Failure Forces a Hard Look at Dams," *Oregonian*, July 28, 1997, Sunrise edition, A6.

2. Thus, the June 28, 2002 *Oregonian* included this shocking headline: "After Waiting Years, Anglers Get Chance to Land a Big One!" The amazing return of large numbers of the huge (up to seventy-pound) summer chinook salmon was an almost complete surprise. Steve King, salmon fishery manager for the Oregon Department of Fish and Wildlife, said simply, "We didn't expect this." It is the first time since 1973 (only two years after the John Day was completed) that the summer chinook run has been large enough to allow sport fishing; 77,700 summer chinook were expected to enter the Columbia between June 1 and July 31. But by June 12, 74,000 had already passed the Bonneville Dam fish ladders. Biologists attribute the large summer chinook run to two factors: Heavy snowpacks and soaking rainfalls in 1998 and 1999 made the Columbia flow cold and fast, giving young salmon a safe trip to the ocean. Second, in the Pacific,

the warm, nutrient-poor currents of the mid-1990s have been replaced by cold, nutrient-rich currents, giving Pacific salmon plenty to eat. Also notable is that about 60 percent of the returning chinook were bred in three Columbia basin hatcheries. Unfortunately, biologists do not expect the upward trend to continue. One way to predict the 2003 run is by counting the number of jacks (male salmon that return a year ahead of schedule). The 2002 jack count at Bonneville Dam was 6,400, down from 14,200 in 2001 and 21,300 in 2000. The full *Oregonian* story by Jonathan Brinkman is available at www.oregonlive.com/news/oregonian/index.ssf?/xml/story.ssf/html_standard.xsl?/base/front_page/102526535877662.xml.

3. Brinkman, "Salmon Failure Forces a Hard Look at Dams," A6.

4. Brinkman, "Salmon Failure Forces a Hard Look at Dams," A6.

5. John Prendergast, "Reconciling Dams and Salmon," *Renewable Resources Journal* 12, no. 4 (winter 1994–1995): 13.

6. Prendergast, "Reconciling Dams and Salmon," 13.

7. Prendergast, "Reconciling Dams and Salmon," 14.

8. Data available at http://sites.state.pa.us/PA_Exec/Fish_Boat/shad01.htm.

SOURCES

Blumm, Michael, Michael Schloessler, and R. Christopher Beckwith. "Beyond the Parity Promise: Struggling to Save the Columbia Basin Salmon in the Mid-1990's." *Environmental Law* 27, no. 1 (1997): 21–126.

Brinkman, Jonathan. "Salmon Failure Forces a Hard Look at Dams." *Oregonian* July 28, 1997, Sunrise edition, A3, A6.

Lackey, Robert T. "Defending Reality." *Fisheries* 26, no. 6 (2001): 26–27.

——. "Salmon and the Endangered Species Act: Troublesome Questions." *Renewable Resources Journal* 19, no. 2 (2001): 6–9.

——. "Pacific Northwest Salmon: Forecasting Their Status in 2100." *Reviews in Fisheries Science* 11, no. 1 (2003): 35–88.

Pacific States Marine Fisheries Commission. "When Salmon Are Damned: Problems for the Columbia Basin's Salmon." Available at www.psmfc.org/habitat/salmondam.html, April 4, 1997.

Prendergast, John. "Reconciling Dams and Salmon." *Renewable Resources Journal* 12, no. 4 (winter 1994–1995): 12–15.

Volkman, John M. "Making Room: The Endangered Species Act and the Columbia River Basin." *Environment* 34, no. 4 (May 1992): 18–20, 37–43.

White, Richard. *The Organic Machine: The Remaking of the Columbia River.* Toronto: HarperCollins Canada, 1995.

14

NOT ON CAPE COD

A proposal to create a "wind farm" off the shore of Cape Cod has bitterly divided regional environmentalists and aroused opposition from the tourism industry. Cape Wind Associates, a privately held company based in Boston, has applied for permits to build a cluster of 170 wind turbines on Horseshoe Shoal, which lies under approximately twenty-five square miles of Nantucket Sound. The turbines would be dispersed over most of the shoal and separated from one another by at least 500 and as much as 900 yards. From Cape Cod, the nearest turbine would be more than three miles offshore; from the island of Martha's Vineyard, the nearest turbine would be more than five miles offshore.

In general, the benefits of wind power are clear and numerous. The most obvious benefit is the lack of air emissions from the turbines. In 1999, the fossil fuels consumed by U.S. electrical utilities generated 7,051,000 tons of nitrous oxides, 11,968,000 tons of sulfur dioxide, and 2,191,576,000 tons of carbon dioxide.[1] The carbon emissions are a major cause of global climate change. Nitrogen oxides and sulfur dioxide are leading causes of acid rain. Ozone caused by the reaction between these gases contributes to increased asthma rates in children. Mercury and other toxic metals released from fossil fuel plants bioaccumulate in fish, leading to health impacts not only on human beings but also on those animals preying on the affected fish. Coal ash is a principal source of radioactive radon gas. In addition to eliminating all these toxic emissions, clean-energy projects reduce the risks and impacts associated with mining, drilling, transporting, and refining fossil fuels.

This particular wind farm, if built as planned, would provide approximately half the electricity used on Cape Cod. Its 420-megawatt capacity would reduce the use of oil to generate electricity in eastern Massachusetts by 112 million gallons annually, preventing the emission of 4,642 tons of sulfur dioxide, 120 tons of carbon monoxide, 1,566 tons of nitrous oxides, more than a million tons of carbon dioxide, and 448 tons of particulates.

The project has been endorsed by a number of prominent environmental and public health organizations, including MASSPIRG, the Conservation Law Foundation, the Union of Concerned Scientists, Greenpeace, Clean Water Action, the American Lung Association (Massachusetts chapter), and the Toxics Action Center. It is also supported by many state and local elected officials. A public opinion poll conducted in October 2002 found that it was favored by a slight majority of residents on the cape and the islands and by two-thirds of other Massachusetts citizens.

But opponents of the project argue that although renewable energy is good, the Cape Wind project would be the wrong facility in the wrong place—"a permanent industrial facility in a pristine natural environment," in the words of the Alliance to Protect Nantucket Sound. The alliance has some prominent allies. Robert F. Kennedy Jr., senior attorney for the Natural Resources Defense Council, argues that the proposed wind farm "is going to injure a very, very valuable tourist industry, and it's going to destroy a resource which is really a part of the commons, it's part of our nation's history, and a part of the maritime and the nautical tradition of Massachusetts."[2] Echoing Kennedy's reference to the commons, the alliance argues that no private corporation should be allowed to exploit Nantucket Sound for its own profit.

For some opponents, a major concern is the impact that the project could have on Cape Cod's $1.5 billion tourism economy. Although they would be painted neutral colors to blend in with the sky, the turbines are massive: At their tips, the blades would reach 426 feet above the water and carry flashing navigational lights. At least in clear weather, many of the turbines would be visible from shore both at day and at night.

Other critics worry about the possible ecological impacts of the turbines. The impact of wind turbines on birds and marine life has not been extensively studied and is largely unknown. Both are important issues in Nantucket Sound, which is an important flyway for migratory birds and a popular recreational fishing ground. Critics also point out that the turbines are, after all, large machines that could burn or leak or collapse into Nantucket Sound.

Finally, opponents of the project are concerned about the hazards the turbines would present to recreational boaters and private pilots. Although the shoal on which the turbines would be built is outside commercial navigation lanes (parts of the shoal are only two feet below mean water levels), the area is very popular with recreational boaters. The local branch of the National Air Traffic Controllers Association has warned that the wind farm would be a "disaster waiting to happen" because of the number of private pilots who fly from the cape to the islands.

DISCUSSION

Environmental economists emphasize the importance of considering externalities in a good decision-making process. Externalities are all those costs that are borne by society at large but not by any of the parties directly involved in an economic activity. External costs can be upstream (such as the impacts of extracting, processing, and transporting fuel to a coal-fired plant) or downstream (such as the impacts of air pollution and ash disposal). To the extent that such external costs are not billed to the generating plant, the cost of electricity to consumers does not reflect the full cost to society of generating electricity.

Much of the social value of "green energy" comes from the dramatic reduction of such external costs both upstream and downstream. However, wind turbines have their own unique externalities, including aesthetic, construction, safety, and biosystem impacts.

Clearly, the Cape Wind project would reduce many externalities associated with generating electricity from fossil fuel. Ironically, however, local residents might not experience these reductions. Consider air pollutants: Because the prevailing winds in the region blow from the west out to sea, the cape itself would derive little benefit from reductions associated with the Cape Wind project. All the major point sources for air pollutants blowing through Massachusetts are too far to the west to be displaced by electricity generated in Nantucket Sound. But local residents would experience most of the new externalities associated with the project, such as the aesthetic and safety impacts.

This unhappy distribution of external costs is unfortunately typical of green energy projects: Although total external costs to society are significantly reduced, local external costs are often increased. Thus, local residents who sincerely favor national migration toward green energy sources may feel justified in opposing local projects because they receive few of the benefits and most of the burdens. This is the classical not-in-my-backyard (NIMBY) problem: We may all want green energy, public transportation, and trash-to-energy recycling, but we want the windmills, rails, and facilities associated with such projects to be built in someone else's backyard.

Despite its advantages, some scientists and policymakers are skeptical that wind power will ever be a significant component of the U.S. energy system and argue that attempts to develop wind power have diverted funds from more pressing energy projects, such as conservation. For example, in 2000 (the last year for which records are available), according to the U.S. Department of Energy, wind power generated $\frac{13}{100}$ of 1 percent of all electricity produced in the United States. However, between 1978 and 1996, wind power generators received $900 million in federal subsidies compared to the $778 million in subsidies received by the natural gas industry (which produces 33 percent of U.S. electricity) in the same period.[3]

QUESTIONS

1. The local branch of the National Air Traffic Controllers Association has declared that the Cape Wind proposal is a "disaster waiting to happen" because of the large number of small planes, many under visual flight rules, that fly in the area. Proponents of the project point to the much larger number of deaths associated with air pollution. Is there any fair and rational way to compare the relative importance of deaths from turbine-related airplane and boating accidents to deaths from diseases associated with air pollutants? Does it matter that flying and boating are typically more voluntary activities than breathing?

2. The potential impacts of the turbines on marine and avian wildlife are largely unknown. Cape Wind points out that its turbines will rotate at only twelve to fifteen revolutions per minute, but the Alliance to Protect Nantucket Sound points out that some migrating birds fly in large formations and often at relatively low speed. Scientists have offered conflicting estimates of the turbines' impacts, but none claim to have proven their case. How should decision makers proceed in the face of such uncertainty?

3. Opponents of the Cape Wind project stress that it is the particular *location* of the project to which they object. Should aesthetic impacts on popular tourist areas be given higher priority than similar impacts on less popular areas? Should aesthetic impacts be considered at all? If so, how can they be weighed and balanced against other kinds of impacts?

4. Proponents of the wind farm point out that one of the individuals who has helped organize the opposition is the retired chief executive officer of a multinational fossil fuel company. But the NIMBY problem is hardly limited to an imagined cabal of former executives: No one wants ugly, smelly, or noisy facilities in their backyard (for what seems to be an unusual exception, see Case 33: The Tooele Weapons Incinerator). As U.S. communities and corporations try to build a green energy system over the next decades, how can decisions about facility siting take the NIMBY reaction into account and yet result in decisions that are socially fair and ecologically responsible?

5. Suppose that you were an adviser to the U.S. Department of Energy. How would you urge it to prioritize expenditures between the promotion of green energy generation technologies (such as wind) and the promotion of energy conservation technologies (such as fuel-efficient cars, improved home insulation, and so on)?

NOTES

1. Energy Information Administration, U.S. Department of Energy, *Estimated Emissions from Fossil-Fueled Steam-Electric Generating Units at U.S. Electric Utilities*, available at www.eia.doe.gov/cneaf/electricity/epav2/html_tables/epav2t22p1.html.

2. Alliance to Protect Nantucket Sound, www.saveoursound.org/localopp.html.

3. For a synopsis of some of the critics arguments, see Marc Morano, "Wind Power: Folly or the Future?" Cybercast News Service, April 1, 2002, available at www.cnsnews.com/Politics/archive/200204/POL20020401b.html.

SOURCES

Alliance to Protect Nantucket Sound. www.saveoursound.org.
Cape Wind Associates. www.capewind.org.

Carlin, John. "Environmental Externalities in Electric Power Markets: Acid Rain, Urban Ozone, and Climate Change." Available at www.eia.doe.gov/cneaf/pubs_html/rea/feature1.html.

Emery, Theo. "Controllers Criticize Cape 'Wind Farm.'" *Burlington Free Press*, July 31, 2002, B2.

Energy Information Administration, U.S. Department of Energy, *Estimated Emissions from Fossil-Fueled Steam-Electric Generating Units at U.S. Electric Utilities*. Available at www.eia.doe.gov/cneaf/electricity/epav2/html_tables/epav2t22p1.html.

Sukiennik, Greg. "Debate Rages over Wind Farm Proposal." *Burlington Free Press*, July 21, 2002, B6.

15

OIL AND ANWR

Reports of surface oil seeps on the North Slope of Alaska began in the early 1900s. Exploration followed quickly on the heels of these reports, and by World War II the evidence for significant oil deposits was strong enough for the government to declare the entire North Slope and the oil it contained reserved for military purposes.

By the 1950s, scientists began to realize the biological riches that the North Slope offered and pressed for the protection of the northeastern portion of the area, which was the least impacted by development. In 1960, President Eisenhower created the 8.9-million-acre Arctic National Wildlife Range "for the purpose of preserving unique wildlife, wilderness and recreational values."[1] In 1980, Congress passed the Alaska National Interest Lands Conservation Act (ANILCA), which doubled the size of the range to 19.8 million acres, renamed it the Arctic National Wildlife Refuge (ANWR), and designated 8 million acres of the area as wilderness.

But ANILCA left the fate of the coastal plain of ANWR, called Section 1002, open. The 1.5 million acres of Section 1002 that abut the Beaufort Sea midway between Prudhoe Bay and the Canadian border contain potentially vast oil deposits but also constitute the biological heart of the refuge. ANILCA mandated studies to determine the size of the oil deposits, the nature of the fish and wildlife resources, and the potential impacts of oil extraction projects. ANILCA further provided that an act of Congress was required to open ANWR to oil and gas development. For the past twenty years, Congress and the White House have taken turns proposing such legislation, and each has rebuffed the other's proposals.

There is considerable uncertainty concerning just how much oil lies beneath ANWR and how much can be economically recovered. The U.S. Geological Survey (USGS) estimates that the deposits contain 7.7 billion barrels of "technically recoverable" oil. At a price of $24 per barrel, 5.4 billion barrels would be economically recoverable; at $30 per barrel, 6.3 billion barrels would be economically recoverable. Americans use 19 million barrels of oil each day, or 7 billion barrels each year. Actual pumping from the ANWR field would likely continue for twenty-five years or more, so using the USGS estimates, ANWR oil is unlikely to provide more than 3 percent of the oil Americans consume in any given year. Proponents of development, however, are more optimistic and cite North Slope production as evidence:

> Developing this tiny sliver of land, which would impact but two *thousand* acres (the size of a regional airport) of the 20-*million* acre ANWR refuge, could yield up to 16 billion barrels of oil. This would equate to *30 years of Middle East imports*, and possibly more. (The North Slope, originally thought to contain nine billion barrels of oil, has to date produced 13 billion barrels.)[2]

Another issue is the distribution of the oil deposits. Prudhoe Bay, to the west of ANWR, taps into one large deposit that allows for a fairly centralized production process. According to the USGS, it is possible that the deposits under ANWR are scattered. If so, recovery of the oil will be more costly and will have more widely distributed environmental impacts.

There is also significant debate about the impact that oil development would have on the biological resources of the coastal plain. The biodiversity and biodensity of the area—often referred to as "America's Serengeti"—are astounding for an area entirely above 70 degrees of latitude. In all, the plain is home to 160 bird, 36 land mammal, 9 marine mammal, and 36 fish species. Of particular importance is the Porcupine caribou herd, consisting of some 130,000 individuals, which migrates to the coastal plain of ANWR each year to give birth. The calving sites of the herd fall within the prime development sites, leading to the concern that development will decrease calf production and increase calf mortality in those that are born, thereby decreasing the overall size of the herd. Proponents of development point to the Central Alaskan caribou herd, which calves each year in the Prudhoe Bay region, the site of a significant oil production facility (the Prudhoe herd has actually grown since drilling began in the area). At stake is not only the herd itself but also the subsistence lifestyle of the Gwich'in people in Canada and the interior of Alaska who depend on the herd.

Also likely to be impacted by oil production are the several hundred musk oxen that reside year-round in Section 1002 and the polar bears who den in the area during winter. Because the environment is so hostile at the edge of the Arctic Ocean, even slight impacts on these animals might lead to increased mortality. Finally, the coastal tundra provides an important food source for birds, including several game species, prior to migration. The potential impacts of development on these animals are unknown.

Beyond these potential development impacts, conservationists are concerned about possible oil spills during production. Together, the oil fields on the western North Slope and the Trans-Alaska Pipeline experience an average of 400 spills per year. While some of these spills involve less than a quart of oil, at least one was catastrophic. The *Exxon Valdez* spill in 1989 killed hundreds of thousands of seabirds and thousands of marine mammals while crippling the fishing industry in the region.

Often overlooked in the public debate between conservationists and developers are the 250 residents of Katovik, an Inupiat village on an island within Section 1002. The Inupiat support development of ANWR oil deposits and believe that the project would bring money to their community. Also supporting development are the majority of Alaskans and several large unions, including the Teamsters and the AFL-CIO. All these groups see the potential for high-paying jobs, but here, too, estimates vary widely. The American Petroleum Institute predicts that opening ANWR could create 700,000 jobs, while the Center for Economic and Policy Research puts the number at about 50,000.

On April 16, 2002, Senators Lisa Murkowski (R-Alaska), Ted Stevens (R-Alaska), and John Breaux (D-Louisiana) introduced legislation that would permit the president to open ANWR to oil recovery operations if he deems such operations to be in the interest of our national and economic security. The legislation included a variety of significant restrictions and provisions. If passed, it would restrict surface disturbances in ANWR to no more than 2,000 acres; extend formal wilderness designation to an additional 1.5 million acres of ANWR; ban the export of oil from the refuge (except, in the event of an embargo, to Israel); extend the U.S.–Israeli oil supply agreement by ten years to 2014; impose seasonal limits to protect denning and migrating of wildlife; require lessees to restore leased land to its prior condition; require the use of "best commercially available technology"; require the use of ice roads, ice pads, and ice airstrips for exploration; prohibit public use or access on all pipeline access and service roads; require "no significant adverse affect" on fish and wildlife; require consolidated facility siting to reduce impacts on the land; and empower the secretary of the interior to close areas of unique character or of special importance to the local community.

Only a year before in the House of Representatives, a bill had been introduced to ban development of Section 1002. That bill included the following findings:

> Americans cherish the continued existence of expansive, unspoiled wilderness ecosystems and wildlife found on their public lands, and feel a strong moral responsibility to protect this wilderness heritage as an enduring resource to bequeath undisturbed to future generations of Americans.[3]

Neither bill passed. The future of ANWR remains to be determined.

DISCUSSION

Those who oppose opening ANWR to oil development typically call for measures to reduce oil use rather than increase oil production or imports. One way to reduce oil use is to raise CAFE (corporate average fuel efficiency) standards for automobiles. The Union of Concerned Scientists has estimated that a significant increase in CAFE standards would eventually save more oil each year than ANWR could produce. But recent attempts to raise CAFE standards have been opposed by the White House. Proponents of drilling in ANWR cite the need for "energy security," by which they mean the need to reduce America's dependence on foreign oil. A recent proposal in Congress to require that 20 percent of the energy produced in the United States come from renewable sources (wind, hydroelectric, solar, and biomass) failed to pass. As Case 13: The John Day Dam shows, U.S. hydroelectric generating capacity is far more likely to shrink than to grow in coming decades. And as Case 14: Not on Cape Cod shows, it is one thing to support green energy in theory but quite a different thing to build particular facilities in particular communities.

QUESTIONS

1. Suppose that you had been an elected official in 2002. Would you have supported either the Senate or the House bill described in this case? How would you have justified your decision both to yourself and to your constituents?

2. On paper, the debate over ANWR is a debate about whether to permit development activities on just 0.01 percent of ANWR, 2,000 out of 20 million acres. Are proponents of oil extraction unfair when they frame the question this way? If so, how?

3. The indigenous Inupiat people who live in Section 1002 account for less than one one-millionth of the U.S. population. Yet they have lived in Section 1002 for generations. What role, if any, should their views have in deciding the future of Section 1002?

4. All parties to the ANWR debate claim to agree that at least *almost all* of ANWR should be protected and preserved. Why? Does wilderness have intrinsic value? If so, what is that value?

5. Compare this case to Case 16: The Grand Staircase. Both involve wilderness preservation. Both involve fossil fuel reserves. Both involve tensions between local residents and national policymakers. Are the moral and ecological issues in the two cases the same? If not, in what significant ways do they differ?

NOTES

1. President Dwight Eisenhower, "Creation of the Arctic National Wildlife Range," Public Land Order 2214, *Federal Register* 25 (December 6, 1960): 12598. For the legislative history of ANWR, see Adam Kolton, "Testimony of Adam Kolton, Arctic Campaign Director, Alaska Wilderness League, before the House Committee on Resources," July 11, 2001, available at http://resourcescommittee. house.gov/107cong/fullcomm/2001july11/kolton.htm#N_6.

2. C. Toohey, "ANWR Equals Thirty Years of Saudi Oil," *Arctic Power*, 1 April 1, 2001, available at www.anwr.org/features/ctoohey.htm.

3. *Arctic Wilderness Act of 2001*, 107th Cong., 1st sess. (2001), H.R. 770 (the full text of the bill is available at www.congress.gov/cgi-bin/query/z?c107:H.R.770).

SOURCES

Congressional Research Service. *Issue Brief for Congress: The Arctic National Wildlife Refuge.* August 1, 2001. Available at http://cnie.org/NLE/CRSreports/Natural/ nrgen-23.cfm.

———. *Issue Brief for Congress: Arctic National Wildlife Refuge: Legislative Issues: Updated May 14, 2002.* Available at www.cnie.org/nle/crsreports/natural/ nrgen-29.pdf.

Energy Stewardship Alliance. *ANWR*. Available at www.anwr.org.

Kolton, Adam. "Testimony of Adam Kolton, Arctic Campaign Director, Alaska Wilderness League, before the House Committee on Resources." July 11, 2001. Available at http://resourcescommittee.house.gov/107cong/fullcomm/2001july11/kolton.htm#N_6.

The Wilderness Society. *Arctic Update: February 2003*. Available at www.tws.org/arctic.

Union of Concerned Scientists. "Will Drilling the Arctic Refuge Really Solve Our Oil Woes?" Available at www.ucsusa.org/clean_energy/renewable_energy/page.cfm?pageID=71.

U.S. Fish and Wildlife Service. www.r7.fws.gov/nwr/arctic/issues1.html.

U.S. Geographic Survey. *Arctic National Wildlife Refuge, 1002 Area, Petroleum Assessment, 1998, Including Economic Analysis*. Available at http://pubs.usgs.gov/fs/fs-0028-01/fs-0028-01.pdf.

16

THE GRAND STAIRCASE

Mining jobs are good jobs, and mining is important to our national economy and to our national security. But we can't have mines everywhere, and we shouldn't have mines that threaten our national treasures.

So declared President Clinton on September 18, 1996, when he announced the establishment of the Grand Staircase–Escalante National Monument (GSE) in southern Utah. President Clinton bypassed Congress by invoking the 1906 Antiquities Act, a pre–World War I law allowing the president to unilaterally declare any federal land of historic or scientific interest to be a national monument—to be regulated so as to protect these interests. In effect, with a stroke of his pen, the president had banned mining in GSE.

The designation provoked an outraged response from residents of Utah and high praise from many environmentalists. In Utah, both the president and Secretary of the Interior Bruce Babbitt were burned in effigy. Utah's congressional delegation vowed to repeal the Antiquities Act. Utah newspapers denounced the decision. The criticism centered on two themes: that the president had peremptorily denied Utah's local control and that environmental protection in GSE would restrict employment in an already economically depressed area.

The GSE includes 1.7 million acres of some of the wildest land remaining in the lower forty-eight United States and was the last area to be mapped in the continental United States. The large elevation and terrain changes in the area—from desert to coniferous forest—provide a large variety of habitats and consequently rich biodiversity. The GSE is also rich in archaeological sites, providing information on ancient Native American cultures and early Mormon settlers and containing significant paleontological finds as well.

But the area, though wild, is certainly not untouched by human activity. Small coal mines operated in the area from the late 1800s into the 1960s. Over sixty oil wells have been drilled within what is now the GSE since 1921. Nevertheless, the area's remoteness and the then-low estimates of its resource deposits effectively discouraged more aggressive exploration and exploitation.

That changed in 1996, when a Dutch-owned company announced plans to open a large-scale coal mining operation in the area. Although there were varying accounts of the quantity and quality of coal in the area, most were very optimistic, and local residents looked forward to the jobs the mine would bring.

DISCUSSION

The proclamation establishing the GSE stated, "Remoteness, limited travel corridors and low visitation have all helped to preserve the monument's important ecological values."[1] Ironically, declaring the GSE a national monument has attracted attention to the area, and visitation has since increased dramatically, virtually ensuring that the three previously cited factors will soon be threatened. Even before any new roads or camping areas were constructed, visitation to the area more than doubled.

Utah's congressional delegation is now pushing for the commercialization of the area in order to bring in tourist dollars in lieu of mining jobs. Representative Jim Hansen of Utah seems to enjoy the irony: "What environmentalists don't understand is that this is going to come back and haunt them. So instead of locking this up so only the birds and bees can see it, they're going to encourage a lot of visitors."[2]

The Bureau of Land Management is currently creating a long-term management plan for the GSE. The plan will need to address motorized vehicle access, including all-terrain vehicles (ATVs), new road construction, and permanent campsite development. Most important, the plan must address how to limit the impact of visitors if the government wishes to preserve the ecological values of the monument.

Twenty-eight percent of all the land in the United States is owned by the federal government, and most of it is west of the Mississippi. In the state of Utah, 64 percent of the land is federal. Although these lands are often utilized by local ranchers, the regulations that control the use of the land are written in Washington, D.C. Recent regulatory changes intended to reduce the utilization and degradation of these public lands have led to increasingly strident calls for local control.

President Clinton's designation of GSE particularly angered the people of Utah because they were not consulted about the plan. The Antiquities Act gives the president unilateral authority to proclaim any federal land as a national monument and to devise regulations to protect the historic or scientific character of the monument. One writer expressed the feelings of Utah citizens this way: "We have had it up to here with the Federal Government. The people born and raised down here feel they know how to handle this land better than people in Washington, or in the Wasatch Front [referring to Salt Lake City]."[3]

Defenders of the president's action point out that federal lands are owned by all Americans, not just those who live near them. It is only right, they argue, that the lands should be used in ways that serve the needs of the larger population (and of future generations) rather than the relatively few people who live near them.

QUESTIONS

1. Some would say that the history of the United States is in large part the history of a people moving into a wilderness. Does the fact that a particular area is still wild make it, ipso facto, historically significant to the American people? In other words, in the sense intended by the 1906 law, is the preservation of relatively pristine wild areas always also the preservation of historically significant areas?

2. Like Case 5: Yellowstone Wolves, Case 8: Matinicus Island, Case 10: The Delhi Sands Fly, Case 13: The John Day Dam, and Case 15: Oil and ANWR, this case raises a perennial question in American politics: To what degree should local communities be able to control the use of nationally owned resources? How does one balance the social value of local autonomy against the ecological values of wilderness preservation or resource conservation?

3. As Case 43: Trading Pollutants illustrates, whether a utility burns high- or low-sulfur coal has important economic and environmental consequences, because sulfur dioxide is the major cause of acid rain and is stringently regulated. There have been conflicting estimates regarding the quality of the coal deposits beneath the GSE. Some reports claim that the coal there has extremely low sulfur content, making it environmentally cleaner than coal from other sites. Other reports are skeptical about the size of the low-sulfur deposits. If you had been an adviser to President Clinton, how would knowing the quality and size of the deposits have affected your advice about mining in the GSE?

4. How do the issues raised by this case differ from the issues raised by Case 15: Oil and ANWR? Does the fact that the "locals" in the ANWR case are indigenous Inupiats give them a stronger claim to a voice in ANWR decisions than can be made by the citizens of Utah for a voice in GSE decisions?

NOTES

1. President, Proclamation, "Establishment of the Grand Staircase–Escalante National Monument, Proclamation 6920," *Federal Register* 61, no. 186 (September 24, 1996): 50221, available at www.ut.blm.gov/monument/Monument_Management/Initial%20Planning/Background/proclamation.html.

2. "Clinton Enters Utah Battle over Fate of Wilderness Area," *New York Times*, September 17, 1996.

3. James Brooke, "New Reserve Sits Animosities in Utah," *New York Times*, October 13, 1996.

SOURCES

Baltezore, Jay. "Frustration, Tourism Up in Kane County." *Salt Lake Times*, October 6, 1996.

Brooke, James. "New Reserve Stirs Animosities in Utah." *New York Times*, October 13, 1996.

———. "Clinton Enters Utah Battle over Fate of Wilderness Area." *New York Times*, September 17, 1996.

"Kaiparowits Coal Is Poor Quality, BLM Report Says." *Salt Lake Times*, May 14, 1997.

"Monument Site Isn't Unique, Say Backers of Oil Drilling." *Salt Lake Times*, April 23, 1997.

"Monument Status May Have Put Escalante in Fatal Spotlight." *Salt Lake Times*, April 28, 1997.

President. Proclamation. "Establishment of the Grand Staircase–Escalante National Monument, Proclamation 6920." *Federal Register* 61, no. 186 (September 24, 1996): 50221–27.

U.S. Bureau of Land Management. "The Grand Staircase–Escalante National Monument: Proposed Management Plan/Final Environmental Impact Statement." July 1999. Available at www.ut.blm.gov/monument/Monument_Management/ Initial%20Planning/feis/feis_introduction.html.

Utah Geological Survey. *A Preliminary Assessment of Energy and Mineral Resources within the Grand Staircase–Escalante National Monument.* January 1997. Available at http://geology.utah.gov/online/c-93/index.htm.

THE MAINE WOODS NATIONAL PARK

The northern portion of Maine holds the largest tract of undeveloped land in the Northeast—approximately 10 million acres. The vast majority of this land is owned by commercial timber companies. Until recently, the stability of northern Maine seemed assured: The timber companies had owned the land and provided employment for generations of families. But the 1980s saw rapid changes in landownership and the subdivision and development of thousands of acres of real estate. Now, in an effort to ensure that the woodlands remain undeveloped, a Massachusetts-based group, RESTORE, is proposing the creation of a 3.2-million-acre national park. The proposed park is described as follows:

> The new National Park would encompass 3.2 million acres, an area larger than Yellowstone and Yosemite combined. The Park would restore native wildlife and ecosystems, protect the headwaters of Maine's major rivers, guarantee public access to the land, provide wilderness recreation on an Alaskan scale, diversify the boom-and-bust local economy, and inspire people across the nation to help save the Maine Woods. The Maine Woods National Park would truly be the "Yellowstone of the East." As a vast core wilderness, the Park would anchor a system of ecological reserves stretching to the Adirondacks on the west, the Central Appalachians on the south, and Canada on the north. Management of the park would be informed by conservation biology. Thus the Maine Woods National Park would be a critical component of preserving biodiversity in the northeastern United States.[1]

Not everyone supports the proposal. Maine's congressional delegation has been outspoken in their opposition to the idea. So have most of Maine's leading politicians. Several towns that would be directly affected by the park have passed resolutions opposing the plan.

In addition to overcoming local opposition, proponents must also find funding. The main source of money under RESTORE's proposal would be the federal government. It is not certain what the cost of acquiring the 3.2 million acres would be, but it is likely to be substantial. One woman has used her own funds to buy land in the hopes of donating it to the federal government if the Maine Woods National Park is created. By 2001, she had purchased 8,513 acres at a cost of $2,925,000.[2]

DISCUSSION

The proposed park would undoubtedly provide protection for much of the land within the park boundaries. However, the effect that such a designation would have on the surrounding region is largely unknown. It is likely that the park would increase development pressures outside the boundaries of the protected area. Hotels, gas stations, and gift shops would spring up to serve the substantial number of tourists who would visit the area. The number of visitors would be substantial, as several million people live within a day's drive of the proposed park.

The extent to which the area within the park would be developed is also unknown and depends entirely on officials of the National Park Service. There is no question that campsites and roads would be developed within the boundaries; the only question is the extent of these "improvements" (for a similar issue, see Case 16: The Grand Staircase).

The proposal seems to involve two underlying assumptions: that logging is inherently bad for the forest and for wildlife and that government ownership is the best way to protect land and wildlife. These assumptions are not shared by most residents in Maine.

A common perception is that all logging has a profoundly negative effect on biodiversity. This perception stems from the early history of logging, the effects of poor forestry practices in the world's tropical forests, and the recent media coverage of old-growth-dependent species in the Pacific Northwest. These factors are not as applicable to the situation in Maine. Forests have been cut several times over since the 1600s, resulting in miniscule amounts of old growth. The temperate forest is more resilient and less species rich than tropical forests. Finally, several scientific studies have shown that responsible forestry is not harmful to biodiversity. And the much-maligned practice of clear-cutting is not widely used in Maine, representing only about 3.5 percent of all harvesting.

One method that has recently been employed to ensure that the woodlands stay undeveloped is the use of easements. The Land Trust Alliance defines an easement as follows: "A legal agreement between a landowner and a land trust that permanently protects open space by limiting the amount and type of development that can take place, but continues to leave the land in private ownership. A conservation easement can also be negotiated between a landowner and a government agency."[3] Conservation easements have been employed to preserve open space in America for over 100 years. As of 2000, 6,225,225 acres of land have been protected by such arrangements.

Conservation easements can be thought of as a contract between a landowner and a nonprofit or government entity. The landowner retains possession of the land and all rights that are not given away by the easement. The easement holder controls those rights bargained for in the easement and the right to enforce these provisions. The conservation easement runs with the land in perpetuity, and all subsequent holders of the burdened land must abide by the easement restrictions. Conservation easements typically are broadly written with the main purpose being the restriction of development. Easements may also provide for the preservation of certain features of the landscape, such as riparian corridors within woodland areas.

Conservation easements that restrict development while allowing for timber production have only recently become popular. Most of these easements also attempt to strike a balance between logging and the protection of wildlife. A recent example of this approach is the acquisition of development rights for an area larger than the state of Rhode Island in northern Maine. The Pingree Family Trust placed 762,192 acres of its forest into a trust managed by the New England Forestry Foundation. Development rights were purchased from the Pingree family for $28,142,316, a price that worked out to about $37 per acre. Money was raised by numerous foundations and gifts from over 1,000 individuals.

The easement attempts to balance the production of timber with the protection of wildlife habitat. The protection of wildlife is accomplished primarily through the establishment of riparian buffer zones. This allows management of the forest to serve both timber production in the upland areas and wildlife management in the riparian areas.

The timber harvesting that does occur on the Pingree lands follows best-management practices as established by a process of "green certification." Under this process, an independent group ensures that all logging is done according to best-management practices, in other words, that the logging follows the precepts of sustainable forestry described here:

> Sustainable forestry means managing all our forests to meet the needs of the present without compromising the ability of future generations to meet their own needs. It means practicing a land stewardship ethic that integrates the growing, nurturing and harvesting of trees for useful products with the conservation of soil, air and water quality and wildlife and fish habitat.[4]

QUESTIONS

1. What would be the best way to preserve the ecological integrity of the Maine woods? Should a national park be created in this area? If it is, should logging be allowed in the park?

2. Some environmental groups, including the Sierra Club, are seeking to end all logging in national forests. Suppose that this were to happen and that the Maine woods were to become a national park. Wood would still need to be purchased somewhere, and much of it would likely be purchased from countries with less stringent environmental protections. Should decisions about U.S. resources management take into consideration the impacts such decisions may have on the ecological integrity of forests outside the United States?

3. To the extent that logging on public lands is prohibited, lumber prices will rise. This would affect markets, such as housing, driving up prices and making the dream of becoming a home owner less realistic for many. To what extent should the indirect economic consequences of resource decisions be considered?

4. To what extent should the federal government be expected to continue to purchase land for national parks? Although land acquisition does not come out of the budget of the National Park Service (NPS), the staffing and maintenance of the park would come from the NPS budget. The budget of the NPS for fiscal year 2002 was $2.3 billion. The National Parks Conservation Association contends that this budget is woefully inadequate to accomplish the many tasks that the agency is charged with and that an additional $600 million would be necessary.

Taking into consideration that federal funding is limited, should any new additions be added to the national park system when the funding for the NPS is inadequate?

5. The vast majority of Maine's woodlands are open to some form of recreation, including hunting, hiking, rafting, snowshoeing, and snowmobiling. Hunting, in particular, is an important part of Maine's culture and is often an important component of putting food on the table. If a national park were created in the area, should hunting be allowed within its confines?

NOTES

1. RESTORE: The North Woods, www.restore.org/Maine/overview.html.

2. "Putting Her Money Where Maine's Woods Are," *New York Times*, August 6, 2001.

3. Land Trust Alliance, "What Is a Conservation Easement?" available at www.lta.org/conserve/easement.htm.

4. American Forest and Paper Association, *Sustainable Forestry Initiative Program* (Washington, D.C.: American Forest and Paper Association, 2000), available at www.afandpa.org/Content/NavigationMenu/Environment_and_Recycling/SFI/Publications1/Current_Publications/Best_Management_Practices_to_Protect_Water_Quality/BMP_Brochure.pdf.

SOURCES

American Forest and Paper Association. *Sustainable Forestry Initiative Program.* Washington, D.C.: American Forest and Paper Association, 2000. Available at www.afandpa.org.

Diehl, Janet, and Thomas S. Barrett. *The Conservation Easement Handbook: Managing Land Conservation and Historic Preservation Easement Programs.* Alexandria, Va.: Trust for Public Land and Land Trust Exchange, 1988.

Gustanski, Julie Ann, and Roderick H. Squires, eds., *Protecting the Land: Conservation Easements Past, Present, and Future.* Washington, D.C.: Island Press, 2000.

Maine Department of Conservation. *The 2001 Biennial Report on the State of the Forest and Progress Report on Forest Sustainability Standards: Report to the Joint Standing Committee of the 120th Legislature on Agriculture, Conservation and Forestry.* Augusta: Maine Department of Conservation, October 11, 2001.

New England Forestry Foundation. "Pingree Forest Partnership Conserving Over 750,000 Acres in Maine." November 2002. Available at www.newenglandforestry. org/projects/pingree.asp.

"Putting Her Money Where Maine's Woods Are." *New York Times*, August 6, 2001.

RESTORE: The North Woods. Available at www.restore.org/Maine/overview.html.

Verry, Elon S., et al. *Riparian Management in Forests of the Continental Eastern United States*. Boca Raton, Fla.: Lewis Publishers, 2000.

Young, Susan. "Maine Land Purchased with Eye on U.S. Park." *Bangor Daily News*, July 10, 2001.

18

OLD GROWTH ON
MOUNT WACHUSETT

Mount Wachusett rises above central Massachusetts only an hour's drive from Boston. With an elevation of only 2,006 feet, Wachusett would be a molehill in the western United States, but in southern New England it has long been an important recreational center. The mountain became popular in 1874, when a three-story hotel, complete with access road, was built on the summit. In 1889, the Massachusetts legislature decided to protect the recreation area by setting aside 2,000 acres for public use.

Ski trails and other improvements were added in the 1930s by the Civilian Conservation Corps. In 1962, the state enlarged the ski runs to cover 450 acres and turned management of facilities over to Wachusett Mountain Associates (WMA), a private business that operated the area under a series of short-term land use permits. In 1977, in order to encourage further development of the facility, the Massachusetts legislature amended state law to allow a long-term lease to be written for the site, and WMA won a thirty-year lease for the period 1981–2011. The lease requires WMA to pay roughly 3 percent of its gross revenues to the state each year in exchange for use of the 450 acres of the parkland. In recent years, the ski area has grossed about $10 million annually and paid the state $300,000 per year.

After winning the lease, WMA made substantial investments, significantly expanding the trails and lifts and base facilities and changing its side of the mountain from a sleepy slope to a bustling alpine attraction. In 1997, 400,000 skiers visited the area. The number of skiers who can be on the slopes at any one time is limited by state regulators to 3,325; given the area's proximity to a large urban population, WMA is often compelled to close its gates and turn skiers away.

In order to increase capacity, WMA proposed further expansion of the ski area. At its own expense, it would build two entirely new trails and widen and lengthen an existing trail. By WMA's calculations, seventeen acres of forest would need to be cleared to accommodate the expansion, which would allow the maximum number of skiers to be increased to 4,125. When the required environmental impact analyses indicated that no threatened or endangered species would be impacted by the plan, it seemed certain that WMA would be able to obtain the necessary permits and begin cutting.

Then an amateur naturalist stumbled across a patch of old-growth forest lying in the path of one of the trails, and the project was put on hold while the extent and character of the old growth was studied. The surveys found that there were several patches of old growth on the mountain, ranging in size from over thirty acres to less then ten acres. Facing uncertain regulatory decisions and growing public protests by environmental groups concerned with protecting the old growth, WMA withdrew its original expansion plan and proposed instead to merely expand existing trails to increase capacity. No old growth would be cut.

Galvanized by their successful efforts to protect the old growth, several environmental groups decided to oppose the new expansion plan as well. The groups argued that state-owned forestlands, old growth or not, should not be cut for the gain of one company, namely, WMA. In reply, WMA pointed out that the land it wished to clear was within its leasehold and would not even involve the full 450 acres allotted to it by its agreement with the state. The new expansion plan was eventually accepted by the state.

DISCUSSION

Many readers may be amused by the idea that an amateur naturalist could "stumble across" an old-growth forest in the middle of a very popular ski area. And if one's image of old growth is drawn from the soaring, majestic redwoods of the Pacific Northwest, the amusement is warranted. But the ecological concept of old growth does not depend on size; rather, it involves the history, geography, and ecological characteristics of a forest community.

To refer to a forest as old growth is to make a statement about the extent to which the natural forest community has been disturbed by human activity or natural disasters. In large part, the distribution of old growth in the United States reflects the pattern and history of European settlement on the continent. New England has seen almost 400 years of settlement, and nearly all its forests were cleared at least once during that period. As a result, there is relatively little old-growth forest in Massachusetts. Many of the areas that are now forested were cleared three or four times. As a result of the decline of regional agriculture, there is actually much more forested land in New England today than there was 100 years ago.

The few surviving pre-European forests in the New England are small and fragmented. They support no endemic wildlife species and rarely contain protected plant species. Their mature trees may be quite old, but they are no larger than much younger trees and have no special scenic signficance. Nearly all are on steep terrain or poor soils. In other words, most of the surviving patches of eastern old growth consist of visually uninspiring, ecologically unimportant clusters of old trees that survived merely because they were not hit by a hurricane and were not worth cutting down for fuel or lumber.

Compare the situation at Mount Wachusett to the Headwaters controversy, which occurred in northern California in the 1990s. There, a 7,000-acre grove of old-growth redwoods, known as the Headwaters grove, had been owned by Pacific Lumber Company. The grove was home to spotted owls and marbled murrelets, two endangered species that are dependent on old growth. In 1985, Pacific Lumber, which had a reputation as an industry model for sustainable forestry, was the object of a hostile and successful takeover. The new owner, who had borrowed heavily to finance the takeover action, promptly doubled (and later tripled) the rate at which Pacific Lumber's forests were logged. He also began planning to harvest the Headwaters grove where the average value of a single tree was estimated to be $100,000. After years of long and bitter controversy, innumerable protests and actions by environmental groups (see Case 21: Monkey-Wrenching), and much debate about the endangered species, the federal government finally purchased the Headwaters Grove for approximately $350 million.

Appropriately or not, eastern old growth does not seem to inspire that kind of loyalty, and it certainly does not receive that kind of protection. But at least for now, the old growth on Mount Wachusett seems safe, and some skiers will continue to be frustrated by locked gates.

QUESTIONS

1. What is the most important characteristic of an old-growth forest? Its age? Its ecological characteristics? Its aesthetic value? Its native species? Whatever your selection, how would you compare a

300-year-old stunted patch of forest to a 2,000-year-old grove of red-woods? Do they have the same value? Is the Headwaters grove more valuable than the old growth on Mount Wachusett?

2. Whether a particular forest is home to endangered species does not always depend on whether it is old growth. Suppose that it was your job to help set acquisition priorities for The Nature Conservancy or for your state or national government. How would you compare the value or importance of a second-growth forest that supported several endangered species to an old-growth forest that harbored no rare or endangered species?

3. Does the value of old growth attach to the individual trees or to the whole community? Some of the smaller parcels of old growth on Mount Wachusett are just collections of trees, indistinguishable in any ecological sense from the new growth around them. Is it important to preserve these parcels?

4. Should states (or the federal government since many ski areas sit on national forestlands) be allowed to lease protected public lands to ski areas? Building a ski area almost always involves cutting montane forest.

5. Many ski areas depend heavily on snow guns to provide a proper base. The guns produce noise pollution and drain water from local streams or ponds. In the spring, all that water runs back down, accelerating soil erosion and reducing surface-water quality. How should authorities balance these and other environmental impacts against the obvious economic and recreational benefits that a ski area brings to a particular region?

6. After WMA decided not to pursue expansion plans that would affect the old growth, it was discovered that some individuals had cut their own "extreme" snowboarding trails right through parcels of old growth, destroying or damaging several of the trees. Old growth, by definition, is irreplaceable. What sort of punishment, if any, would be appropriate for the individuals who vandalized Mount Wachusett's rare trees?

SOURCES

Allen, Scott. "A New Look at Old Growth." *Boston Globe*, November 29, 1998.
"Alternative to Old-Growth-Forest Ski Trail Eyed." *Worcester Telegram and Gazette*, March 16, 1996.
California Resources Agency. Headwaters home page: http://ceres.ca.gov/cra/headwaters.html (or http://resources.ca.gov/headwaters.html).

Cohen, Michael. "A Question of Balance—Ski Area Expansion Has Residents Worried." *Boston Globe,* June 14, 1998.

Dawson, Bill. "Redwood Management Pact Reached; U.S, California Cut Deal with Maxxam." *Houston Chronicle,* February 28, 1998.

Diringer, Eliot. "Cutting a Deal on Redwoods: A Tangled Tale of Trees, Takeovers, and a Texas S&L." *San Francisco Chronicle,* September 4, 1998.

Harris, David. *The Last Stand: The War between Wall Street and Main Street over California's Ancient Redwoods.* San Francisco: Sierra Club Books, 1997.

"Illegal Trails Cleared at Mt. Wachusett; Sierra Club Wants State to End Lease." *Boston Globe,* June 7, 1998.

Miller, Norman. "Forest Study Under Way at Mt. Wachusett." *Worcester Telegram and Gazette,* May 1, 1996.

———. "Wachusett Axes Proposed Trail, Ski Area Bows to Furor over Trees." *Worcester Telegram and Gazette,* May 1, 1996.

Monahan, John. "Wachusett Ski Area to Repair Damaged Trees." *Worcester Telegram and Gazette,* November 15, 1996.

Sheehan, Nancy. "East Faces West on Mountain." *Worcester Telegram and Gazette,* February 1, 1996.

"Ski Area Must Conduct Additional Studies." *Boston Globe,* August 30, 1998.

Snell, George. "Wachusett-Area Chamber Begins Effort to Win Ski Area Expansion." *Worcester Telegram and Gazette,* December 3, 1998.

Vannase Hangen Brustlin, Inc. *Draft Environmental Impact Report: Ski Area Improvements.* Vols. 1 and 2. Watertown, Mass.: Vannase Hangen Brustlin, Inc., 1995.

———. *Historical Forest Ecology Report: Wachusett Mountain Ski Area.* Watertown, Mass.: Vannase Hangen Brustlin, Inc., 1996.

———. *Supplemental Final Environmental Impact Report. Ski Area Improvements.* Vols. 1 and 2. Watertown, Mass.: Vannase Hangen Brustlin, Inc., 1999.

19

MASSACHUSETTS QUESTION ONE

In 1995, Massachusetts, the third most densely populated state in the nation, had thriving populations of black bear, beaver, and deer. It also had a growing population of bobcats. According to state officials, these animals had prospered because of wise management by the Massachusetts Department of Fisheries and Wildlife (MDFW). According to a coalition of environmental and animal rights activists, the animals had prospered despite MDFW management. On November 5, 1996, by a 64 percent majority, Massachusetts voters adopted by referendum the Massachusetts Wildlife Protection Act, popularly known as Question One. The referendum was opposed by every state agency dealing with environmental issues.

Question One mandated dramatic changes in the methods used to manage wildlife in Massachusetts. It also restructured the MDFW's governing board. Two of its provisions were especially controversial. First, except for common mouse and rat traps, the use of traps "designed to capture and hold a fur-bearing mammal by gripping the mammal's leg or body part" was prohibited. Second, the use of dogs to hunt or control bears or bobcats was also prohibited. According to state wildlife biologists, these methods were crucial for effective management of fur-bearing animals, and banning them would lead to a dramatic increase in conflicts between the animals and their human neighbors.[1] These conflicts, the MDFW predicted, "will alter the public view of wildlife from an intrinsically valuable part of our world to a pest." (Proponents of the referendum called this the "If we don't kill them, you won't love them" argument.)

Among the harmful effects of the act predicted by its opponents, these four received the most publicity in preelection debates:

1. *Increased risk of drinking water contamination.* Giardia and other waterborne parasites can be spread from beaver feces through public drinking water supplies. This was especially important in Massachusetts, which relied on "soft" technology (watershed protection rather than chemical treatment) to manage forty-seven of its drinking water reservoirs.
2. *Increased threat of disease to humans and domestic animals.* Raccoon rabies and roundworm were among the diseases mentioned in this connection.
3. *Increased coyote attacks on humans, pets, and farm animals.* The MDFW had received more than 100 reports of coyote attacks in 1994, none involving humans. Opponents of Question One argued that the referendum left no effective method to control coyote populations.
4. *Increased numbers of confrontations between humans and black bears.* In 1995, the MDFW logged a record 100 confrontations. Critics of Question One argued that bear populations would soon outgrow their natural food supply, forcing them to scavenge food from human sources and making more confrontations inevitable.

Opponents of Question One also adduced economic arguments. In 1994, raccoons caused more than $2 million in property damage. Deer and other wildlife caused about $3 million in crop damage. And beavers caused tens of thousands of dollars of damage to roadways and reservoirs.

Proponents of the act did not deny that some of these consequences might result *if animal populations increased dramatically*; rather, they argued that dogs and leg traps could be replaced by other, less cruel and equally effective control measures, such as box traps and nets. If these other measures did not suffice in a particular case to achieve "protection from threats to human health and safety," the act would allow state and federal departments of health (but not city or country authorities or private landowners) to use the prohibited traps.

Question One also changed the composition of the MDFW's governing board. Before Question One, the board had seven members. Of these, five represented geographic districts in the state, and each must have held a fishing, trapping, or hunting license for at least five years. At least one of these five must also be involved in some sort of agriculture. Of the remaining two members, one must be a wildlife biologist and the other an expert on nongame species.

Proponents of the referendum argued that since less than 3 percent of Massachusetts residents hunt, fish, or trap, the MDFW board disenfranchised more than 97 percent of the state's residents, including all 47 percent of the state residents who "enjoy wildlife nonconsumptively through activities such as photography, hiking, and bird-watching."

Opponents of the referendum responded to this constituency argument with an economic one: Almost all the MDFW's budget is funded by fishing, hunting, and trapping license fees, and those citizens who fund the budget should control its use.

DISCUSSION

In the few years since Question One was adopted, some but not all of the opponents' predictions seem to have been validated. Coyote attacks on domestic animals have more than doubled, and three attacks on children (none fatal) have been reported. Confrontations with black bears have increased more than fourfold; in some state campgrounds, confrontations are now a daily event. The state's beaver population has grown from 24,000 in 1996 to 70,000 in 2000. There is no evidence of an increase in the incidence of waterborne parasitic disease, but some municipal wells have been closed because of groundwater contamination from new beaver colonies. Some cities, such as Worcester, have abandoned "soft" drinking water technology (such as watershed protection, including beaver control) and built chemical treatment facilities. Annual road repair costs due to beaver activity have jumped from thousands to millions of dollars.

On the other hand, in private conversations, state park and campground employees are quick to point out that almost all confrontations between humans and bears are the fault of the humans: Many hikers and campers are careless about food storage and trash disposal; some even think it cute, contrary to all state regulations, to feed the bears—in effect, training them to invade campgrounds. Road repair costs due to beaver activities will eventually drop as roads through wetlands are rebuilt to accommodate higher water levels. As to coyote attacks, everyone seems to agree that people who live near coyotes should not leave small pets or children outdoors unattended.

QUESTIONS

1. Question One exempts rat and mouse traps from its ban on traps that grasp any portion of an animal's body. No doubt, this exception was politically expedient. But is it morally defensible? A home owner may use a leg trap to remove a mouse from her basement but not to remove a chipmunk from her attic. A farmer can trap rats in his barn but not coyotes in his chicken coop or beavers in his horse pond. The rat, the mouse, the chipmunk, the coyote, and the beaver all suffer slow and painful deaths. What justifies their different treatment under the law?

2. Is it true that the state residents who fund the MDFW should have a majority of seats on its board? In some other contexts, this argument would be plainly silly: Who would claim that 80 percent of federal officials should be drawn from the 10 percent of the U.S. population who provide 80 percent of federal tax revenues? The argument used by Question One's proponents seems equally weak: If the fact that I hunt or fish does not qualify me as an expert in wildlife management, neither does the fact that I hike or bird-watch. But then what *is* a proper procedure for selecting citizen members of environmentally important public boards, such as the MDFW board?

3. City public health and animal control officers in Massachusetts have repeatedly expressed their frustration that Question One reserves the authority to use banned traps only to state and federal authorities. In July 2000, the law was amended by the Massachusetts legislature to give local boards of health the authority to issue ten-day permits to trap beaver or muskrat in emergency situations threatening drinking water wells or pumping stations, sewage beds or septic systems, roads, railways, electrical generation plants, natural gas or telephone distribution systems, or hazardous waste storage or disposal facilities. Why might the referendum's proponents have preferred a centralized management process? Should more authority be vested in local governments?

4. Feeding bears creates "problem" or "nuisance" animals. These bears, conditioned to look for handouts from humans, can end up in conflict with people. The result of these conflicts is often that the "nuisance" bear is killed. What should be the penalty for feeding bears?

5. How are "fur-bearing pests" controlled in your town or on your campus?

NOTE

1. For example, state park rangers had long used leashed dogs to discourage black bears from visiting campgrounds and picnic areas. The practice, although effective, is now prohibited.

SOURCES

Primary legal and regulatory documents and links to a variety of public and private groups concerned with Question One issues can be found on the Massachusetts Department of Fish and Wildlife site at www.state.ma.us/dfwele/dfw/dfw_beaver_law.htm.

Other links and materials can be found at the site of the Massachusetts Department of Public Health at www.state.ma.us/dph/beha/beavers/beavh.htm and the Massachusetts Executive Office of Environmental Affairs at www.state.ma.us/envir. An especially good collection of links is maintained at www.state.ma.us/dfwele/Links/lnk_toc.htm.

20

LEOPOLD AND TRAPS

Aldo Leopold is best known for writing *A Sand County Almanac*, a work that has earned him a reputation as one of the greatest nature writers in U.S. history. In Curt Meine's biography of Leopold, Meine describes an incident that occurred when Leopold was only seventeen and then quotes from a letter Leopold wrote to his mother about it:

> Aldo came upon a trapped muskrat trying to swim to an escape. After much difficulty, he managed to release the muskrat. He took the trap, and continued on until he came to a second trap, this one containing a muskrat several weeks dead. He took the second trap. A week later, Aldo returned and found a third trap and a third muskrat, dead half the winter. [In a letter to his mother, Aldo wrote], So you see, I have the three traps on my hands, which of course I will by no means give back to the person who traps in the breeding season, and much less if he leaves the carcasses to rot.[1]

DISCUSSION

At the time these events took place, Leopold was attending the elite Lawrenceville Preparatory School in New Jersey. Meine describes this incident as an example of Leopold's "ecological conscience." The person who set the traps would more likely describe it as a crime. Young Leopold stole the traps. The theft was not triggered by moral outrage over muskrat killing: Leopold was a lifelong hunter, and *A Sand County Almanac* abounds with tales of hunting trips. Leopold was upset by two offenses against his conservationist attitudes: trapping during breeding season and letting a trapped animal rot. Both offenses reduce the number of animals available to hunters and trappers who will use them wisely.

QUESTIONS

1. Compare Leopold's behavior to that of the lobstermen in Case 8: Matinicus Island. In each case, we see illegal (or "extrajudicial") means used to protect a common resource (muskrat or lobster) from excessive or wasteful exploitation. But the lobstermen cut traps only as a *last* resort; first, they send a warning. Leopold made no effort to send a warning; he took the traps as a *first* resort. Even if illegal behavior is sometimes justified in defense of environmental values, should it not be a last resort?

2. Was Leopold's theft morally justified by the behavior of the trap owner? Does it matter that the traps probably belonged to someone whose economic and social status was far below young Leopold's?

3. If you encountered a trap holding a long-dead animal, what would you do? Would you steal it as Leopold did? If you encountered a trap set out of season, what would you do? Would you contact a game warden? Would you steal the trap?

4. If you believe that trapping animals in the wild is *always* morally wrong, would you be morally justified in stealing even traps that are set legally? If you did, would you feel obliged to step forward—like the Sea Shepherd Conservation Society in Case 6: Reykjavík Raiders—and accept legal responsibility for your actions?

5. It is often difficult to make good decisions about whether to attempt to police another person's behavior. If your friends drop candy wrappers or cigarette butts on the ground, do you correct them? Should you? If your roommate habitually leaves a desk lamp burning, do you mention it? Do you unplug it? Do you eventually steal the lightbulb? These are small decisions about small matters. But each of us makes dozens of small decisions every day, and the cumulative consequences of such decisions for the environment may be quite large. To what extent should we try to improve the environmental performance of friends or strangers in our everyday lives?

NOTE

1. Curt Meine, *Aldo Leopold: His Life and Work* (Madison: University of Wisconsin Press, 1991), 37.

SOURCES

Aldo Leopold Foundation. "Biography of Aldo Leopold." Available at www.aldoleopold.org/Biography/Biography.htm.

Meine, Curt. *Aldo Leopold: His Life and Work*. Madison: University of Wisconsin Press, 1991.

21

MONKEY-WRENCHING

One of its best-known advocates and practitioners describes monkey-wrenching this way:

> Monkeywrenching, ecological sabotage, ecotage, ecodefense, or "night work"—these are all terms for the destruction of machines or property that are used to destroy the natural world. Monkeywrenching includes such acts as pulling up survey stakes, putting sand in the crankcases of bulldozers, rendering dirt roads in wild places impassable to vehicles, cutting down billboards, and removing and destroying trap lines. . . . It is not major industrial sabotage; it is not revolutionary.[1]

Whether monkey-wrenching includes major industrial sabotage is perhaps a terminological point. Certainly the whalers (see Case 6: Reykjavík Raiders) who lost ships and factories in Norway and Iceland might claim it does. So might the owners of Colorado's Vail Ski Resort after suffering a $12 million arson loss for which the Earth Liberation Front claimed credit.[2] Still, the activity most commonly associated with monkey-wrenching seems to be tree spiking. Here are some typical reports:

> October 1984, Eugene, Oregon: The *Register-Guard* received a letter stating that sixty-three pounds of spikes, about 1,000 twenty-penny nails, had been driven into trees that were part of a proposed sale in Oregon's Hardesty Mountain area. On investigating, the U.S. Forest

Service discovered that one of the claims was true and spent thousands of dollars removing the spikes.[3]

August 11, 1993, Spokane, Washington: Five Earth First! members were convicted of tree spiking, destruction of federal property, and conspiracy. They were sentenced to jail terms ranging from seventeen months to sixty days and ordered to pay $19,639 in damages.[4]

June 4, 1993, Missoula, Montana: Two individuals pleaded guilty to charges of spiking trees in Idaho and agreed to testify against three others. The men said they put metal spikes in trees to hinder a timber sale in the Clearwater National Forest.[5]

October 1995, Williams, Oregon: Thirty tree spikes were discovered by a Boise Cascade crew after a logger broke his chainsaw on a sixteen-inch spike.[6]

June 28, 1996, Lyons, Oregon: Twelve-inch steel and ceramic tree spikes in logs from the Santiam Canyon timber sale destroyed the blades of a veneer lathe at the Freres Lumber Company. No one was injured.[7]

DISCUSSION

Few environmentalists would question the need for wood, which is a basic, renewable resource. In fact, by replacing slow-growing mature trees with fast-growing young trees, proper logging practices can increase a forest's ability to serve as a carbon sink and thus help slow global warming. Many people believe, however, that the need for lumber can and should be met without cutting old-growth, virgin woodlands. Some of them act on that belief by spiking trees.

Proponents of spiking believe that their actions deter logging in multiple ways. They believe that the publicity their actions attract will help save the forests they defend. They believe that their actions can help embarrass "mainstream" environmental groups into doing more to save forests. And they believe that timber companies, most of which operate on very slim profit margins, will be deterred from cutting trees that have been spiked because of the potential risks.

Tree spiking is straightforward. Nails or rods are hammered into the trunk of a tree at or above the level where the tree would be cut by a saw. Usually, the tree is then marked as spiked, or an appropriate organization (such as the Forest Service or a timber company) is informed about the spiking. The marking or notice is important: If a spiked tree is cut, the logger may be severely injured by a broken, flailing saw chain. For this reason, *Ecodefense: A Field Guide to Monkeywrenching* recommends driving the spikes at a sufficient height to ensure that the logger's saw cannot hit the spikes. Even if a tree is spiked in such a way that it can be safely cut, it will have lost much of its economic value because it cannot be safely milled: When hit by the even faster and more powerful saw and plane blades in lumber and plywood mills, spikes can cause catastrophic mechanical damage. Thus, unless the spikes are removed, the tree cannot be safely cut or easily sold. The ceramic spikes used in the previously mentioned example from Lyons, Oregon, are becoming more common because they are invisible to magnetic metal detectors and hence extremely difficult to find and remove.

The federal government's response to spiking actions was to add a rider to the Anti-Drug Abuse Act of 1988 (Public Law 100-690). With the rider, the law states,

> Whoever ... (2) with the intent to obstruct or harass the harvesting of timber, or (3) with reckless disregard to the risk that another person will be placed in danger of death or bodily injury ... uses a hazardous or injurious device on Federal land, or on an Indian Reservation ... shall be punished under subsection (b).

Subsection (b) spells out the penalties: for damage exceeding $10,000 to the property of any individual, fines or imprisonment for up to ten years.

QUESTIONS

1. Compare this case to the others in this volume that involve lawbreaking: Case 6: Reykjavík Raiders, Case 7: High-Seas Fish Wars, Case 8: Matinicus Island, Case 20: Leopold and Traps, and Case 22: Saving Mink, Killing Voles. In which of these was the behavior justified? In which was it not? What are the important differences between the cases in which it was justified and the cases in which it was not?
2. As noted in the discussion of Case 11: Mr. Cone's Woodpeckers, federal law does not permit individual or groups to bid for logging rights on public lands unless they are in fact going to cut the trees. Does this make sense? Should the law be amended at least to permit such groups to bid on cutting rights when old-growth forest is involved?

3. Is it morally acceptable to spike old-growth trees on public lands? If it is, do the spikers have a duty to mark the spiked trees and notify authorities in order to minimize the risk or injuring or killing loggers? Is it ethical to use ceramic spikes?

4. Do the individuals who spike trees have a moral duty to turn themselves in and accept legal or financial responsibility for any damages that they have caused? (On this point, compare Case 6: Reykjavík Raiders.)

5. Is it easier to justify tree spiking on federal land, which in theory belongs to all Americans, including the spikers, than on privately owned land?

NOTES

1. Dave Foreman, *Confessions of an Eco-Warrior* (New York: Harmony Books, 1991).

2. Daniel Glick and Sarah Van Boven, "Fire on the Mountain," *Newsweek*, November 2, 1998, 46.

3. Barry R. Clausen, "Testimony before the House Subcommittee on Crime, in the matter of Ecoterrorism," June 9, 1998.

4. Neal Hall, "U.S. Tree-Spiker Sentences 'Surprisingly' Stiff," *Vancouver Sun*, 17, August 1993.

5. "Two Plead Guilty to Spiking Trees to Stop Sales in Idaho," *Oregonian*, June 5, 1993.

6. Eric Gorski, "15 Arrested in Sugarloaf Timber Sale Protest," *Oregonian*, September 12, 1995.

7. "Tree Spikes Found at Controversial Old-Growth Sale," *Corvallis Gazette-Times*, July 19, 1996.

SOURCES

Foreman, Dave. *Confessions of an Eco-Warrior*. New York: Harmony Books, 1991.

Foreman, Dave, and Bill Haywood, eds. *Ecodefense: A Field Guide to Monkeywrenching*. Chico, Calif.: Abbzug Press, 1993.

Gorski, Eric. "15 Arrested in Sugarloaf Timber Sale Protest." *Oregonian*, September 12, 1995.

Hall, Neal. "U.S. Tree-Spiker Sentences 'Surprisingly' Stiff." *Vancouver Sun*, August 17, 1993.

Hargrove, Eugene. "Ecological Sabotage: Pranks or Terrorism?" *Environmental*

Ethics 4, no. 4 (1982): 291–92.

Headwaters Forest Coalition. www.headwatersforest.org.

Malanowski, Jamie. "Monkey-Wrenching Around." *Nation* 244, no. 17 (1987): 568.

Manes, Christopher. *Green Rage: Radical Environmentalism and the Unmaking of Civilization*. Boston: Little, Brown, 1990.

Martin, Michael. "Ecosabotage and Civil Disobedience." *Environmental Ethics* 12 (1990): 291–310.

Savage, J. A. "Radical Environmentalists: Sabotage in the Name of Ecology." *Business and Society Review*, no. 58 (summer 1986): 35–37.

Steinhart, Peter. "Respecting the Law." *Audubon* 89 (November 1987): 10–13.

"Tree Spikes Found at Controversial Old-Growth Sale." *Corvallis Gazette-Times*, July 19, 1996.

"Two Plead Guilty to Spiking Trees to Stop Sales in Idaho." *Oregonian*, June 5, 1993.

22

SAVING MINK,
KILLING VOLES

In early August 1998, animal rights activists cut through wire fences of a mink farm in Crow Hill, England, and released 6,500 mink in the surrounding countryside. A spokesman for the Animal Liberation Front (ALF) took credit for the release and defended it, stating, "Certainly some people may disagree with it, but the mink which have been shot and killed, had they remained where they were, would have been killed in a barbarous manner to make fur coats which nobody needs."[1]

As the ALF spokesperson's statement acknowledges, the majority of the newly freed animals never got very far from the farm. Some refused to leave their cages. Many returned to the farm on their own. Cars took a heavy toll of the mink that wandered away. And nearby townspeople quickly organized hunting parties in an effort to finish off the survivors.

The hunting parties were motivated by memories of the effects of prior mink releases in the United Kingdom: Domestic animals, pets, and poultry have been killed by newly liberated mink in recent years. Cumulatively, mink releases in Britain have hurt fisheries and now threaten the endangered water vole.

The spokesman for the ALF said the released minks could be expected to "disperse" into an existing wild mink population already numbering in the tens of thousands—all of them descended from former mink-farm escapees.

DISCUSSION

A recent editorial in the *Chicago Tribune* suggested that those responsible for releasing minks from a mink ranch in Iowa be charged with animal cruelty. The newspaper contended that releasing mink during ALF raids was like releasing aquatic animals into the corn and soybean fields of Iowa: The animals had little chance to survive and would likely die a worse death than their captive kin. "It is true that the fate of ranch-raised minks is to be killed so that someone can strip them of their pelts," the editorial noted, "but does anyone think dying of stress or being run over by a pickup truck is a more beneficent or humane end?"

Minks are not native to Britain. The first animals were imported in 1922 to start a mink farm. When released, the mink are an interloper in local U.K. ecosystems. But since 1922, escaped and deliberately released minks have colonized approximately a third of all British waterways. Predation by the minks is blamed for the localized extinction of indigenous water vole populations. The water vole, known to children worldwide as "Ratty" in Kenneth Grahame's *Wind in the Willows*, has been steadily declining since the 1940s. Experts fear that, under pressure from increasing numbers of minks, it may be extinct within the next decade.

On November 23, 2000, England outlawed mink farming with the Fur Farming (Prohibition) Act. Since that date, "keeping of animals solely or primarily for slaughter for the value of their fur" is prohibited.[2] England has not, of course, banned the keeping of animals solely or primarily for slaughter for the value of their meat. Perhaps the British government believes that it is worse to kill animals for their skin than for their flesh. Or perhaps the government simply fears the adverse ecological impact of additional mink releases.

Several of the cases in this volume raise issues about "exotic" or "interloper" species. In this connection, it may be useful to compare this case to Case 23: Have You Seen This Fish?, Case 24: Australian Cats, and Case 25: Hawaiian Feral Pigs.

QUESTIONS

1. From a moral point of view, are the issues raised by mink farms any different than the issues raised by cattle farms or commercial catfish

farms? Is raising an animal for its fur more reprehensible then raising an animal for its flesh? Are there any persuasive moral arguments that would justify a ban on fur farming but still allow other forms of commercial animal utilization?

2. Exotic species raise a number of interesting and difficult ethical and ecological issues. Compare this case to Case 23: Have You Seen This Fish? Do the activists who repeatedly released mink in the United Kingdom have a stronger justification for their raids than the individual who dumped the northern snakehead into U.S. waterways? Is there a moral difference between releasing animals in order to "save" them and releasing them for other purposes? Is there an ecological difference?

3. Reread the last paragraph of the discussion in Case 6: Reykjavík Raiders. How does the ALF mink release compare to the other instances of lawbreaking presented in this volume? Is it morally justified? Should the mink releasers have turned themselves in to authorities?

4. Given the lasting popularity of Kenneth Grahame's *Wind in the Willows*, it is easy to understand why the water vole—a rodent related to mice and rats—has received so much sympathetic attention.[3] But sympathy and ecology are not necessarily identical. British experts believe that the mink, if not hindered by lethal human intervention, will be able to displace and ultimately eliminate the vole. What kind of ecological factors should policymakers consider in order to determine whether this would be a bad thing? Should humans *always* attempt to prevent interloper species from displacing native species?

5. Suppose that mink had once been native to the United Kingdom but had been hunted to extinction in the eighteenth century. Would they then have a "right" to return, even at the expense of the vole? (In connection with this question, compare Case 5: Yellowstone Wolves and Case 26: Tasmanian Tigers.)

6. Is there a moral difference between raising mink for fur and raising mink to test the effects of polychlorinated biphenyls (PCBs) on wildlife? A laboratory in Michigan used mink to study the effects of PCBs on wildlife—an important question for setting Environmental Protection Agency Superfund cleanup goals. The lab was the target of an ALF attack. In addition to freeing the mink, the raiders smashed lab computers, destroying several years of data. Is it more difficult to justify this attack than to justify attacks on fur farms?

NOTES

1. Fawn Vrazo, "Freedom or Fur Coat? Minks Go Wild," *Seattle Times*, August 12, 1998.
2. *Fur Farming (Prohibition) Act of 2000*, 200 Chapter 33.
3. A recent story on the BBC featured the lead, "Save Ratty! Water voles are part of Britain's heritage," available at www.bbc.co.uk/norfolk/your/extra/watervoles.shtml.

SOURCES

British Broadcasting Corporation. "Pressure On to Save the Declining Water Vole." January 12, 2003. Available at www.bbc.co.uk/norfolk/your/extra/watervoles.shtml.
Chicago Tribune. "Pressure On to Save the Declining Water Vole." August 27, 2002.
Gibbs, Geoffrey. "'Bring in Hounds' Call As Some Minks Head Home." *Guardian,* September 12, 1998. Available at www.guardian.co.uk/fur/Story/0,2763,208264,00.html.
Vrazo, Fawn. "Freedom or Fur Coat? Minks Go Wild." *Seattle Times*, August 12, 1998.

23

HAVE YOU SEEN THIS FISH?

It looks and reads just like an FBI "Most Wanted" poster.[1] Neatly centered around a color photograph of a large, snakelike fish, the text reads:

Northern Snakehead
Distinguishing Features
Long Dorsal fin * small head * large mouth * big teeth
length up to 40 inches * weight up to 15 pounds
HAVE YOU SEEN THIS FISH?
The northern snakehead from China is not native to
Maryland waters and could cause serious problems if
introduced into our ecosystem.
If you come across this fish,
PLEASE DO NOT RELEASE.
Please **KILL** this fish by cutting/bleeding
as it can survive out
of water for several days and **REPORT** all catches to
Maryland Department of Natural Resources
Fisheries Service. Thank You.
Phone: 410 260 8320
TTY: 410 260 8835
Toll Free: 1 877 620 8DNR (8367) Ext 8320
E-mail: customerservice@dnr.state.md.us

The northern snakehead has certainly impressed the media. *National Geographic* describes it as "an air-breathing, land-crawling, voracious predator."[2] A CNN feature began by asking, "What has a head like a snake, a mouth full of teeth, a long dorsal fin, and the ability to live out of water and waddle around for days at a time?"[3] *CBS Evening News* was even more dramatic, leading its July 2, 2002, story with, "No one is sure how many of them are out there, but every one of them is wanted, not dead or alive—just dead."[4] Other stories promptly dubbed the creature "FrankenFish."

Channa argus is indeed an impressive predator. It has a primitive but effective lung and can live on land for up to four days (longer in wet, muddy conditions). It can also walk ("wiggle" would be more accurate) and travel as far as 100 yards across land in the right conditions. It reaches three feet in length and fifteen pounds in weight and grows rapidly. A voracious top-level predator, it has no natural enemies and can consume fish up to one-third as long as its own body. According to experts at the U.S. Geological Survey (USGS), it might be able to destroy or displace the native top predators in many North American waterways. "You're talking about a total rearrangement of the food chain when you introduce a top predator like this," said an ichthyologist with the USGS in Florida.[5] *Channa argus* is also a prodigious breeder. Mature females lay as many as 15,000 eggs and breed as many as five times per year. Both parents guard the newly hatched larvae in a protected nest. But the snakehead, a native of China, where it is considered a delicacy, is not an alien from outer space. It cannot tolerate salinity and thus will not threaten species or ecosystems in the Chesapeake Bay region.

On May 18, 2002, an angler caught an eighteen-inch northern snakehead in a small pond in Crofton, Maryland, about twenty miles northeast of Washington, D.C. Not knowing what the fish was, he photographed it and released it. By early June, the Maryland Department of Natural Resources (DNR) had identified the fish from the photographs: *Channa argus*. It was not the first live snakehead taken in U.S. waters: Single specimens have been caught in half a dozen other states, including Virginia, Massachusetts, and Washington. But when another angler caught a twenty-six-inch snakehead in the same pond on June 30, alarms went off: The second fish was six inches longer than the specimen photographed in May. As a biologist with the Maryland DNR noted rhetorically, "Either the fish grew eight inches in a few weeks or we have more than one in the pond. Our biggest fear is that they'll reproduce."[6]

Aggressive investigation by the Maryland DNR quickly determined that there were exactly two fish in the pond in the summer of 2000. That was when the two snakeheads were dumped into the pond by a Maryland resident who had purchased the live fish at a market in New York. (He told authorities that he had intended to make a soup but changed his mind and released the fish.) After the second fish was caught in 2002, Maryland authorities immediately sandbagged the 100-yard channel leading from the pond to the Little Patuxent River and launched a publicity campaign to enlist local anglers in their attempt to catch and kill any more fish that might be in the pond. The critical question was whether the original two were male and female and, if so, whether they had bred. DNR officials got that answer in mid-July, when they netted more than 100 young snakeheads (apparently hatched in spring 2002 and measuring up to four-and-a-half inches long) in the pond.[7]

The DNR's immediate goal was simple: "eradication as expediently as possible."[8] But eradication would not be easy: The pond is too clogged with weeds to use either netting or electroshock. On July 19, a twelve-member panel of scientists advised Maryland to poison the pond with rotonene. Rotonene, which is absorbed through the gills and disrupts oxygen flow, is extracted from the roots of tropical plants and eventually degrades, leaving no long-term toxins. In tests conducted on July 23 at the University of Maryland, the rotonene was "highly effective" on three- to four-inch juvenile snakeheads captured from the pond. Experts hoped it would kill the adults as well but were prepared to drain and filter the entire four-acre pond if necessary.

On September 4, 2002, DNR employees poisoned the pond with rotonene. Over the next few days, more than 1,000 juvenile and six adult snakeheads were recovered. All were dead, as were sentinel fish released at multiple locations in the pond to monitor the rotonene's toxicity. In a press release on September 17, officials declared, "The application of rotonene was successful and has killed all the fish in the pond." The next day, the DNR treated the pond with potassium permanganate to neutralize any poison remaining in the pond.

For DNR Director Schwaab, the lesson is clear: "Perhaps most importantly, this situation again points out the responsibility we all share to refrain from purposeful release of fish to our waterways and to take great care to prevent even accidental introductions of non-native bait, plants or other species."[9] Federal officials have responded as well. On September 21, 2002, the secretary of the interior added all twenty-eight known snakehead species to the list of injurious species. The listing makes it illegal to import the fish into the United States and to transport the fish across state lines.

DISCUSSION

Invasive marine species can disrupt native ecosystems in many ways. They can decrease the biodiversity of a system by driving native plant or animal species to extinction. They can degrade water quality, contribute to soil erosion, or even clog waterways. Other invasive species that are of particular concern in North America include the zebra mussel (a small mussel native to the Caspian and Black Seas) and the nutria (a beaverlike rodent native to Argentina and Chile). The nutria has destroyed millions of acres of wetlands along the Atlantic and Gulf coasts, the Great Lakes, and the Pacific Northwest by destroying the roots of marine plants that hold the wetlands substrata together.

Nevertheless, exotic marine species are a very old problem. Several studies of major U.S. waterways have reached the same conclusion: at least 139 nonindigenous algae, plants, invertebrates, fishes, and fish pathogens (including the zebra and quagga mussels, sea lamprey, Eurasian water milfoil, purple loosestrife, and common carp) have been introduced into the Great Lakes alone since the 1830s;[10] about one new species a year has been introduced to the Chesapeake Bay system since the mid-nineteenth century;[11] and about one new species per year has been introduced to the Hudson River system since 1840.[12]

So-called exotic, feral, newcomer, or interloper species are at the center of many environmental controversies. In this volume, they appear in Case 22: Saving Mink, Killing Voles, Case 24: Australian Cats, and Case 25: Hawaiian Feral Pigs. But as either a conceptual or an empirical matter, it is not easy to say exactly which species deserve such a designation. Clearly, our first, intuitive understanding of the concept makes some appeal to the notion of human involvement: A species that reaches a new biosystem under its own power or by the action of "natural" systems is not an interloper; a species imported by human settlers is. But this distinction is fraught with difficulties, not the least of which is its implicit assumption that whatever humans do is, ipso facto, not natural.

The intuitive assumption is rather more complex: To most people, efforts to reintroduce species to habitats in which they once thrived (see Case 5: Yellowstone Wolves and Case 26: Tasmanian Tigers) seem very different than efforts to introduce new species to habitats in which they have never thrived—yet both involve human agency. In most cases, this may be because humans were involved in the past disappearance of the species to be reintroduced. But this need not be the case. Suppose that the last regional colony of a particular variety of marmot had been obliterated by the explosion of

Mount Saint Helens on May 18, 1980. And suppose that now, the mountain's alpine ecosystem having restored itself, the U.S. Forest Service were to reintroduce marmots to Mount Saint Helens using animals captured on Mount Rainier. It would seem absurd to regard these reintroduced marmots as interlopers simply because their 1980 disappearance had been caused by natural rather than human action.

QUESTIONS

1. What does this case have in common with the other exotic species cases (Case 5: Yellowstone Wolves and Case 26: Tasmanian Tigers) in this volume? How is it different?
2. When comparing the ethical and public policy questions raised by the cases of different exotic species in this volume, which factors seem most or least important to you? The kind and degree of human agency involved, for example, whether the release was accidental or deliberate? Well- or malevolently intentioned? The impacts of the introduced species on native species, on the ecosystem, or on human social and economic systems? How long the introduced species has been in the ecosystem? The extent to which the ecosystem had already been altered by human activity? The relative rarity or uniqueness of the ecosystem? Why are the factors you select important? Is there a moral or policy theory that explains your selections?
3. Exactly what are the criteria for regarding a particular species as an interloper in a particular biosystem? Are *exotic, feral, newcomer*, and *interloper* simply empirical terms, or does each involve a set (perhaps even a different set) of value judgments?
4. Assuming that the concept of being an exotic species can be made clear, is it also useful? That is, does knowing that a particular species is exotic in a particular ecosystem help us make better moral or public policy decisions regarding either the species or the ecosystem?
5. The person who released the original pair of northern snakeheads into the Crofton pond has been identified and has admitted releasing the fish. But because the Maryland statute banning the release of exotic species has a two-year statute of limitations, he cannot be criminally charged. Should the statute of limitations for such actions be longer than two years? How long?

6. Reread the comments of Director Schwaab. Is the responsibility he articulates ethically serious? Should it be legally serious as well? Should individuals who deliberately or accidentally release an alien species into a new ecosystem be statutorily responsible for the costs associated with control and eradication efforts? If control and eradication efforts fail, how can one be held accountable for long-term damages that may be beyond estimation?

7. The northern snakehead is considered a delicacy in China. Some might say that if it manages to spread and drive out the native top predator species in some North American lakes and rivers, it has only proven itself to be "more fit" under "nature's laws." What moral or ecological considerations justify the Maryland DNR's immediate decision to eradicate the fish as expeditiously as possible? Does it have as much "right" to a niche in the Crofton pond or the Little Patuxent River as any other species?

8. Poisoning the pond with rotonene has apparently eliminated the snakehead. It also killed every other fish in the pond. Is so much destruction justified to eliminate a single species?

NOTES

1. The poster is available at www.dnr.state.md.us/fisheries/fishingreport.

2. Hillary Mayell, "Maryland Wages War on Invasive Walking Fish," *National Geographic News* (online ed.), July 2, 2002, available at http://news.nationalgeographic.com/news/2002/07/0702_020702_snakehead.html.

3. "Wanted: Snakehead," *CNN News Online*, July 12, 2002, available at http://fyi.cnn.com/2002/fyi/news/07/12/news.for.you.

4. "Wanted Dead: Voracious Walking Fish," *CBS Evening News*, July 3, 2002, available at www.cbsnews.com/stories/2002/07/03/eveningnews/main514182.shtml.

5. Walter Courtenay, quoted in "Scientists Suggest Poisoning Alien Fish," *CNN News Online*, July 20, 2002, available at www.cnn.com/2002/US/07/20/alien.fish.ap.

6. Mayell, "Maryland Wages War on Invasive Walking Fish."

7. "Scientists Suggest Poisoning Alien Fish."

8. Eric Schwaab, "Director's Corner," July 2002, available at www.dnr.state.md.us/fisheries.

9. Schwaab, "Director's Corner."

10. E. L. Mills, J. H. Leach, J. T. Carlton, and C. L. Secor, "Exotic Species and the Integrity of the Great Lakes: Lessons from the Past," *Bioscience* 44, no. 10 (1994): 666–76. See also the same authors' "Exotic Species in the Great Lakes: A

History of Biotic Crises and Anthropogenic Introductions," Great Lakes Fishery Commission: Research Completion Report 117 (Brockport, N.Y.: National Aquatic Nuisance Species Clearinghouse, 1991).
11. Mills et al., "Exotic Species and the Integrity of the Great Lakes."
12. E. L. Mills, M. D. Scheuerell, D. L. Strayer, and J. T. Carlton, "Exotic Species in the Hudson River Basin: A History of Invasions and Introductions," *Estuaries* 19, no. 4 (1996): 814–23.

SOURCES

Mayell, Hillary. "Maryland Wages War on Invasive Walking Fish." *National Geographic News* (online ed.), July 2, 2002. Available at http://news.nationalgeographic.com/news/2002/07/0702_020702_snakehead.html.
Schwaab, Eric. "Director's Corner." July 2002. Available at www.dnr.state.md.us/fisheries.
"Scientists Suggest Poisoning Alien Fish." *CNN News Online*, July 20, 2002. Available at www.cnn.com/2002/US/07/20/alien.fish.ap.
Snakehead Scientific Advisory Panel. *First Report to the Maryland Secretary of Natural Resources.* July 26, 2002. Available at www.dnr.state.md.us/irc/ssap_report.html.
"Wanted Dead: Voracious Walking Fish." *CBS Evening News*, July 3, 2002. Available at www.cbsnews.com/stories/2002/07/03/eveningnews/main514182.shtml.
"Wanted: Snakehead." *CNN News Online*, July 12, 2002. Available at http://fyi.cnn.com/2002/fyi/news/07/12/news.for.you.

24

AUSTRALIAN CATS

I am calling today for the total eradication of cats in Australia!

—Richard Evans, member of the Australian Parliament[1]

The common house cat is at the center of a major environmental controversy in Australia. Cats are being blamed for the extinction or decline of many endemic species of animals throughout Australia, a continent with a particularly high proportion of unique endemics (that is, animals that are both native and unique to Australia).

Cats were first introduced into Australia by English settlers in the eighteenth century. At that time, Australia and Antarctica were the only continents on Earth that did not have any members of the felid family. During the nineteenth century, large numbers of cats were deliberately released into the wild in an attempt to control mice and rabbits, which had also been imported to Australia from elsewhere. Today, feral cats are found in all Australian habitats except for a few of the wettest rain forests. Wildlife experts estimate that there are now about 18 million feral cats in Australia, more than six times the number kept as pets. Some experts say they are the most destructive of all the nonnative species in Australia. If Evans has his way, pet cats will be eliminated, too. The only difference between feral cats and pet cats, he said, is "one meal." His proposal would require that all pet cats be neutered, ensuring their elimination within ten years.[2]

The cat's formidable skills as a predator, including its stealth and its ability to kill animals as large as itself, have gotten it into trouble with both environmentalists and the government. Under the Australian Endangered Species Protection Act of 1992, feral cats qualify as a "key threatening process" for two independent reasons: their predation of endangered and vulnerable species and their role as a biological vector spreading parasites and diseases to endangered and vulnerable species. As a result, Australia's Endangered Species Advisory Committee mandated the development of a "threat abatement plan" to protect the endangered and vulnerable species threatened by feral cats.

It seems very unlikely that the final abatement plan will call for the complete eradication of feral cats—not because eradication is regarded as undesirable but because it is regarded as unfortunately impossible. According to the National Feral Animal Control Program, the eradication of feral cats is well beyond the capacity of available techniques and resources because the species is so well established across such a vast area.

There is also some public resistance to the abatement plan, and not just from urban cat lovers. As the draft plan notes, "Aboriginal people recognize introduced animals as part of the landscape and see them as newcomers rather than as feral. . . . [The feral cat] is also a preferred food item for some groups. With the decline and extinction of many arid zone mammals . . . introduced mammals are viewed as a welcome addition to their diet."[3]

DISCUSSION

The general issues raised by exotic species are discussed in Case 23: Have You Seen This Fish? This case adds a new dimension to those issues: the interestingly different understandings of "exotic" held by Euro-Australians and Aboriginals. Case 25: Hawaiian Feral Pigs also illustrates the ways in which native peoples may be more concerned to protect interlopers than their more recently arrived fellow citizens.

QUESTIONS

1. In what ways are the issues raised by this case similar to the issues raised by the other exotic species cases in Case 22: Saving Mink, Killing Voles, Case 23: Have You Seen This Fish?, and Case 25: Hawaiian Feral Pigs? In what ways are they different?

2. Compare the Australian government's description of feral cats to the Aboriginal peoples' description. Can both descriptions be correct? Is one better or more true than the other? Is it morally relevant that, unlike the Aboriginal peoples, the European population of Australia is itself entirely composed of "newcomers"?

3. Are the ethical issues in this case affected in any way by the fact that the cat, unlike the exotic species in the other cases, is a "domestic" animal? Are they affected by the fact that the domestic cat is itself the product of thousands of years of deliberate human breeding?

4. Obviously, Mr. Evans believes that as long as cats are kept as pets, they will escape into the wild and exacerbate the problems caused by feral cats. Is this a sufficient reason to justify eliminating Australia's domestic cats by requiring that all be neutered?

5. In 1996, the Australian government released into the environment a virus intended to kill many of its 150 million wild rabbits. Rabbits were themselves introduced to the Australian wild by early European settlers. Suppose that a virus is discovered or designed that, after extensive testing, seems to infect and kill only feral cats. And suppose that a vaccine is available that will protect domestic cats from the virus. Should Australia release this new virus as well?

NOTES

1. "Australia Urged to Wipe Out Its Cats," *Seattle Times*, October 17, 1996, available at http://archives.seattletimes.nwsource.com/cgi-bin/texis.cgi/web/vortex/display?slug=cats&date=19961017&query=Australia.

2. "Australia Urged to Wipe Out Its Cats."

3. Australian National Feral Animal Control Program, *Draft Threat Abatement Plan for Predation by Feral Cats*, available at www.anca.gov.au/plants/threaten/cats/1.htm.

SOURCES

Australian National Feral Animal Control Program. *Draft Threat Abatement Plan for Predation by Feral Cats*. Available at www.anca.gov.au/plants/threaten/cats/1.htm.
"Australia Urged to Wipe Out Its Cats." *Seattle Times*, October 17, 1996. Available at http://archives.seattletimes.nwsource.com/cgi-bin/texis.cgi/web/vortex/display?slug=cats&date=19961017&query=Australia.

25

HAWAIIAN FERAL PIGS

The smaller ones came with the first Polynesian explorers, crossing the open Pacific at least fifteen centuries ago. They were the first hoofed animals ever to set foot on the Hawaiian islands, the world's most isolated landmasses. More than a millennium later, the larger ones came with European settlers. The smaller Asian pigs interbred with the larger European boars. The new breed prospered—and it escaped. Today, with abundant food, a perfect climate, no natural predators, and no significant natural competitors, *Sus scrofa*, the wild Hawaiian pig, flourishes on all five islands.

For ecologists concerned about saving some of the most fragile and unique ecosystems on Earth, that is the problem. The pigs are prodigious eaters. Their hooves crush native plant species that evolved over millions of years in the absence of any such animal. Omnivores, they eat the nestlings of ground-nesting tropical birds. Their wallows create ideal breeding ponds for alien mosquitoes that carry avian malaria, against which native Hawaiian birds have no resistance. They also love to root (one ecologist has called them "living rototillers"), and wherever they annihilate patches of native vegetation, faster-growing alien plants, such as Himalayan ginger, invade and dominate. Perhaps worst, *Sus scrofa* is especially fond of the cores of giant tree ferns. Tree ferns are a favored nesting place for many tropical bird species but grow slowly and are difficult to replace. Half of Hawaii's native bird species had gone extinct by 2000, and the wild pig is widely regarded as the single most important cause. But for the last twenty years, hunters, government agencies, and environmental groups have been locked in a bitter dispute about how to control the animals. Front and center in the dispute is The Nature Conservancy's Kamakou Preserve on Molokai.

Molokai is the least densely settled of the big islands. It is home to only about 7,000 human inhabitants, most of whom are of Polynesian descent and many of whom have hunted wild pigs for generations. The island is spectacularly beautiful and contains some of the rarest and most interesting ecosystems in the world.

The Nature Conservancy (TNC) owns several preserves on Molokai. Each is home (sometimes the last and only home) to many unique plant and animal species. The Kamakou Preserve was acquired in 1982. It includes lush rain forests and high mountains. It is home to a rare variety of native Hawaiian bird species, some of which (such as the *kakawahie*) survive nowhere else. The preserve abuts other wild areas managed by the Hawaiian Department of Land and National Resources (DLNR) and the U.S. National Park Service (NPS). Collectively, they are a priceless ecological resource.

In the 1960s, DLNR and NPS began a variety of programs to control the wild pigs. Their goal was not eradication but a reduction in numbers sufficient to protect the ecosystem from excessive damage. For the pigs, it was not a happy development: All the control measures (trapping, snaring, and hunting) are lethal. But to DLNR and NPS ecologists, the choice seemed simple: Stop the pigs, which are neither rare nor endangered, or lose bird and plant species, which are both.

Since its founding, TNC has defined its core mission as the preservation of important ecosystems. At the Kamakou Preserve, TNC members and volunteers have spent hundreds of thousands of hours carefully patrolling to remove alien plants, destroy alien insect nests, and so on. In 1989, TNC decided that the existing pig control measures were inadequate: Many parts of the preserve were so remote, for example, that hunters could not be induced to hunt pigs in them. It launched an aggressive new control program using snares. The snares were extremely effective. Between 1989 and 1992, more than 300 wild pigs were killed, and tree fern destruction fell by almost half.

But the snares quickly became controversial. Snares are indiscriminate and will kill a hunting dog as surely as a wild pig. Molokai natives, who use dogs to hunt the pig, soon organized opposition to the snaring program. Snares are also cruel, as animals caught in them often die slowly, sometimes of starvation rather than asphyxiation. In 1993, at the invitation of local hunting organizations, two members of People for the Ethical Treatment of Animals (PETA) secretly entered the Kamakou Preserve. They were Alex

Pacheco (then PETA president) and David Barnes (a PETA staff member of Hawaiian ancestry). Over the next fourteen days, they photographed dead pigs and goats, collected skulls, and destroyed more than 700 TNC snares. Their report, subtitled "Hell in Paradise," is gruesome. It began thus:

> A hunter on the island of Molokai Hawaii came upon a pregnant pig caught in a snare trap, still alive. Maggots filled her open, bleeding neck, where the wire noose had eaten through to her trachea. She was totally dehydrated; obviously she had been there many days. The torn-up ground around her told of her frantic thrashing that had only tightened the noose further. She . . . was one more victim of The Nature Conservancy's (TNC) monstrous program to annihilate the free-roaming pigs of Hawaii, pigs brought here by the Polynesians 1,500 years ago . . .
>
> TNC has set itself up as a judge, arbitrarily deciding who shall live and die so as to recreate the "biodiversity" of a certain moment in time. But the Earth is not a static theme park; it is a living, changing organism, and the animals' capacity for pain and their right to live out their lives are not trivialities, but major considerations. Help us fight TNC's plan![1]

The daily log kept by Pacheco and Barnes is equally vivid. Here are excerpts from two of the entries:

> DAY 6 At one station next to each snare that had been tripped were piles of bones. The skulls were tagged and surveying tape was wrapped around them. . . . Next station, more bones, skulls. More snares TNC had set long ago and just left.
>
> DAY 14 One station had 30 snares, almost all had skulls and bones, the vegetation was gone around them all. It must have been quite a scene when all these animals were starving to death here in "paradise."[2]

Weeks later, PETA launched a national campaign calling for a boycott against TNC until the snaring program was stopped.[3] Later that year, partly in response to public demonstrations organized by PETA and local groups, the Hawaiian state legislature asked (but did not order) that DLNR, NPS, and TNC abandon snaring and use other methods to control the wild pig.

A Hawaiian hunting group opposed to snaring offers this comment:

> The fact of the matter is that the majority of the trapped animals are snared in a manner that allows them to survive for days and sometimes weeks. They are subjected to a living death of dehydration, starvation, infection and being eaten alive by the insect larvae that hatch in the gaping cuts inflicted by the

snare and subsequently spread into the eyes, nostrils and mouth of the captured animal. The dependent young that have no choice except to remain with the mother, suffer the same slow death of dehydration and starvation.[4]

The snares are not monitored, and in most areas managed by TNC, NPS, and DLNR, they are checked only every several months. Between 1995 and 2000, TNC spent $85,000 to develop a radio telemetry snare that would send a signal revealing its location, allowing TNC staff to quickly dispatch snared pigs. The system proved impractical because of the numbers of snares (there are thousands on the islands) and the signal-blocking terrain features.

But along with hunting and fencing (with one-way pig gates), TNC still uses unattended steel snares. It believes that it has no other option. Hawaii's native plants and animals reflect its uniquely isolated evolutionary history. It has only two native mammals (a bat and a seal), no native reptiles, and no native land amphibians. Over time, with no selective pressure from large predatory mammals, some native birds lost the ability to fly. Having evolved on islands without grazing animals, many native plants evolved root and stem structures that cannot recover from grazing. The hoofed animals that were introduced to the island (pigs, goats, sheep, and deer) are especially damaging. According to TNC, "These hoofed animals inflict catastrophic damage by trampling vegetation, browsing, and rooting up the tender shoots of young plants, opening the way for other aggressive invasive plant and animal pests."[5]

DISCUSSION

At the dawn of the twenty-first century, Hawaii's island ecosystems are a still a fantastically rich and complex web of plants and animals indigenous to the islands, plants and animals transplanted by Polynesians, and plants and animals imported by Europeans. But all seem to agree that the ecosystems are not as rich or complex as they were only a few decades ago. And most seem to agree that *Sus scrofa* is one of the important causes driving the change.

In the title of this case, we referred to the wild Hawaiian pig as "feral." This is technically correct: *feral* (from the Latin *ferus*) simply means "wild" or "untamed." It is the term most commonly used in the public literature regarding the pig. But from an ecological perspective, what is most important about the pig is not that it is wild but that is an "interloper" or "exotic" in the Hawaiian ecosystem.

As noted in the discussions of Case 23: Have You Seen This Fish? and Case 24: Australian Cats, the concept of an exotic, alien, or interloper species is more complex than it may seem. This may be especially true in Hawaii, where the only truly native species are those that landed or evolved before the arrival of the first Polynesians. Neither TNC nor any other environmental group intends or aspires to restore a pre-Polynesian ecosystem on any part of the Hawaiian islands. But TNC, with the support of other groups and agencies, does hope, as far as it is possible, to restore a pre-European ecosystem in some of its Hawaiian preserves.

In TNC's view, the pre-European Hawaiian ecosystems have special value—values sufficient to justify not only the time and effort required to restore them but also the painful killing of the wild pigs who threaten them.

In PETA's view, the project could hardly be more wrong: It is using immoral means—a "monstrous program to annihilate the free-roaming pigs of Hawaii"—to pursue an ecologically silly goal: a "a static theme park."

The mostly Polynesian hunters on Molokai have a range of views, but at least three beliefs seem to be widely shared. First, the wild pig should not be eradicated from the entire island. Second, controlling wild pig populations in the ecological reserves may be necessary to save endangered bird and plant species. Third, means other than unmonitored steel snares (which are cruel to pigs and dangerous to dogs) should be used.

QUESTIONS

1. TNC believes that Hawaii's pre-European island ecosystems, to the extent that they can be restored, have very special value. Do they? What is that value? Is it sufficient to justify killing members of interloper species such as the wild pig? Is it sufficient to justify killing such animals slowly and painfully?

2. PETA asserts that it would be better to eradicate the wild pig from Molokai once and for all than to "control" them indefinitely by the use of cruel and painful methods. Eradication would clearly not please island natives, who have hunted and eaten the pigs for generations. Is eradication morally preferable to control? Is eradication morally preferable to control programs relying on snares?

3. Molokai's hunters obviously believe that their dogs are more valuable than the wild pig: They use their dogs, after all, to help them kill the

pigs. Is their view morally justified? To their owners, the hunting dog obviously has more extrinsic or instrumental value than the hunted pig. Does the dog have more intrinsic or inherent value?

4. How do the issues raised by this case differ from the issues raised by the other cases involving alien or interloper species, such as Case 22: Saving Mink, Killing Voles, Case 23: Have You Seen This Fish?, and Case 24: Australian Cats?

5. Why is killing wild pigs on Molokai so controversial but killing northern snakeheads in Maryland so uncontroversial? Both are interlopers. Both are regarded as delicacies by those who eat them. Both threaten substantial ecological havoc, including the extermination of native species. Both can suffer. Is the crucial difference simply the use of snares, or is it simply more acceptable to kill a fish than to kill a mammal?

6. Suppose that the snares could be modified so that they invariably caused a quick death. They would then be much more dangerous to dogs, who are usually accompanied by their owners and can now be freed when accidentally caught. Would such snares be morally preferable to the ones now in use?

7. Suppose that a variety of the swine flu virus could be modified to render it highly lethal to swine but nonpathogenic to other animals, including humans. And suppose that there were a vaccine to guard against the virus's escape into other populations. Would it be morally justifiable to release the virus on Molokai in the hope of eradicating the island's pigs?

8. According to Aldo Leopold, "A thing is right when it tends to preserve the integrity, stability, and beauty of the biotic community. It is wrong when it tends otherwise." [6] If Leopold is correct, what should TNC do regarding the wild pigs in the Kamakou Preserve?

NOTES

1. "A Research and Investigative Report: Hell in Paradise," *PETA News* 8, no. 2 (1993), available at www.halehaku.com/peta.html.

2. "A Research and Investigative Report."

3. As of January 2003, PETA publications still advised readers not to donate to TNC. See Carla Bennett, "Find Out Where Your Donations Are Going," available at www.peta.org/liv/c/23.html.

4. Halehaku, "A Comment on Steel Snares," available at www.halehaku.com/ informationonsnares.html.

5. The Nature Conservancy, "Hawaii's Natural History," available at http://nature. org/wherewework/northamerica/states/hawaii/science/art2412.html.

6. Aldo Leopold, *A Sand County Almanac; With Essays on Conservation from Round River* (New York: Oxford University Press, 1966).

SOURCES

Campbell, Faith Thompson. "Killer Pigs, Vines and Fungi: Alien Species Threaten Native Ecosystems." *Endangered Species Technical Bulletin* 19, no. 5 (October 1994): 3–5.

Halehaku. "A Comment on Steel Snares." Available at www.halehaku.com/ informationonsnares.html.

Modavi, Neghin. "Mediation of Environmental Conflicts in Hawaii: Win-Win or Co-Optation?" *Sociological Perspectives* 39, no. 2 (1996): 301–16.

Mueller-Dombois, Dieter, Kent W. Bridges, and Hampton L. Carson, eds. *Island Ecosystems: Biological Organization in Selected Hawaiian Communities*. Strouds- burg, Pa.: Hutchinson Ross, 1981.

The Nature Conservancy. "Hawaii's Natural History." Available at http://nature.org/ wherewework/northamerica/states/hawaii/science/art2412.html.

People for the Ethical Treatment of Animals. "A Research and Investigative Report: Hell in Paradise." *PETA News* 8, no. 2 (1993). Available at www.halehaku.com/peta. html.

Royte, Elizabeth. "Hawaii's Vanishing Species." *National Geographic* 188, no. 3 (September 1995): 2–37.

26

TASMANIAN TIGERS

It has been almost seventy years since anyone has seen a live Tasmanian tiger. But scientists at the Australian Museum in Sydney are hoping that within a decade the animal will be reborn and new generations will be able to witness one of the world's most intriguing carnivores.

The Tasmanian tiger, or thylacine (*Thylacinus cynocephalus*), was a marsupial carnivore. Two feet high at the shoulders and six feet long from nose to tail, the thylacine was the region's largest predator until its extinction. Its name is derived from the distinctive tigerlike stripes along its hindquarters despite the fact that the thylacine resembles a large wolf more closely than a cat.

At one time, the thylacine roamed the wilds of Australia, New Guinea, and Tasmania. Nearly 6,000 years ago, it was driven out of Australia and New Guinea when the human tribes then native to those islands introduced dogs to their ecosystems. The eventual colonization of Tasmania by Europeans and the introduction of sheep in 1924 sealed the thylacine's fate. A bounty on the animal was instituted by the Van Diemens Land Company in 1830 and by the Tasmanian Parliament in 1888. Although the government bounty was repealed in 1909, the thylacine never recovered. The last known thylacine was captured in 1933 and died in the Hobart Zoo on July 9, 1936.[1]

Now scientists are attempting to map the thylacine's genome and re-create its DNA sequence by using preserved specimens. Their most important resource is a six-month-old pup that has been preserved in alcohol since 1866. Fragments of thylacine DNA have already been replicated, and the researchers are working to create a complete genetic library. Once the genome has been completely mapped, scientists will construct a full set of thylacine chromosomes. The chromosomes will then be inserted into a host marsupial oocyte from which the nuclear DNA has been removed. If all goes well, the fertilized egg will then be implanted into the uterus of a surrogate animal, most likely a Tasmanian devil, where it will gestate. In due course, the cloned thylacine will be delivered at full term by the surrogate.

Even if one or several individual animals can be produced, restoring a viable thylacine population will still be a serious challenge. Because there are only a handful of specimens to provide DNA, it will be extremely difficult to achieve a significant degree of genetic diversity in a laboratory-produced population of the animals. It may also be impossible to train the animals to live in the wild since scientists have little understanding of the social and predatory skills that might once have been taught to thylacine pups by their elders.

DISCUSSION

Mike Archer, director of the Australian Museum, regards the project as an effort to undo past wrongs, an act of morally obligatory restoration ecology. In his words, the project seeks "to redress our immoral actions when we willfully and wrongly exterminated this animal." As to the morality of using genetic reconstruction and cloning techniques, his view seems to be that the *technical means* by which restoration projects are accomplished do not raise any independent ethical issues. Indeed, he argues that we have a duty to employ such means in the interests of restoration goals: "Most people agree that the 'immoral act' was the extermination of the Tasmanian tiger in the first place; to bring it back, if we can, would be to me a *moral imperative* aimed at undoing that black act." Indeed, Archer claims that the project will even relieve Australian national guilt: "The Tasmanian tiger is an iconic Australian animal. It's woven in a complex web of guilt, because Australians made it extinct. We need to lift this burden."[2]

Some others in the government are less than enthusiastic about the project. An official of the Tasmanian Department of Primary Industries, Water and Environment, Parks and Wildlife, for example, is particularly concerned about the expense of the cloning attempt: "Even if cloning were possible, it should be asked whether such effort and expense is justifiable when many other species are currently threatened with extinction, and when we allow the same processes that threaten habitats and wildlife to continue."[3] Neither the technology nor the project are unique; however, a similar project is under way in the United States to clone the extinct Bucardo, a mountain goat once native to the Pyrenees.

QUESTIONS

1. How legitimate is the concern that resource-intensive efforts to restore extinct species will divert scarce resources from environmental protection programs and habitat restoration projects aimed at protecting multiple living species?

2. Is the museum director correct in asserting that Earth's present human community has a moral obligation to undo the ecological damage inflicted by previous generations? If we do have such a moral obligation, how far back into the past does it extend? Many scientists have theorized, for example, that the human inhabitants of Pleistocene-era North America helped exterminate the megafauna (mastodons, giant sloths, and so on) of their time through overhunting. Supposing that sufficient genetic material for some of these species could be recovered, would we be morally obligated to bring them back?

3. Compare the issues raised by this case to the issues raised in Case 27: Golden Rice. Is it easier to justify the use of genetic manipulation to bring back extinct species than to modify existing species?

4. Is the ability to establish a viable population of the thylacine crucial to the morality of creating single individuals? Would it be moral to produce just a few of the animals for scientific and educational purposes even if a population of wild thylacines could not be restored?

5. Some religious groups in Tasmania have accused the museum scientists of "playing God." The phrase is not uncommon in debates about genetic engineering, but what exactly does the criticism mean? Suppose it is meant to assert that there are some ways in which humans should never tinker with nature (such as by using genetic technologies to restore lost species or to create new species). Is there any truth in the claim? Or suppose that the religious groups simply mean to accuse the researchers of excessive hubris. Is the accusation fair?

6. Both this case and Case 5: Yellowstone Wolves involve attempts to restore a top predator species to an ecosystem from which it has been absent for almost a century. Does the fact that the thylacine is extinct raise moral issues not presented by Case 5? Does the use of genetic technologies raise such issues?

7. Do the other species now in the ecosystem to which the thylacine might be restored have any rights or interests that should be considered as the project moves forward?

8. Now that you have read this case, go back and reread the "true but twisted" version in the preface. Would it be professionally unethical for a journalist to write this case up along the lines of the paragraph in the preface? (For related issues about professional responsibility in journalism, see question 3 in Case 35: Bhopal and Case 38: Scientific Integrity at EPA.)

NOTES

1. Department of Primary Industries, Water and Environment, Government of Tasmania, *Tasmanian Tiger*, August 2002, available at www.dpiwe.tas.gov.au/inter.nsf/ WebPages/BHAN-53777B?open.

2. James Meek, "Special Report: The Ethics of Genetics. Scientists Pledge to Clone Extinct Tasmanian Tiger," *Guardian*, May 29, 2002, available at www.guardian.co. uk/genes/article/0,2763,723868,00.html.

3. Meek, "Special Report."

SOURCES

Australian Museum. "Australia's Thylacine: A Conversation with Professor Mike Archer, Director of the Australian Museum." *The Australian Museum Online*. 2002. Available at www.austmus.gov.au/thylacine/archer.htm.

"Bringing Back the Tiger." *ABC News*. August 22, 2002. Available at http://more. abcnews.go.com/sections/science/dailynews/cloning_tasmaniantiger000822.html.

Holloway, Grant. "Cloning to Revive Extinct Species." CNN. May 28, 2002. Available at www.cnn.com/2002/WORLD/asiapcf/auspac/05/28/aust.thylacines.

Meek, James. "Scientists Pledge to Clone Extinct Tasmanian Tiger." *Guardian*, May 29, 2002. Available at www.guardian.co.uk/genes/article/0,2763,723868,00. html.

Tasmanian Department of Primary Industries, Water and Environment. *Tasmanian Tiger*. August 2002. Available at www.dpiwe.tas.gov.au/inter.nsf/WebPages/ BHAN-53777B?open.

Weidensaul, Scott. "Raising the Dead." *Audubon*. May 2002. Available at http:// magazine.audubon.org/features0205/thylacine.html.

27

GOLDEN RICE

Vitamin A deficiency is a serious and widespread problem in the developing world, leading to blindness and increased risk of infectious disease for approximately 400 million people worldwide. In the hopes of ameliorating the problem, researchers at the Swiss Federal Institute of Technology created a genetically engineered strain of rice: golden rice. To create golden rice, the researchers first added a daffodil gene to their rice's genome. Then to enhance iron absorption, the researchers removed the gene that codes for phytate.

The Swiss institute has turned the golden rice over to the International Rice Institute, which will employ traditional breeding techniques to produce rice varieties best adapted to particular geographic areas. These varieties will then be distributed to farmers on an ability-to-pay basis, with those most in need receiving the rice free of charge.

Golden rice will not eliminate vitamin A deficiency by itself. Consumed in normal quantities as a staple food, it contains less than a quarter the amount of vitamin A recommended by most authorities as a daily requirement. But there is no doubt that adding vitamin A to one of the world's most important staple crops will provide health benefits to millions of malnourished people whose vitamin A intake is on the margins.

DISCUSSION

The creators of golden rice hoped that their plant would be easily accepted because of its potential benefits to so many of the world's poorest persons. As one writer expressed the hope in 1999, "Because the potential benefits seem great and the potential health and environmental risks small, . . . the new rice strain may draw less opposition from the critics of genetically engineered foods than other modified crop plants now being marketed."[1] Both the scientists' and the writer's optimism has proven to be naive.

Critics of golden rice, including Greenpeace, contend that the rice is a cheap substitute for serious efforts to eliminate the causes of vitamin A deficiency: poverty and inadequate diet. According to Dr. Vandana Shiva, "The lower cost, [more] accessible and safer alternative to genetically engineered rice is to increase biodiversity in agriculture."[2] Vitamin A, the critics point out, can be found in a variety of food plants, including green leafy vegetables, eggs, milk, and meat. These alternative sources of vitamin A, the critics argue, are being threatened by genetically engineered foods. Proponents reply that the vitamin content of eggs, milk, and meat is irrelevant to the hundreds of millions of poor who cannot afford these foods.

Some part of the debate is clearly political and is being conducted with an eye on plants other than golden rice. To both proponents and opponents of genetically modified foodstuffs, golden rice is seen as the "gateway organism"—the plant that will give genetic engineering a kindly face. Widespread acceptance of golden rice, both groups believe, would establish a legal and psychological precedent that would open world marketplaces to a much broader range of genetically modified organisms (GMOs). Vandana Shiva writes, "Genetically engineered vitamin A rice is now being used as a Trojan horse to push genetically engineered crops and foods."[3]

Proponents of golden rice also frame their arguments in moral and political terms. In a particularly scathing article, Dr. Ingo Potrykus, the principal scientist behind the creation of golden rice, comes close to accusing GMO critics of crimes against humanity:

> The GMO opposition often demands that scientists be held responsible for their actions. At the same time, however, they sidestep responsibility for the harm they cause to the disadvantaged and poor with their creation of a most hostile atmosphere against GMOs in Europe and elsewhere. In my judgment, hindering a person's access to life- or sight-saving food is criminal. To do this to millions of children is so criminal that it should not be tolerated by any society.[4]

Greenpeace's answer is just as blunt:

"Golden Rice" containing provitamin A will not solve the problem of malnutrition in developing countries. . . . A normal daily intake of 300 grams of rice would, at best, provide 8 percent of the vitamin A needed daily. . . . It is clear from these calculations that the GE [genetic engineering] industry is making false promises about "Golden Rice." . . . This whole project is actually based on what can only be characterized as intentional deception.[5]

Clearly, one's attitude toward golden rice might be affected by one's citizenship and nutritional status. The United Nations Development Program, in a report on genetically modified foods, offered this observation: "Western consumers naturally focus on potential allergic reactions and other food safety issues. People in developing countries, however, may be more interested in better crop yields, nutrition, or the reduced need to spray pesticides that can sicken farmers."[6]

But it is one thing to observe that the concerns of consumers in Europe and America may be different than the concerns of poor persons in developing countries. It is more difficult to decide how those different concerns should be balanced. Proponents of golden rice accuse critics of imposing Western priorities on malnourished Africans and Asians. Critics accuse the proponents of putting the lives and ecosystems of Third World peoples at risk to serve their own Western scientific hubris. Some African scientists believe that much of the present debate is misplaced. For example, while suggesting that "the millions of dollars being wasted each year by antibiotech activists elsewhere could go a long way to help build badly needed capacity for agbiotech research in Africa," Jesse Machuka goes on to conclude that "biotechnology for Africa should mostly be done in Africa and mostly by Africans themselves."[7]

QUESTIONS

1. In terms of the moral and ecological issues it presents, does golden rice differ significantly from Bt corn, which has been genetically modified to render it immune to a commonly used synthetic pesticide?
2. Is it true, as Dr. Potrykus charges, that the environmental groups that oppose genetically engineered crops such as golden rice are responsible for denying life-prolonging or life-saving nutrition to millions of the world's poorest people?

3. Is it true, as Greenpeace charges, that the promotion of golden rice can only be characterized as intentional deception?

4. Like Case 26: Tasmanian Tigers, this case raises issues about the release of genetically engineered organisms into the environment. What principles should govern such releases?

NOTES

1. Trisha Gura, "New Genes Boost Rice Nutrients," *Science* 285 (August 13, 1999): 994.

2. Vandana Shiva, "Genetically Engineered Vitamin 'A' Rice: A Blind Approach to Blindness Prevention," February 14, 2000, available at www.biotech-info.net/blind_rice.html.

3. Shiva, "Genetically Engineered Vitamin 'A' Rice."

4. Ingo Potrykus, "Golden Rice and Beyond," *Plant Physiology* 125 (March 2001): 1160.

5. Greenpeace, "Genetically Engineered 'Golden Rice' Is Fool's Gold," Greenpeace Statement, February 9, 2001, available at www.biotech-info.net/fools_gold.html.

6. United Nations Development Program, "Press Release: Although Controversial, GMOs Could Be Breakthrough Technology for Developing Countries," Human Development Report, 2001, available at www.undp.org/hdr2001.

7. Jesse Machuka, "Agricultural Biotechnology for Africa: African Scientists and Farmers Must Feed Their Own People," *Plant Physiology* 126 (May 2001): 19, available at www.plantphysiol.org/cgi/content/full/126/1/16?maxtoshow=&HITS=10&hits=10&RESULTFORMAT=&searchid=QID_NOT_SET&stored_search=&FIRSTINDEX=0&volume=126&firstpage=16.

SOURCES

American Society of Plant Biologists. *Genetically Modified Crops: What Do Scientists Say?* Rockville, Md.: American Society of Plant Biologists, 2001.

Greenpeace. "Genetically Engineered 'Golden Rice' Is Fool's Gold." Greenpeace Statement. February 9, 2001. Available at www.biotech-info.net/fools_gold.html.

Guerinot, Mary Lou. "The Green Revolution Strikes Gold." *Science* 287 (January 14, 2000): 241–43.

Gura, Trisha. "New Genes Boost Rice Nutrients." *Science* 285 (August 13, 1999): 994–95.

Machuka, Jesse. "Agricultural Biotechnology for Africa: African Scientists and Farmers Must Feed Their Own People." *Plant Physiology* 126 (May 2001):

16–19. Available at www.plantphysiol.org/cgi/content/full/126/1/16?maxtoshow= &HITS=10&hits=10&RESULTFORMAT=&searchid=QID_NOT_SET& stored_search=&FIRSTINDEX=0&volume=126&firstpage=16.

Potrykus, Ingo. "Golden Rice and Beyond." *Plant Physiology* 125 (March 2001): 1157–61. Available at www.plantphysiol.org/cgi/content/full/125/3/1157? maxtoshow=&HITS=10&hits=10&RESULTFORMAT=&searchid=QID_ NOT_SET&stored_search=&FIRSTINDEX=0&volume=125&firstpage= 1157.

Shiva, Vandana. "Genetically Engineered Vitamin 'A' Rice: A Blind Approach to Blindness Prevention," February 14, 2000. Available at www.biotech-info.net/blind_rice. html.

United Nations Development Program. "Press Release: Although Controversial, GMOs Could Be Breakthrough Technology for Developing Countries." Human Development Report. 2001. Available at www.undp.org/hdr2001.

Wambugu, Florence. "Why Africa Needs Agricultural Biotech." *Nature* 400 (1999): 15–16.

"Zambia Affirms Rejection of Genetically Modified Food." CNN. September 3, 2002.

28

ANCIENT APPLES, DANGEROUS WORK

Americans love their apples and eat about fifty pounds of them per person per year. But in the global economy, all is not well for New England apple growers. China has planted millions of acres of apple trees and is slowly moving into the Far East's fresh-fruit market, threatening the growers in the U.S. Pacific Northwest who currently supply that market. As a result, western U.S. growers are trying to enter eastern U.S. markets. "It's a domino effect," said the owner of one of New Hampshire's largest orchards. "Over the long haul, that'll be a serious, serious problem for us."

Chinese apples have already pushed the price of cider apples into the loss column for many American growers. "The price was so low this past year that we left thousands of bushels on the ground," said Ezekiel Goodband, manager at Alyson's Apple Orchard in Walpole, New Hampshire. "We would have lost money picking them up."

But do not look for Alyson's to fold. Alyson's Apple Orchard is one of a growing number of orchards specializing in varieties that have not been grown commercially for generations. In addition to peaches, plums, grapes, and pears, Alyson's grows and markets forty-six varieties of apples, twenty-two of which are "heirloom" varieties such as Hudson's Golden Gem, Cornish Gilliflower, Dolgo Crab, Callville Blanc de Hiver, and Maiden's Blush. In its nursery, Alyson's preserves nearly 1,000 other heirloom varieties. This treasure trove of genetic diversity may prove particularly important to an industry that has concentrated nearly all its production on just half a dozen varieties, leaving itself potentially susceptible to new pests and disease.

Alyson's fruit does not qualify as organic under the new National Organic Rule promulgated by the U.S. Department of Agriculture (USDA) on October 21, 2002. That rule, which is expected to replace current private and state rules, restricts the labels "Organic" and "100 Percent Organic" to foods produced without antibiotics, avicides, chemical fertilizers, fungicides, genetic modification, herbicides, hormones, insecticides, molluscicides, radiation, or rodenticides. Alyson's managers use small quantities of synthetic chemicals as a component of their integrated crop management (ICM) strategy. Alyson's describes its ecological policy as follows:

> We employ Integrated Crop Management (ICM) methods because we believe this to be the most environmentally responsible method of growing tree fruit—even superior to organic methods. . . . ICM gradually enhances the complexity of the orchard's ecology. . . . We have adopted a system of cultivation common in Europe, but rarely seen in the northeast. It calls for high density planting of dwarf trees—approximately 600–725 per acre—and intensive cultivation by hand. More akin to gardening than tree culture, this method requires skill and attention to detail, and produces trees which bear fruit sooner than in a conventional orchard. Visitors are surprised to see trout thriving in our irrigation ponds. These ponds supply and recycle the orchard's irrigation water. Trout are like canaries in a coal mine; if the water is not pure, they will not survive. Even more sensitive frog and amphibian populations abound in our ponds, and birds by the hundreds nest in our trees. Natural predators for pests, they provide a barometer for the health of the orchard ecosystem.[1]

First planted in 1982, Alyson's is clearly an economic success story. In addition to its wonderful fruits, it offers cooking classes, orchard outings, rustic or modern accommodations, facilities for special events, and a wide range of other products and services. It also seems to be an environmental success story. Its ICM methods are state of the art, and its nursery program is wonderful. Finally, Alyson's is a social success: As a major employer with good employee relations and a participant in local school-to-work and other programs, it is respected as a good community citizen.

DISCUSSION

Alyson's is a small, regional player in an industry increasingly dominated by global giants, but, at least for social ecologists, it illustrates some interesting issues about food production. Alyson's strives to be economically, ecologically, and socially responsible. Despite its failure to earn USDA organic certification, Alyson's seems to be successful on all three counts. So do many small organic growers. At Jim Cochran's organic strawberry farm in California, for example, workers get a union wage, a pension, and medical benefits. In an interview with *U. S. News & World Report*, Cochran put it this way: "I've always felt that labor issues were just as important as environmental and food safety issues. What's the point of growing 'clean' product when the people who perform the labor are being forced to live in terrible conditions?"[2]

Unfortunately, according to state and federal inspectors, Cochran's attitudes are not shared by many of the larger farms whose produce also carries the USDA "Organic" label. At Willamette River Organics, one of Oregon's largest organic farms, workers claim that they were forced to buy company tools, charged for bunk space even on days they were given no work, and cheated out of some of their (already subminimum) wages by managers who undercounted their pickings. State labor inspectors described the situation as "typical." Willamette River Organics denies the claims; according to the company's vice president, Greg Pile, "I give these men jobs, but people think that because you have an organic field that the workers should all be sitting around in lounge chairs."[3]

In many large agricultural states, labor inspectors are able to visit only about 1 percent of commercial farms each year. Ironically, precisely because they do *not* expose workers to toxic chemicals, organic enterprises are inspected less frequently.

The "antisweatshop" movement in the United States suggests that many consumers are concerned not only about the quality of the products they purchase but also about the way a manufacturer treats the workers who make the products. Indeed, many U.S. colleges and other organizations have adopted purchasing and licensing codes that commit them to buying and selling only apparel that has been certified as "sweat-free." In a curious way, the USDA "Organic" and the U.S. Agricultural Service "Sweat-Free" standards are perfect complements: The former deals only with a product's *quality* (such as no pesticides), the latter only with its *social origins* (such as no sweated labor). Consumers who would like to purchase foods that have been produced in a way which respects both social and ecological values will find little to guide them in the current marketplace. Some growers, like Jim Cochran, agree and hope that the criteria for organic certification will be broadened to include ethical labor standards.

QUESTIONS

1. Should the USDA expand the criteria for organic certification to include such concerns as fair wages and safe working conditions for agricultural workers? Are these concerns "ecological" issues?
2. In an increasingly global economy, should U.S. public policies have as one of their goals the preservation of relatively small, regional agricultural concerns such as Alyson's? If so, what would such policies look like?
3. Should efforts to support local and regional agricultural enterprises be tied to improved environmental performance by those firms? For example, should policy supports for small dairy farms be linked to their adoption of methane-from-manure capture technology?
4. Suppose that a campus food service was able to procure most of its fresh fruit and vegetables from vendors such as Alyson's but at an increased cost (for a typical cafeteria meal plan) of $80 per student per semester. Would you support such a change?

NOTES

1. Alyson's Orchard website, "Using Applied Ecology," 2003, available at www.alysonsorchard.com/integrated_crop_management.html.
2. Kit R. Roane, "Ripe for Abuse," *U.S. News & World Report*, April 22, 2002, 32.
3. Roane, "Ripe for Abuse," 32.

SOURCES

Alyson's Orchard. www.alysonsorchard.com/index.html.
"Apple Farmers Face Losses." *Concord Eagle-Tribune*, July 31, 2000. Available at www.eagletribune.com/news/stories/20000731/BU_001.htm.

Cowley, Geoffrey. "Certified Organic: New Government Rules Will Define *Organic.*" *Newsweek,* September 30, 2002, 50–55. Available at www.theorganicreport.com/pages/9_newsweek_(9_30_02)_certified_organic_.cfm?redirect=yes.

Political Economy Research Center. "Private Solutions—Ancient Apples." Available at www.perc.org/privatesolutions/apples.html.

Roane, Kit R. "Ripe for Abuse." *U.S. News & World Report,* April 22, 2002, 30, 32.

29

MOSQUITOES, DISEASE, AND DDT

Each year, 1,124,000 people die from malaria. An additional 42,280,000 people are chronically afflicted by the disease, which causes recurring chills, fevers, and anemia. The vast majority of these individuals live in developing nations, primarily in Africa. Many are too sickened to carry on vital subsistence activities. The lowly mosquito is responsible for transmitting this disease and dozens of others to humans across the world. Dengue fever infects 653,000 annually, causing fever, pain in the joints, rash, and hemorrhaging; it has no specific treatment and kills 21,000 people each year.

The most effective method of controlling these diseases is controlling the vector, that is, killing the mosquitoes before they can transfer the disease. In turn, the most effective method of killing mosquitoes is DDT. To date, no other pesticide has proven to be as effective, as nontoxic to humans, and as inexpensive to produce. DDT's toxicity to humans is so low that it is common practice to dip sleeping nets in DDT. During World War II, it was credited with saving the lives of hundreds of thousands of allied soldiers fighting in the Pacific. Immediately after the war, it became the most widely used pesticide in history—not only by public health authorities but also by U.S. farmers from coast to coast.

But if DDT was the most effective and (for humans) least toxic pesticide ever discovered, it is also the most persistent. Once applied, it remains in the environment for months or years. It bioaccumulates in fatty tissue. As it moves up the food chain, from little fish to bigger fish and then to eagles and ospreys, for example, it becomes biomagnified. The resulting environmental dangers of DDT were famously explained by Rachel Carson in her landmark book *Silent Spring*:

> For the first time in the history of the world, every human being is now subjected to contact with dangerous chemicals, from the moment of conception until death. In the less than two decades of their use, the synthetic pesticides have been so thoroughly distributed throughout the animate and inanimate world that they occur virtually everywhere. They have been recovered from most of the major river systems and even from streams of groundwater flowing unseen through the earth. Residues of these chemicals linger in soil to which they may have been applied a dozen years before. They have entered and lodged in the bodies of fish, birds, reptiles, and domestic and wild animals so universally that scientists carrying on animal experiments find it almost impossible to locate subjects free from such contamination. They have been found in fish in remote mountain lakes, in earthworms burrowing in soil, in the eggs of birds—and in man himself. For these chemicals are now stored in the bodies of the vast majority of human beings, regardless of age. They occur in the mother's milk, and probably in the tissues of the unborn child.[1]

Silent Spring has been credited with being the motivating force behind the eventual banning of DDT in the United States, and the elimination of DDT is believed by nearly all experts to be the single most important factor behind the recovery of endangered birds of prey, most notably the bald eagle.

Nevertheless, at the end of 2002, twenty-four countries severely impacted by malaria and other tropical diseases still relied on DDT as their primary weapon against the diseases responsible for much death and suffering. Now, however, there is an international movement to end the use of DDT worldwide.

DISCUSSION

The United States experiences much less mosquito-related disease and death than many other countries. In part, this is due to the country's excellent medical system and to the surveillance activities of the Centers for Disease Control and Prevention (CDC). But in large part, it is also due simply to climate. With the exception of some areas in the southern portion of the country, malaria-bearing mosquitoes cannot survive in the United States.

The vast majority of U.S. citizens who contract malaria or other tropical diseases contract them while traveling abroad.

But the United States does face increasingly common outbreaks of other mosquito-borne diseases carried by other species of mosquitoes. Headlines in the summer of 2002 called attention to the West Nile virus, which killed 241 of the 3,852 people who were known to have contracted the disease—some as far north as New England. Eastern equine encephalitis is becoming more common and ranging across more of North America. Even dengue fever has begun to appear in some parts of Florida.

The CDC advocates aggressive mosquito control measures to combat West Nile virus. Effective mosquito control involves multiple efforts: habitat reduction (draining standing water), pesticides, and integrated pest management (IPM), which uses natural predators to suppress mosquito populations by introducing fish that prefer mosquito larvae and building bat boxes to encourage these predators. Although IPM is useful and important, it has not supplanted the use of pesticides.

QUESTIONS

1. Should DDT be banned worldwide because of its long-range ecological damage? As long as public health authorities in some developing countries believe that they need DDT, should they be permitted to import and use it?
2. Under U.S. law, pesticides that are not permitted to be *used* in the United States can still be manufactured in this country and *exported* for use elsewhere. In fact, a large fraction of the world's DDT is now manufactured in countries, including the United States, that ban its use. Is this an example of environmental racism?
3. With pesticides, there seems to be a systematic trade-off between *environmental persistence* and *acute toxicity*. The families of chemical agents that degrade quickly, thus reducing the risk of bioaccumulation or biomagnification, are also much more toxic to humans who are exposed to them. Deaths due to accidental pesticide poisoning, for example, increased dramatically in the United States when DDT was replaced by newer, less persistent chemicals. In much of the U.S. agricultural sector, the persons most likely to be exposed to pesticides are migrant workers. Is it fair that these poorest members of society

bear the health costs associated with eliminating DDT's environmental effects?

4. DDT was once used to kill head and body lice, a rapidly growing nuisance for American schoolchildren. It is far less likely to cause neurological damage than the medicines now available in the United States. It is also far more effective. Should an exception be made to permit the use of DDT by prescription for lice? Or would this inevitably lead to cries that "if it's safe enough for our children, it's safe enough for our corn!"

NOTE

1. Rachel Carson, *Silent Spring* (Boston: Houghton Mifflin, 1962), 15–16. For a flattering but largely fair account of the origin and impact of *Silent Spring*, see Natural Resources Defense Council, "The Story of Silent Spring," available at www.nrdc.org/health/pesticides/hcarson.asp.

SOURCES

Carson, Rachel. *Silent Spring*. Boston: Houghton Mifflin, 1962.

Centers for Disease Control, Division of Vector-Borne Infectious Diseases. *Epidemic/Epizootic West Nile Virus in the United States: Revised Guidelines for Surveillance, Prevention and Control*. April 2001. Available at www.cdc.gov/ncidod/dvbid/westnile/resources/wnv-guidelines-apr-2001.pdf.

———. *West Nile Virus Basics*. November 2002. Available at www.cdc.gov/ncidod/dvbid/westnile/index.htm.

Code of Federal Regulations, Title 40, Chapter 1—Environmental Protection Agency, Subchapter E—Pesticide Programs (2003). Available at www.epa.gov/docs/epacfr40/chapt-I.info/subch-E.htm.

Federal Insecticide, Fungicide, and Rodenticide Act. 7 U.S.C. § 136(o) (1996). A summary of the law is available at http://css.snre.umich.edu/css_doc/FIFRA.pdf. The full text is available at www4.law.cornell.edu/uscode/7/ch6.html.

Pesticide Management Education Program. *Risk-Benefit Balancing under FIFRA*. Ithaca, N.Y.: Cornell University, 1997. Available at http://pmep.cce.cornell.edu/issues/risk-benefit-fifra.html.

World Health Organization. *Action Plan for the Reduction of Reliance on DDT in Disease Vector Control*. 2001. Available at www.who.int/water_sanitation_health/Documents/DDT/ddt.pdf.

World Health Organization, Special Programme for Research and Training in Tropical Diseases. *Dengue Disease Information.* Available at www.who.int/tdr/diseases/dengue/diseaseinfo.htm.

——. *Malaria Disease Information.* Available at www.who.int/tdr/diseases/malaria/diseaseinfo.htm.

30

A BREATH OF
FRESH AIR

B y comparison to any other industrialized democracy, Japan is not a liti-
gious society. Still less is it a society where citizens routinely sue public
officials. Nevertheless, between 1982 and 1999, 500 residents of Kawasaki
waged a prolonged legal battle with the Japanese government over responsibility for pollution-related illnesses. All had suffered health damage as a result of the pollution, and many had died before the case was finally settled. It
is an interesting story that raises important questions about development,
unintended consequences, and public responsibility.

Kawasaki is part of the Keihin industrial belt in Kanagawa prefecture, the
heartland of Japanese industry. Its rows of factory smokestacks were considered to be a symbol of economic development. During the post–World War
II industrial recovery, Kanagawa prefecture developed a 3,430,00-square-
meter industrial park in and near Kawasaki that was occupied by petroleum
companies involved in Japan's postwar shift from coal to petroleum. Roads
and highways to support the rapid industrial growth were built and expanded. Between 1950 and 1969, total road mileage increased by 544 percent (from 135,444 to 872,688 kilometers). In the same period, the number
of cars, buses, and trucks using the roads increased by 24,252 percent (from
38,325 to 9,294,605). Auto emissions grew correspondingly, and Kawasaki
residents soon suffered from poor air quality due to vehicle exhaust and factory emissions.

Kawasaki's main highways are routes 1, 15, 132, and 409 and the Yokohama-Haneda Expressway. All were built before 1954, when there was no the Department of Environment (in Japan or the United States), and no attempt was made to assess their impact on air quality. But their impact has been dramatic.

The most important emissions related to the highways are hydrocarbons, nitrogen oxides, carbon monoxide, and suspended particulate matter. Around Kawasaki's highways, all these emissions are present at levels deemed harmful. Hydrocarbons are a major component of smog, which irritates the eyes, damages the lungs, and aggravates respiratory problems. Nitrogen oxides are precursors to both ozone and acid rain. Carbon monoxide reduces the flow of oxygen in the bloodstream and is particularly dangerous to persons with heart disease. Suspended particulates can cause lung damage and aggravate existing respiratory problems.

In 1998, air in residential neighborhoods abutting Kawasaki's highways rarely met national air quality standards despite the fact that, in 1992, the government had lowered the standards in response to growing awareness of the environmental and health problems caused by the air pollution. Southern Kawasaki did not once meet the nitrogen dioxide standard between 1988 and 1998.

The number of children qualifying for subsidies under the Kawasaki Childhood Asthma Medical Subsidy Ordinance increased sixfold, from 839 to 5,125, between 1972 and 1998. By September 1999, 5,869 people had been qualified as Kawasaki pollution patients, entitling them to free medical care, medical transportation, compensation to bereaved relatives, and funeral costs. By the end of 2001, 1,828 of them had died.

On May 20, 1999, the Tokyo High Court officially accepted a mediated settlement between the surviving Kawasaki plaintiffs and the government. The terms of the settlement provide the following:

1. The government will spend about 400 billion yen (U.S.$3.3 billion) to upgrade the expressways in Kawasaki in order to improve traffic flow and reduce emissions.
2. The government and the Metropolitan Expressway Public Corporation accept, as a guide to future road administration, that there is a causal relationship between nitrogen dioxide and suspended particulate matter and damage to human health.
3. The government and the expressway operator are to make serious efforts to meet existing environmental standards.

4. The government and corporation are to make efforts to survey the quality of air in the area, including measuring the amount of suspended particulate matter present.

5. The plaintiffs, the Construction Ministry, and the expressway operator are to set up a liaison committee to examine ways to improve the environment in the area.

6. The plaintiffs are to abandon all claims, including for compensation, against the government and the expressway operator.

The settlement is silent on the question of whether the government bears any responsibility for the health problems caused by automobile emissions in Kawasaki.

Since Kawasaki is built around its roads and factories, it is not clear how government officials will be able to bring air quality in the area into compliance with national standards anytime soon. The roads are crucial to the Japanese economy, and closing them would be economically ruinous to millions of citizens. Traffic can be diverted from the expressway by increasing the (already high) tolls, but this would only increase traffic on and pollution from already congested alternative routes.

In the short term, some have proposed that the government provide free air filtration systems to residents in affected neighborhoods. At a cost of approximately $500 per unit, the systems can remove 99.97 percent of all particles down to 0.3 micron, removing dust, pollens, and dust allergens. But with approximately 200,000 households affected, this would cost $100 million and would do little to reduce levels of nitrogen dioxide, carbon monoxide, or hydrocarbons.

Some government consultants have proposed moving parts of the highway system underground and then using industrial scrubbers to treat tunnel exhaust fumes before releasing them into the atmosphere. But such a project would be extraordinarily expensive and yield only marginal improvement for ambient air quality.

In the long term, most seem to agree that the only real solution will be to replace existing vehicles with extremely low-emission (ELE) vehicles, such as the gas–electric hybrid. The Toyota Prius, for example, averages seventy miles per gallon in Japanese tests and emits only about one-tenth the nitrogen oxides, carbon monoxide, and hydrocarbons of the vehicles it replaces. Unfortunately, the hybrid is expensive—prohibitively so for the average Japanese family.

One young Japanese professional from Kawasaki (who does not wish to be named) summed up the current situation this way:

> The government had to build the highways to stimulate our economy and support millions of people. The government made believe that pollution did not exist. The government should admit that it failed to protect people who live close to the roads. If the government cannot admit the truth, then all laws will be nonsense to us. The government could say that there are high concentrations of air pollution near the highways, which may make some people sick, but ultimately, some people have to live in this area. Rich people live outbound. People who do not have much money live close to the highways. The government should support those people in some way. But this policy discriminates between rich and poor, and seems unjust to residents who live in the area. As to the settlement between the plaintiffs and the government . . . I did not go through the paper work for the trial, I do not have any significant symptom due to the pollution, and I have not lost any family members, but thanks to the people who fought for all these long years, I will have cleaner air and a better transportation system.

DISCUSSION

Unintended consequences seem to be a ubiquitous feature of human interaction with their environment. The major highway systems built in Japan and the United States after World War II were intended to support economic development and improve the quality of citizens' lives. In both those respects, they were largely successful. But when added to the pollutants already present in urban industrial centers from factories and other major point sources, emissions from the trucks and automobiles using those highways have sickened or killed tens of thousands of mostly working-class people. Two obvious questions that arise are, Who is responsible? and What should be done about it?

In Japan, the road system itself—as a set of legal entities receiving both tax and toll revenue—has been held responsible. In Kawasaki, Tokyo, and other major cities, the expressway systems are now legally compelled to provide various kinds of relief and compensation to pollution victims. To the extent that such payments are funded from toll revenues, the system seems to reflect the principle that those who cause pollution should pay for the effects of the pollution. But vehicles are not the only source of air pollution, and not all drivers use the toll roads. In addition, Japanese courts have repeatedly refused to hold vehicle manufacturers responsible for pollution effects, reasoning that the manufacturers have no way to control where or how often their products are used.

In the long run, the only really adequate solutions would seem to be greater reliance on public transportation and the transition to ELE vehicles for private use. That transition can be accelerated by reducing the now very large (often 100 percent) price differential between ELE vehicles and comparable regular models. One way to do this is by raising the cost of traditional vehicle ownership, either directly (such as with sales taxes based on pollution performance, higher fuel taxes, or stiffer emission inspection programs) or indirectly (such as by raising fleet mileage standards and hence production costs). The second way to do this is to lower the cost of ELE vehicle ownership, again either directly (such as with publicly funded subsidies to ELE purchasers) or indirectly (such as providing some benefit to ELE producers).

In the context of American energy policy, using subsidies to promote the purchase of environmentally preferable products is common. In one way or another, such subsidies are available for products ranging from compact fluorescent lightbulbs to energy-efficient home windows. Disincentive programs are less common, though a "gas guzzler" tax applied to the purchase of particularly fuel-inefficient vehicles would be an example.

Finally, it is worth mentioning that no vehicle is less polluting than a bicycle. In some European cities, local governments have been quite successful in encouraging large numbers of their residents to use bicycles for much of their urban travel. The most successful of such programs are integrated with local public transportation systems, so that, for example, one finds ample and secure bicycle parking space at every train and bus station.

QUESTIONS

1. Are urban residents whose health has been damaged by air pollution entitled to any special kind of relief or compensation? If so, who should pay for it?
2. What, if anything, should the federal or state governments in the United States do to encourage people to purchase ELE vehicles rather than traditional vehicles?
3. What could your city or town do to encourage bicycle use for short-range travel?
4. If you own a car, when was the last time you chose to use a bicycle or a bus instead?

SOURCES

The primary sources for this case, which were drafted by Ms. Yasuyo Maruyama, are Japanese government documents, legal papers, and press accounts; they are not available in English translation. We list here some English-language sources that the interested reader may find helpful.

"Agency to Tackle Worst Pollution Cases." Asahi News Agency. October 15, 1998.

"Air Pollution Case Settled as Others Fume." *The Daily Yomiuri*, May 21, 1999.

"Companies Apologize for Kawasaki Air Pollution," *Mainichi Daily News*, December 26, 1999.

Japanese Ministry of Justice. Some materials related to the Kawasaki case are available at www.moj.go.jp/index.html.

"Japan: Kawasaki Pollution Victims, Government Settle 17-Year Suit." *Malaysia General News*, May 14, 1999.

Japan Times. Several articles related to the case are available at www.japantimes.co.jp/start.htm.

"Kawasaki Pollution Suit Finally Settled." Asian News Service. May 20, 1999.

Mainichi Daily News. Several articles dealing with pollution-related litigation and vehicle emissions are available at http://mdn.mainichi.co.jp.

"State, Road Corporation Appeal Kawasaki Pollution Decision." Japan Economic Newswire. August 5, 1999.

"A Victory for Victims of Pollution." *Japan Times*, August 8, 1998.

31

THE DARK SKIES ORDINANCE

Ketchum Ordinance 743 [abridged]

AN ORDINANCE OF THE CITY OF KETCHUM, IDAHO, TO BE KNOWN AS THE "DARK SKIES ORDINANCE" . . .

WHEREAS, unnecessary and improperly designed light fixtures cause glare, light pollution and wasted resources; and,

WHEREAS, glare and light pollution can result in: hazardous circulation conditions for all modes of transportation; the diminishing ability to view the night sky; light trespass; and, unattractive townscape; and,

WHEREAS, the people who live in and near Ketchum value the natural environment, including the beauty and high quality of the night sky; and,

WHEREAS, the City of Ketchum is a destination resort community, economically dependent upon tourists and part-time residents, and is dependent upon its natural resources and environment to attract tourists and part-time residents; and,

WHEREAS, the City of Ketchum desires to protect the health, safety and welfare of the general public, and to protect the night sky that adds to the quality of life and economic well-being of the City; and,

WHEREAS, these regulations for exterior lighting will not sacrifice the safety of our citizens or visitors, or the security of property, but instead will result in safer, efficient and more cost-effective lighting.

NOW, THEREFORE, BE IT ORDAINED BY THE MAYOR AND CITY COUNCIL OF THE CITY OF KETCHUM, IDAHO:

SECTION 1—GENERAL PROVISIONS

1.1 Title—This Ordinance . . . may be cited as the Ketchum Dark Skies Ordinance.

1.2 Purposes—The general purpose of this Ordinance is to protect and promote the public health, safety and welfare, the quality of life, and the ability to view the night sky. . . .

1.3 Scope—All exterior lighting installed after the effective date of this Ordinance in any and all zoning districts in the City of Ketchum shall be in conformance with the requirements established by this Ordinance . . .

   b. All existing exterior commercial lighting that is not in conformance with this Ordinance shall be brought into conformance with this Ordinance within twelve months. . . .

   d. All existing exterior residential lighting . . . is required to be brought into conformance with this Ordinance within two years. . . .

SECTION 2—DEFINITIONS

2.1 Area Light—Light that produces over 1,800 lumens [approximately the output of a 90-watt incandescent bulb] . . .

2.15 Full Cut-Off Fixtures—Fixtures, as installed, that are designed or shielded in such a manner that all light rays emitted by the fixture . . . are projected below a horizontal plane running through the lowest point on the fixture where light is emitted.

2.22 Light Pollution—Any adverse effect of man-made light including, but not limited to, light trespass, uplighting, the uncomfortable distraction to the eye, or any man-made light that diminishes the ability to view the night sky. Often used to denote urban sky glow.

2.23 Light Trespass—Light falling where it is not wanted or needed, generally caused by a light on a property that shines onto the property of others.

2.26 Luminaire—The complete lighting unit, including the lamp, the fixture, and other parts.

2.34 Uplighting—Lighting that is directed in such a manner as to shine light rays above the horizontal plane.

SECTION 3—CRITERIA

3.2 All exterior lighting shall be full cut-off fixtures with the light source fully shielded, with the following exceptions:

b. Luminaires that have a maximum output of 1,000 lumens per fixture, regardless of number of bulbs (equal to one 60-watt incandescent light), may be partially shielded, provided the bulb is not visible, and the fixture has an opaque top to keep light from shining directly up.

e. Sensor activated lighting may be unshielded provided it is located in such a manner as to prevent direct glare and lighting into properties of others or into a public right-of-way, and provided the light is set to only go on when activated and to go off within five minutes after activation has ceased, and the light shall not be triggered by activity off the property.

3.3 Light Trespass—All existing and/or new exterior lighting shall not cause light trespass and shall be such as to protect adjacent properties from glare and excessive lighting.

3.6 Area Lights—All area lights, including streetlights and parking-area lighting, shall be full cut-off fixtures . . . All freestanding area lights within a residential zone, except streetlights, shall be mounted at a height equal to or less than the value 3 + (D/3), where D is the distance in feet to the nearest property boundary.

3.8 Uplighting—Uplighting is prohibited in all zoning districts. . . .

SECTION 5—THE CITY'S ROLE

5.1 The City of Ketchum will commit to changing all lighting within the City rights-of-way and on City-owned property to meet the requirements of this Ordinance. . . .

SECTION 6—VIOLATIONS, LEGAL ACTIONS AND PENALTIES

6.2 Penalty—A violation of this Ordinance, or any provision thereof, shall be punishable by a civil penalty of one hundred dollars ($100) and each day of violation . . . shall constitute a separate offense for the purpose of calculating the civil penalty.

DISCUSSION

This ordinance was passed by the city council of Ketchum, Idaho, on June 21, 1999. Other dark sky regulations have been adopted in Texas, Maine, New Mexico, and parts of Arizona. Some apply only to highways and state-owned properties; others, like Ketchum's, apply to private properties as well. In Canada, the province of Ontario has set aside 5,000 acres of wilderness—the Torrance Barrens Conservation Reserve—as a "dark sky preserve."

In tourist-friendly Ketchum, it seems likely that the dark skies ordinance will promote both aesthetic and economic values. Sometimes, however, the choices are more complex. Springfield, Vermont, is a small, economically depressed city with 9,500 residents. Springfield is also known as the birthplace of amateur astronomy: Its thirty-acre Stellafane Observatory is home to the world's only reflecting turret telescope. The sky at Stellafane is so dark that the Milky Way, invisible from most U.S. cities, looks like a bright cloud. Stellafane's annual convention attracts more than 2,000 professional and amateur astronomers from around the world.

Springfield residents were bitterly divided by a state proposal to site a new 350-bed prison just four miles from the observatory. In the end, with hundreds of good jobs and almost $8 million in additional state incentives at stake, residents voted to accept the prison (and its dazzling all-night lighting) by a vote of 1,633 to 1,564. In the months following the vote, the Department of Corrections adopted design changes to reduce the facility's light pollution.

In a small but interesting way, one part of the debate over dark sky ordinances echoes an issue that arises regarding nuclear technology, namely, a conflict between *expert* and *public* perceptions of risk. Just as it seems fair to say that a majority (but by no means all) of relevant technical experts believe that nuclear power plants can be operated safely, so it seems fair to say that a majority (but by no means all) of relevant technical experts believe that dark sky restrictions can be implemented without compromising public safety. Indeed, just as some experts believe that nuclear electrical generation is safer than coal, when compared on a "total fuel cycle" basis (which includes mining and transportation fatalities), so some experts argue that dark skies actually enhance public safety. In both cases, however, the large majority of private citizens assess the risks differently: They feel safer with coal power than with nuclear technology, and they feel safer with bright outdoor lighting than with dimmer, shielded lighting. According to risk psychologists, such discordance between "expert" and "public" risk perception is very common. Other examples include the discrepancy between expert and public perceptions of the risk of airplane travel (versus the risk of travel in private automobiles) and the risk of adverse reactions to vaccines (versus the risk of infectious disease).

QUESTIONS

1. How should public authorities balance technical expertise against discordant public perceptions in matters of health and safety?

2. Is it fair to restrict people's use of their own private property in order that the night sky is more visible to others? Is this kind of restriction a "taking" in the sense explained in Case 9: Taking Lake Tahoe? Suppose that you and your family were in the habit of playing basketball in the late evening and that you had invested $15,000 to pave a small outdoor court and install lighting. Should the fact that you can longer use this property for its intended purpose entitle you to compensation?

3. Is it fair to require private property owners to bear the costs of replacing existing exterior lighting equipment so that others can better enjoy the night sky? Does it matter whether the property is a business or a private residence? (In this connection, compare Case 40: Plumbing Matters.)

4. Would this ordinance be less reasonable if the community's economy did not rely heavily on revenue from tourism?

5. Is the night sky a natural resource that should be protected?

SOURCES

City of Ketchum, Idaho. Ordinance Number 743. Available at www.scn.org/darksky/code/id/ketcdrlo.html.
Harrington, Philip S. "Dark-Sky Observing Site Directory." Available at http://65.18.168.153/dssd.htm.
International Dark Sky Association. www.darksky.org/index.html.
———. *U.S.A. Municipal Outdoor Lighting Regulations by State.* Available at www.darksky.org/ordsregs/usamunis.html.
Stahl, Greg. "Dark Skies Forecast." *Idaho Mountain Express*, March 15, 2000. Available at www.mtexpress.com/2000/03-15-00/3-15lights.htm.

32

THE ANSWER IS
BLOWING IN
THE WIND

Sometimes conservation measures simply involve reviving old ideas. In response to soaring energy prices and rolling blackouts in California, many home owners rediscovered the humble clothesline. For an investment of as little as $10, a typical household could save hundreds of dollars per year.

But some of the Californians who attempted this simple conversion were in for a nasty shock: Clotheslines are banned in many communities. The villains behind the ban are not a cabal of appliance manufacturers or even the members of an overzealous city zoning board; rather, they are home-owner associations that had written deed covenants to protect their property values. In large, planned developments, it is common for each deed to contain restrictions called covenants. Home owners purchasing property in such developments agree to abide by the restrictions or face fines or eviction.

Here is an example of one such covenant:

No exterior clothesline shall be erected or maintained on any Lot nor shall there be any drying or laundering of clothes outside of the structure if such laundering or clothes drying would be visible from any street or other Lot.[1]

DISCUSSION

Certainly, restrictions such as this give an indication of the degree to which Americans are concerned with property values. But they also involve aesthetic and other issues. Many home owners want to live and raise children in a neat, aesthetically pleasing environment. Many people are willing to accept deed restrictions in the belief that they will help ensure that they will be able to raise their family in such an environment.

Deed restrictions banning clotheslines are certainly not the worst environmental offenders found in American households. Americans apply 70 million pounds of pesticides and a vastly larger quantity of synthetic fertilizers to their lawns each year, much of which ends up polluting groundwater and surface water. Americans purchase 200 million strands of Christmas lights each year, enough to "wrap around the earth almost 23 times and consume enough electricity during the holiday season to power all of the homes in Vermont or Wyoming for an entire year."[2]

In a society where few people have the time or inclination to iron their laundry, old-fashioned clotheslines may not work for all laundry: Some of the clothes may still need to go into the dryer. Clotheslines are not practical everywhere and in every season, but especially in dry, sunny climates, even throwing the towels and sheets out "on the line" can produce impressive energy savings.

QUESTIONS

This case can be usefully compared to Case 40: Plumbing Matters.

1. When writing deed restrictions for housing developments, how should aesthetics be balanced against environmental impacts?
2. To what extent should individual decisions about individually small but collectively significant matters be subject to public regulation? No one strand of Christmas lights will cause global warming, but collectively they use an enormous amount of energy.
3. Should people who do not have the time or resources to use natural pest management methods be forced to accept brown, patchy lawns in order to reduce the amount of pollutants introduced into the environment?
4. California's 2000–2002 energy crisis had serious environmental consequences (see Case 13: The John Day Dam). Under such circumstances, should courts or other authorities have voided or at least temporarily suspended deed restrictions banning energy-saving practices such as the use of clotheslines?

NOTES

1. Such deed restrictions can cover an astounding variety of issues: exterior color schemes, acceptable roofing materials, landscaping style, contributions to shared recreational facilities, pet ownership, and even whether children are allowed to live in the neighborhood.

2. Edison Electric Institute, "Holiday Lights Continue to Blaze in the U.S., Causing Demand for Power to Grow 5 Percent," December 19, 2002, available at www.eei.org/issues/news/releases/021220.htm.

SOURCES

Amended and Restated Declaration of Covenants, Conditions and Restrictions (Stonebriar, California). Available at www.smcsd.org/Stonebriar/stonebriarCCRs2.pdf.

Edison Electric Institute. "Holiday Lights Continue to Blaze in the U.S., Causing Demand for Power to Grow 5 Percent." December 19, 2002. Available at www.eei.org/issues/news/releases/021220.htm.

Project Laundry List. www.laundrylist.org.

33

THE TOOELE WEAPONS INCINERATOR

Tooele County, Utah, comprises about 7,000 square miles of arid land—about the size of New Jersey. With the third-highest per capita income in Utah, it has well-financed schools, new fire-fighting and ambulance equipment, and a state-of-the-art emergency alarm and evacuation system. Only fifty miles southwest of Salt Lake City, Tooele is prosperous and growing.

One factor behind the county's prosperity is its unusual number of toxic waste storage and disposal facilities. These include two commercial hazardous waste incinerators, a commercial hazardous waste dump, a storage facility for radioactive wastes from uranium processing and atomic bomb production, the Dugway Proving Ground (until 1969 the chief site for open-air testing of biological weapons), and the Tooele Army Depot Chemical Weapons Incinerator.

The depot is located just ten miles north of the town of Tooele. In 1996, it held 13,616 tons of chemical weapons, approximately 40 percent of the country's total inventory. The chemicals included modern nerve agents such as VX and GB and older blister agents such as mustard gas. They were stored both in bulk tanks and in more than a million individual weapons, including artillery shells, mines, rockets, and bombs.

In 1985, Congress mandated that all chemical munitions and warfare agents be destroyed by 2004. On January 13, 1993, the United States signed the Chemical Weapons Convention, an international agreement that obliges signatories to destroy all chemical weapons in their possession within ten years of signing. The Tooele incineration facility, built at a cost of $400 million, was designed to destroy all on-site weapons by 2003. The plant itself is then supposed to be dismantled. The total cost for the destruction of all chemical weapons in the U.S. inventory is estimated at $12 billion. This is a description of the incineration process at Tooele:

> The chemical agent, metal parts, and explosive components are disassembled, then destroyed separately to ensure safe and complete destruction. . . . Weapons are loaded onto a conveyor and sent to a special thick-walled explosive containment room. Here, automated equipment punctures and drains the chemical agent. . . . Explosive components go directly to a deactivation furnace. . . . Drained chemicals are stored in tanks for later disposal in an incinerator designed for liquids. The metal parts remaining from these weapons are thermally decontaminated in a metal parts furnace, and other remaining materials are destroyed in yet another incinerator. Ash and decontaminated metal parts are packaged and transported to an approved landfill. The liquid brine resulting from the treatment of exhaust gases in the pollution control system is dried to reduce its volume and then sent to a landfill.[1]

Critics of the incineration process do not oppose the elimination of the weapons but have charged that the process exposes too many people to danger, especially since most of the chemicals are colorless, odorless, and tasteless but can lead to collapse within seconds and death within minutes after inhalation. Even very low exposures can have significant nonlethal health effects. In support of their view, critics cite the statement of a former chief incinerator safety officer alleging that the plant's design is flawed and potentially unsafe.[2]

According to the National Research Council, incineration is the safest disposal method for chemical weapons, and the risks from continued storage would be greater than the risks of on-site disposal. Many of the weapons were manufactured in the 1940s and 1950s, and during a 1993 inventory, 1,510 of them were discovered to be leaking. But critics argue that incineration and continued storage of active toxic agents are not the only alternatives. A coalition of activists living near chemical weapon storage sites has argued that the drained chemical agents should be chemically neutralized and then put back into storage until a disposal method safer than incineration is available.

Tooele itself seems utterly unfazed by the facility. A public hearing on the incinerator plan in 1996 drew only four local citizens.

DISCUSSION

Chemical neutralization of the toxic agents might be sufficient to comply with the Chemical Weapons Convention. The risks posed by leaks in individual weapons would be eliminated by either incineration or neutralization since both processes are designed to destroy the original toxic agent. The dispute regarding disposal methods thus seems to turn on a balance of uncertainties: on the one hand, the uncertain risks of design or operations failure during the few years the incinerator will operate and, on the other hand, the uncertain risks of design or operations failure during the period in which an alternative chemical neutralization process would be conducted plus whatever risks would be associated with the storage and eventual destruction of the neutralized agents. It is easy to say that, in situations of uncertainty, decision makers should always prefer the safest course. But as this case illustrates, it is often far from clear which course is safest. On November 20, 2002, the U.S. Department of Defense announced that chemical munitions at the U.S. Army's Blue Grass Army Depot will be destroyed on-site using chemical neutralization followed by supercritical water oxidation. Organized public opposition to incineration played an important role in shaping the decision.[3]

QUESTIONS

1. Suppose that the signatory obligations of the United States under the Chemical Weapons Convention would not be satisfied by the neutralization and storage proposal. Would that fact be a decisive consideration, sufficient to justify using the incineration technology now available?
2. Is it fair to leave all or even any of the burdens and hazards of chemical weapons disposal to future generations? Supposing that the weapons helped deter or contain international conflicts in the latter half of the twentieth century, it would seem that the persons who benefited from the weapons existence are those generations now alive. Whatever the risks associated with destroying the weapons, does the principle of benefit–burden concordance entail that present rather than future generations should therefore bear those risks?
3. Some scholars argue that the disproportionate concentration of noxious and hazardous facilities in poor and nonwhite areas is the result of environmental racism. Prosperous Tooele might seem to be an anomaly on this view. Is it? More generally, what principles and procedures might be

used to distribute such facilities is a morally and socially equitable way? (In this last connection, compare Case 14: Not on Cape Cod.)

NOTES

1. Tim Weiner, "Secrecy Lifted on Destroying Chemical Arms," *New York Times*, January 23, 1996.

2. Keith Schneider, "Unbridled Inspector or Unsafe Incinerator?" *New York Times*, September 27, 1994.

3. Chemical Weapons Working Group, "Pentagon's Final Environmental Statement on Kentucky Chemical Weapons Destruction Released," December 29, 2002, available at www.cwwg.org/pr_12.29.02kyfeis.html.

SOURCES

Allen, Scott. "Army Disposal of Poison Gas Is Under Fire." *Boston Globe*, October 10, 1994.

Brooke, James. "So Far, So Good, as Chemical Weapons Are Burned in Utah, Officials Say." *New York Times*, April 13, 1998.

Chemical Weapons Working Group. "Pentagon's Final Environmental Statement on Kentucky Chemical Weapons Destruction Released." December 29, 2002. Available at www.cwwg.org/pr_12.29.02kyfeis.html.

Israelsen, Brent. "Tooele Incinerator: Violation Records Authentic." *Salt Lake Tribune*, December 28, 2001.

Lee, Gary. "Dispute Delays Burning of Nerve Gas." *Washington Post*, October 12, 1994.

Munro, Nancy K., et al. "Toxicity of the Organophosphate Chemical Warfare Agents GA, GB, and VX: Implications for Public Protection." *Environmental Health Perspectives* 102, no. 1 (1994): 18–38.

Schneider, Keith. "Unbridled Inspector or Unsafe Incinerator?" *New York Times*, September 27, 1994.

———. "Unfazed, a Utah Town Prepares to Burn a Toxic Piece of the Past." *New York Times*, October 23, 1994.

Weiner, Tim. "Secrecy Lifted on Destroying Chemical Arms." *New York Times*, January 23, 1996.

34

THE TOXIC LAGOON

I magine that you are an environmentally and socially responsible entrepreneur interested in buying one of the many formerly state-owned enterprises now being sold by the new democratic governments in central and eastern Europe. The following advertisement—which accurately describes an entirely nonfictional facility—catches your eye:

FOR SALE TO PRIVATE INVESTOR

Toxic industrial sludge lagoon: Uncovered, unlined, built on sandy soil. 0.6-acre surface, approximately 2 meters deep, with soil retaining wall approximately 5 meters high and 3.5 meters thick. Contains 140,000 tons of liquid waste. Toxins include trivalent chromium, assorted metals, organic solvents, and biological agents. Almost full, has overflowed several times in recent years. Leachate has been contaminating underground aquifer for at least a decade. In continuous use since 1979.

Free with purchase of lagoon: Radom Leather Tannery, established 1972. Currently starved for capital and struggling for markets. Outmoded infrastructure, substandard wastewater treatment facility. 430 employees. Numerous environmental and occupational health problems.

DISCUSSION

The grim legacy of environmental degradation in Poland (and other central European states) under communist rule has been exhaustively documented in the past decade. Since democratization, both technical and popular publications have described the state economies' toxic legacy in painful detail: suffocating air in major urban areas, levels of particulates and sulfur dioxide vastly higher than those in the European Union or the United States, severe erosion of historical buildings and monuments, dangerous soil and aquifer contamination with heavy metals and volatile organics, and rivers too polluted even for industrial use.

Following democratization in 1989, the new Polish government faced an extraordinarily difficult pair of challenges: first, to pursue an aggressive environmental agenda and, second and simultaneously, to privatize a mostly state-owned economy without massive unemployment and social dislocation. Either task would be daunting alone. This case illustrates the ways in which these two goals can conflict. Clearly, the best environmental solution is to close the tannery. Just as clearly, the worst social solution is to eliminate 430 jobs in an already economically depressed city.

It seems extremely unlikely that *any* private investor will purchase the tannery as long as the purchase involves the toxic lagoon. Bluntly stated, no one is likely to want to assume responsibility for one of the worst ground- and water-contamination sites in Europe. But if the government sells the tannery without the lagoon, then the government—or perhaps, locals fear, the city of Radom—will be responsible for the site. (Radom, it should be noted, is certainly not an environmental backwater: With assistance from the U.S. Agency for International Development, it is home to a state-of-the-art landfill gas recycling program.)

QUESTIONS

1. Suppose that you were a social ecologist interested in simultaneously ameliorating Poland's toxic legacy and improving its social and economic circumstances. How would you recommend that authorities handle the tannery issue? Would your advice be any different if you were a deep ecologist, an animal rights advocate, or (perhaps particularly appropriate in Poland) a Catholic scholar committed to the ecological ethics articulated in Case 39: Peace with All of Creation?

2. Compare this case to Case 37: DRUMET Poland—A Different Approach. Both are set in the same social, political, and economic context. Yet DRUMET is clearly a social and ecological success story, and the present case is a social dilemma and an ecological disaster. What might have accounted for such different outcomes in these two cases?

3. Compare this case to Case 35: Bhopal. The cases are set in very different social, political, and economic contexts, yet each is a tragedy. What do the cases have in common that might have served as a warning of future problems?

4. Suppose that Polish authorities were to ask permission to load the lagoon's 140,000 tons of toxic liquid waste into secure containers and ship it to Tooele (see Case 33: The Tooele Weapons Incinerator) for destruction at the U.S. Army's chemical weapons incinerator. If you were a resident of Tooele or of one of the ports or cities through which the waste containers would travel, would you be willing to consider the plan? Suppose that when the Tooele incinerator is no longer needed for munitions disposal, a European entrepreneur offered to purchase it for $1, with a plan to reassemble it in Radom. Would you be willing to consider that plan?

SOURCE

Szejnwald Brown, Halina, David Angel, and Patrick G. Derr. *Effective Environmental Regulation: Learning from Poland's Experience*. Westport, Conn.: Praeger, 2000.

35

BHOPAL

The cinders of the funeral pyres at Bhopal are still warm, and the mass graves still fresh, but the media prostitutes of the corporations have already begun their homilies in defense of industrialism and its uncounted horrors. . . . The corporate vampires are guilty of greed, plunder, murder, slavery, extermination and devastation.[1]

The image is powerful: The multinational corporation as a First World vampire sucking life and profit from helpless Third World countries. The body count, if uncertain, is catastrophic: half a million persons exposed, hundreds of thousands sickened, tens of thousands maimed for life, and 2,000 to 6,000 dead (because of mass cremations and burials, the final count will never be known). However, the image notwithstanding, this much is clear: More will be needed to prevent another Bhopal than wooden stakes or rings of garlic.

Union Carbide India Limited (UCIL) built its pesticide plant at Bhopal in 1969 to supply cheap agricultural chemicals for India's Green Revolution. When the disaster happened on December 2, 1984, the plant was under entirely Indian management. The last American employee had left almost two years before.[2]

The Union Carbide Version:[3] Like most "foreign" enterprises in India, UCIL was (at the insistence of the Indian government) a "joint venture" in which the foreign partner(s) was permitted only a minority position. A quarter of its stock was held by the Indian government, about half by Indian nationals, and the remaining quarter by the U.S.-based Union Carbide Corporation (UCC).

Although immediately reported in the popular press as an industrial accident, the Bhopal disaster was the result of deliberate sabotage. Late on the evening of December 2, an angry employee had removed a pressure gauge from a methyl isocyanite (MIC) storage tank, attached a hose, and turned on the water. Perhaps it was only his intention to destroy the batch of pesticide being manufactured from the MIC, but every technical employee at the plant was supposed to know that MIC must *never* be mixed with water. Within hours, the toxic cloud released from the tank had killed thousands and injured hundreds of thousands more, many permanently.

Before the event, there had been only one fatal accident in the plant's fifteen-year history: A single worker had been killed while performing routine maintenance. UCIL had built the facility to the same safety standards used by UCC at its U.S. plants, incorporating multiple, redundant engineering and procedural controls. And UCC plants using MIC in the United States had excellent safety records.

At the time of the accident, UCIL's Indian managers had shut down the MIC refrigeration unit in an effort to boost sagging profits. Both the gas scrubber and the flare tower—devices designed to neutralize or burn any escaping MIC—were also shut down and waiting for repairs. Two years before the disaster, UCC safety inspectors had recommended changes to a fourth safety system: a water curtain designed to react any MIC escaping the other three systems. UCIL management ignored the recommendations. Finally, when the MIC began to escape on December 2, the entire on-site management team was, in violation of explicit safety regulations, off together on a tea break.[4]

UCC immediately accepted moral responsibility for the disaster and promised compensation and relief, but local government officials would not permit UCC officials to interview plant mangers, deliver aid, or assist survivors. The governor of Madhya Pradesh found it more useful to condemn UCC than to deliver relief to the suffering and flatly rejected UCC's offer of $5 million in immediate relief money.

The DOW Chemical/Public Record Version:[5] At the time of the disaster, UCC owned 50.99 percent of UCIL.[6] At least four members of UCIL's board of directors were senior UCC executives. UCIL's annual budgets, major capital expenditures, policy decisions, operating manuals, and company reports were all subject to approval by UCC corporate headquarters, and

UCC control and ownership was hardly inadvertent: The MIC production facility had been added to the plant in 1975 precisely to enable UCC to retain ownership. On January 1, 1974, India had enacted the Foreign Exchange and Regulation Act (FERA), which required all foreign equity holdings to be reduced to no more than 40 percent. But FERA included a statutory exemption for certain kinds of high technology, and UCC promptly submitted a proposal to produce MIC at its Bhopal plant, thereby qualifying the plant for the exemption. Since FERA prohibited any foreign equity holdings larger than 51 percent, UCC reduced its previous 60 percent holding to 50.99 percent and retained its ownership of UCIL.

At the time of the disaster, Union Carbide owned and operated a sister MIC plant in Institute, West Virginia. This plant had computerized warning and monitoring systems; the Bhopal facility used manual gauges. Emergency evacuation plans were in place at the Institute facility; none existed at Bhopal. Safety systems at the Institute plant were scrupulously maintained; of the four systems at Bhopal, one was shut down to save money, two were broken, and the fourth was improperly designed. At the time of the disaster, Bhopal's MIC tank number 610 was filled above recommended capacity, and the reserve tank, which was supposed to be available to handle any excess MIC, was itself already filled with MIC.

The Aftermath: Multiple investigations after the disaster by Indian authorities, international scientific teams, and private environmental groups found that the plant was "an accident waiting to happen." Most damning was the report by a team of UCC safety experts who had inspected the UCIL facility in May 1982 for UCC management in the United States. Their report warned UCC of a "potential for the release of toxic materials" and a "runaway reaction" due to "equipment failure, operating problems, or maintenance problems." The report mentions "deficiencies in safety valve and instrument maintenance programs" and warns that "filter cleaning operations are performed without slip-blinding process. Leaking valves could create serious exposure during this process." In all, the experts reported a total of sixty-one hazards, of which at least thirty were major, including eleven specifically related to the MIC units.

Later that year, UCIL disconnected its public siren from its internal alarms, putatively so that employees could respond to "routine minor leaks" without "unnecessarily" frightening the surrounding populace. Had local residents been given even enough warning to place a wet towel over their faces and flee, thousands of casualties might have been averted.

Union Carbide no longer exists. Sixteen years after the disaster, on February 6, 2001, it was purchased by Dow Chemical. Prior to the purchase, Dow conducted an investigation to determine whether it would thereby acquire any liability related to Bhopal. Dow concluded that it would acquire absolutely no responsibility for either the tragedy or the Bhopal site. According to Dow management, this conclusion was based on the following factors:

1. On February 14, 1989, the Indian government signed a settlement agreement with UCC and UCIL accepting $470 million as compensation for all claims relating to the incident.
2. On October 3, 1991, the Supreme Court of India upheld the settlement and concluded that the amount was just, equitable, and reasonable. The court also found the government of India responsible for any future claims that might exceed the settlement and ordered it to purchase a group medical insurance policy to cover the 100,000 citizens of Bhopal in case of future illnesses.
3. On October 4, 1993, the U.S. Supreme Court reaffirmed earlier U.S. court rulings that the only country with jurisdiction in the case against UCC on matters relating to the Bhopal tragedy was India.
4. In November 1994, UCC sold its remaining interest in UCIL to MacLeod Russel (India) Ltd of Calcutta (later renamed Eveready Industries India Ltd [EIIL]). EIIL took possession of the land under lease from the government of Madhya Pradesh.
5. In 1998, the government of Madhya Pradesh revoked the EIIL lease for the Bhopal site and reclaimed the property "as is," stating that it would take responsibility for managing any future cleanup or remediation work required at the site.

Accordingly, in the view of Dow chemical, when it acquired UCC in February 2001, it inherited "no responsibility whatsoever" in relation to the Bhopal tragedy. Not everyone agrees with Dow's judgment.[7]

DISCUSSION

Foreign corporations involved in constructing potentially hazardous facilities in India during the 1960s and 1970s faced many difficult choices. The facility's location, ownership, design, management, employment practices, and production capacity are all subject to negotiation within the context of a complex set of legal restrictions and political interests.[8] The FERA law plainly threatened UCC's ownership and control of its UCIL subsidiary. In response to that threat, UCC backward-integrated the facility by adding MIC manufacturing capability to the facility.

Having retained ownership by adding dangerous technology, could UCC deny responsibility for the eventual disaster by blaming local Indian managers? It is not as easy a question as it may seem. A quick and simple "no" smacks of colonial disdain for Indian competence. India has fine universities and excellent scientists and engineers—indeed, such excellent scientists and engineers that corporations in developed countries are continually engaged in attempting to lure them away. It has fine businessmen as well, and it is justly proud to call itself "the world's largest democracy." It has designed and constructed nuclear weapons. Obviously, Indian nationals have the technical and managerial skills to operate a pesticide manufacturing facility using MIC.

The nagging question is, Were the Indian managers *prevented* from using those skills by budgets and operating procedures dictated by UCC, or were they merely following local business norms? And even if the latter, why did UCC not follow up on its own experts' safety audit by compelling UCIL to make needed improvements? Why was the siren disconnected? Why was the MIC refrigeration unit allowed to be shut down for financial reasons? Why were the other safety systems not repaired? Why did MIC production continue *without* functioning safety systems? Why did UCC amend UCIL operating procedures so that it could use pipe-flushing procedures (according to most technical investigations, the ultimate cause of the disaster) that were banned in U.S. facilities? It is not easy to avoid the conclusion that UCC safety procedures involved a double standard: one for facilities in rich countries and another for facilities in poorer countries.

The vampire image portrayed in this case's opening quote is dramatic, but it is falsely monolithic. Multinationals have a very wide range of environmental, health, and safety (EHS) policies. One leading American chemical company has long taken the position that unless it can be assured of "cradle-to-grave" control of a business venture's EHS performance, it will not participate in the venture. E. I. DuPont de Nemours will not build, own, or operate a facility unless it is confident that it can make a profit while operating the facility at U.S. EHS standards. With its superb health and safety record, it is virtually certain that DuPont will never experience a Bhopal. (As a sector, according to the U.S. Bureau of Labor Statistics, U.S. chemical workers experience one-tenth as many occupational injuries and illnesses as U.S. industrial workers generally and DuPont workers only one-tenth of the chemical sector norm.) But developing countries, whose markets may not suffice to support a facility operated at DuPont's EHS standards, are eager for technology transfer. If DuPont says no, some other firm will say yes.

Former chief executive officer of Union Carbide Warren Anderson has retired to his estate in Bridgehampton, New York, where he is regularly picketed by protesters holding placards reading, "Warren, shouldn't you be in India?"[9] In early 2002, Indian courts ordered India's Central Bureau of Investigation to expedite Anderson's extradition to face criminal charges, including the culpable homicide of more than 8,000 persons. In December 2002, the formal extradition papers were delivered to India's minister of external affairs. As of March 2003, the minister had not presented the request to U.S. authorities.

Finally, there is the question of Dow's position. At the time of the disaster, Dow had absolutely no connection with the facility or with any of the companies or entities linked to the incident. When it purchased what remained of UCC in 2001, UCC no longer owned the Bhopal facility. Further, Dow believed—on the basis of Supreme Court decisions in both India and the United States—that UCC had entirely discharged its liabilities. But even Dow acknowledges that there is a distinct "humanitarian question": "Can Dow, in its role as a corporate citizen, help to address any of the present day needs which are apparent in Bhopal?"[10]

QUESTIONS

1. Was UCC responsible for the Bhopal disaster? What should it have done in 1982, when its inspection team found serious safety problems at the plant? Should it have repaired the safety systems even if this meant taking a financial loss on its UCIL holdings? If it did not repair the systems and knew that they were inadequate, did its continued involvement with the facility constitute immoral profiteering from an unsafe operation?

2. What are the pros and cons of DuPont's joint venture policy from an *environmental* perspective? From an *international development* perspective? Does the policy unfairly restrain economic and technological development in poorer nations? Suppose that the majority of

multinational corporations involved in high-technology enterprises were to adopt the same policy. Would this be a good thing?

3. Reporting the Bhopal disaster was no picnic for journalists. On one side was a major corporation willing to spend millions of dollars to spin sabotage theories, deny ownership, and blame local management. On the other side was a set of local politicians and regulatory officials who had failed to enforce their own building, safety, and inspection codes and were in the middle of an election year. No one told the whole truth. If you were a journalist, how might your reporting have been affected by your own prejudices regarding multinational corporations or developing countries? Do you have such prejudices?

4. Should corporate executives be held personally and criminally responsible for deaths caused by corporate neglect of EHS standards? Should Warren Anderson face homicide charges in India?

5. What moral responsibility does Dow Chemical have toward the still-suffering survivors of the Bhopal disaster?

6. What moral responsibility does the government of India have toward the still-suffering survivors of the Bhopal disaster?

NOTES

1. George Bradford, "We All Live in Bhopal," *Fifth Estate* 19, no. 4 (winter 1985): 319.

2. Some material regarding Indian development and regulatory practices is derived from Halina Szejnwald Brown, Patrick G. Derr, Ortwin Renn, and Allen L. White, *Corporate Environmentalism in a Global Economy* (Westport, Conn.: Quorum Books, 1993).

3. For an eminently readable Union Carbide version of the story that is particularly rich in technical and scientific details, see Lisa H. Newton and Catherine L. Dillingham, *Watersheds 2: Ten Cases in Environmental Ethics* (Belmont, Calif.: Wadsworth, 1996), chapter 3.

4. Ashok Kalelkar, "Investigation of Large-Magnitude Incidents: Bhopal as a Case Study," paper presented at the Institution of Chemical Engineers' Conference on Preventing Major Chemical Accidents, London, May 1988, 21.

5. The most comprehensive source of materials related to the disaster are the depositions, complaints, answers, and reports filed with the U.S. District Court for the Southern District of New York in the matter of *Bano, Bi, Kumar, Norton, Khan, et al. v. Union Carbide Corporation and Warren Anderson*. See particularly the Revised Complaint, Index No. 99 Civ. 11329 (JFK) Southern District of New York.

6. *Statement of the Dow Chemical Company regarding the Bhopal Tragedy*, May 19, 2003. "When the disaster occurred, the Bhopal plant was operated by Union Carbide India Limited (UCIL), a 51% affiliate of Union Carbide Corporation." The statement is available at www.bhopal.com/position.htm.

7. An excellent portal to the activist campaign to hold Dow responsible for the Bhopal aftermath can be found at www.mad-dow-disease.com.

8. For a detailed account of this process, see Brown et al., *Corporate Environmentalism in a Global Economy*, chapters 3–5.

9. An entire network of organizations seems to be devoted to supporting Anderson's extradition to India. For a look at a typical group, see www.bhopal.net/welcome2.html.

10. *Statement of the Dow Chemical Company regarding the Bhopal Tragedy.*

SOURCES

Bradford, George. "We All Live in Bhopal." *Fifth Estate* 19, no. 4 (winter 1985): 319.

Kalelkar, Ashok. "Investigation of Large-Magnitude Incidents: Bhopal as a Case Study." Paper presented at the Institution of Chemical Engineers' Conference on Preventing Major Chemical Accidents, London, May 1988.

Kurzman, Dan. *A Killing Wind: Inside Union Carbide and the Bhopal Catastrophe.* New York: McGraw-Hill, 1987.

Statement of the Dow Chemical Company regarding the Bhopal Tragedy. May 19, 2003. Available at www.bhopal.com/position.htm.

Szejnwald Brown, Halina, Patrick G. Derr, Ortwin Renn, and Allen L. White. *Corporate Environmentalism in a Global Economy.* Westport, Conn.: Quorum Books, 1993.

Weir, David. *The Bhopal Syndrome: Pesticides, Environment, and Health.* San Francisco: Sierra Club Books, 1987.

36

CERES AND CORPORATE RESPONSIBILITY

Environmental degradation has many causes, but many people would be inclined to put corporations, especially big multinationals, at the top of their list of environmental villains. Although many corporations have earned their bad reputations, a growing number of companies have decided to embrace environmental values. The reasons are several: Some are convinced that "it pays to be green" in the marketplace, others have found that reducing pollution saves them money, many have found that energy and materials efficiencies improve the bottom line, and some really want to be good global citizens.

As a result of these changing corporate attitudes, a number of formal initiatives have emerged in recent years to help corporations adopt and implement higher environmental standards. Two of the most impressive are the Greening of Industry Network[1] and the ISO 14000 certification program.[2] A third is CERES—the Coalition for Environmentally Responsible Economies. Corporate members of CERES commit themselves to implementing the CERES principles. We reprint the principles here:

OUR WORK: THE CERES PRINCIPLES

By endorsing the CERES Principles, companies not only formalize their dedication to environmental awareness and accountability, but also actively commit to an ongoing process of continuous improvement, dialogue and comprehensive, systematic public reporting. Endorsing companies have access to the diverse array of experts in our network, from investors to policy analysts, energy experts, scientists, and others.

Principles

Protection of the Biosphere

We will reduce and make continual progress toward eliminating the release of any substance that may cause environmental damage to the air, water, or the earth or its inhabitants. We will safeguard all habitats affected by our operations and will protect open spaces and wilderness, while preserving biodiversity.

Sustainable Use of Natural Resources

We will make sustainable use of renewable natural resources, such as water, soils and forests. We will conserve non-renewable natural resources through efficient use and careful planning.

Reduction and Disposal of Wastes

We will reduce and where possible eliminate waste through source reduction and recycling. All waste will be handled and disposed of through safe and responsible methods.

Energy Conservation

We will conserve energy and improve the energy efficiency of our internal operations and of the goods and services we sell. We will make every effort to use environmentally safe and sustainable energy sources.

Risk Reduction

We will strive to minimize the environmental, health and safety risks to our employees and the communities in which we operate through safe technologies, facilities and operating procedures, and by being prepared for emergencies.

Safe Products and Services

We will reduce and where possible eliminate the use, manufacture or sale of products and services that cause environmental damage or health or safety hazards. We will inform our customers of the environmental impacts of our products or services and try to correct unsafe use.

Environmental Restoration

We will promptly and responsibly correct conditions we have caused that endanger health, safety or the environment. To the extent feasible, we will redress injuries we have caused to persons or damage we have caused to the environment and will restore the environment.

Informing the Public

We will inform in a timely manner everyone who may be affected by conditions caused by our company that might endanger health, safety or the environment. We will regularly seek advice and counsel through dialogue with persons in communities near our facilities. We will not take any action against employees for reporting dangerous incidents or conditions to management or to appropriate authorities.

Management Commitment

We will implement these Principles and sustain a process that ensures that the Board of Directors and Chief Executive Officer are fully informed about pertinent environmental issues and are fully responsible for environmental policy. In selecting our Board of Directors, we will consider demonstrated environmental commitment as a factor.

Audits and Reports

We will conduct an annual self-evaluation of our progress in implementing these Principles. We will support the timely creation of generally accepted environmental audit procedures. We will annually complete the CERES Report, which will be made available to the public.[3]

DISCUSSION

Traditionally, corporations have understood their primary duty to be to their shareholders. The legal, fiduciary duty of corporate officers is to maximize profits for the shareholders. But some academic and corporate leaders are now suggesting that this fiduciary duty be expanded to include a "triple bottom line," that includes environmental and community impacts as well as profits. For example, many argue that corporations should examine the costs to the community and to the environment of closing manufacturing plants in the United States and moving to countries with lower wages and weaker environmental regulations. Advocates of this approach argue that by making decisions on the basis of the triple bottom line, corporations will increase their profits in the long run. Indeed, by looking to improve environmental practices, several companies have been able to increase their bottom line. For example, short-term investments in energy efficiency can reduce long-term energy costs and decrease greenhouse gases and air pollution.

Unfortunately, however, the three components of a triple bottom line do not always agree. Not every investment in community welfare or environmental protection will return a profit. And when they do not, the consequences for a publicly owned company are as simple as they are brutal: Stock prices will fall, and investors willing to eliminate the company's socially and environmentally beneficial policies will acquire ownership, eliminate the policies, and profit in the bargain.

But public ownership can work both ways. One benefit of the CERES principles is that they allow investors to be better informed about the environmental practices of the companies in which they invest. Many investment houses now offer "socially responsible" investment portfolios.[4] In addition to a quantitative analysis of the company's profit, social investing examines more qualitative analyses, such as environmental or social principles. During the 1980s, many investors put pressure on companies to withdraw from doing business in South Africa in an attempt to pressure the South African government to end apartheid. Almost every U.S.-based corporation ultimately divested of South Africa.

When a corporation praises itself for adhering to strict environmental principles while actually continuing to do business as usual, its behavior is called "greenwashing." Some groups have pointed to Exxon's donation of $9 million to protect tigers (their corporate symbol) as an example of greenwashing, citing Exxon's efforts to open the Arctic National Wildlife Refuge for oil drilling as proof of corporate hypocrisy. But the money donated by Exxon clearly did help protect the endangered tiger.

QUESTIONS

1. A few of the CERES principles are mandated by U.S. law, such as some of the requirements listed under "Environmental Restoration." Should all the principles be made mandatory?

2. Notice that the CERES principles are "locality blind" in that they oblige a member to implement the same environmental standards whether its facilities and operations are sited in a developing country or in the United States or the European Union. Some scholars argue that if this obligation is taken literally, it would simply obstruct economic and technological development in many poorer countries (in this context, compare Case 35: Bhopal). Others argue that foreign workers and ecosystems deserve the same respect as U.S. workers and ecosystems and that corporations that fail to show such respect deserve to be called "corporate vampires." Should U.S. companies working overseas be required to meet U.S. environmental standards?

3. As a stockholder, would you prefer that the board of directors of a given company adopt a long-term business strategy that takes into consideration environmental principles or a shorter-term strategy that focuses on quarterly earnings? How likely do you think it is that a truly green company could compete economically?

4. Should universities urge the companies in which their endowment funds are invested to become CERES members? Should the trustees of public (for example, state and county) pension funds do the same?

5. Directors often focus on quarterly earnings as an indicator of whether they are fulfilling their fiduciary duty to shareholders. Should their focus be broadened to incorporate a triple bottom line? Should the law governing directors' fiduciary responsibilities be changed to include corporate impacts on communities and environments?

6. There are several investment companies that invest only in "socially responsible" companies. Is the emergence and growth of these funds likely to influence corporate behavior?

7. The reporting requirements in the CERES principles are intended to eliminate greenwashing by requiring that companies report not only their environmental goals but also their actual practices. Do the requirements seem strong enough? Other things being equal, would the fact that a corporation was a CERES member incline you to put more trust in its stated environmental policies?

8. Notice that the CERES principle "Informing the Public" protects employee whistle-blowers who report dangerous incidents or conditions to *management* or to *appropriate authorities* but not to the *media*. Is this an important lacuna? Is it a reasonable one?

9. Is greenwashing an ethical public relations strategy? Should it be banned as a kind of false advertising? If so, how could the ban be enforced?

NOTES

1. For information about the Greening of Industry Network (GIN), see www.greeningofindustry.org. Note: GIN sponsors several international conferences each year, typically in the United States, Europe, and Asia. The network has a well-deserved reputation for welcoming interested undergraduate and graduate students at its events.

2. The best introduction to the ISO 14000 standards is *ISO 14000—Meet the Whole Family*, written by ISO/TC 207, the ISO technical committee responsible for developing and maintaining the 14000 family of standards. The document is available free from the International Organization for Standardization at www.isoeasy.org/iso14000.pdf. More information about this and other ISO programs is available at www.iso.ch/iso/en/ISOOnline.frontpage. The American National Standards Institute (ANSI) also has a website devoted to ISO 14000: www.ansi.org/public/iso14000/default.htm. A variety of materials concerning the involvement of nongovernmental organizations (NGOs) in the ISO 14000 development process can be accessed through the ISO 14000 NGO Initiative at www.ecologia.org/iso14000.

3. Available at www.ceres.org/our_work/principles.htm.

4. An excellent "first stop" for exploring the rapidly growing world of socially responsible investing is www.socialinvest.org.

SOURCES

American National Standards Institute. *ISO 14000*. Available at www.ansi.org/public/iso14000/default.htm.

Coalition for Environmentally Responsible Economies. *Our Work: The CERES Principles*. Available at www.ceres.org/our_work/principles.htm.

Greening of Industry Network. www.greeningofindustry.org.

ISO Technical Committee 207. *ISO 14000—Meet the Whole Family*. Available at www.isoeasy.org/iso14000.pdf.

37

DRUMET POLAND— A DIFFERENT APPROACH

Wloclawek, Poland, is a city of 120,000 located 100 miles northwest of Warsaw. DRUMET is one of four major industries in Wloclawek, the others being a fertilizer manufacturer, a paint manufacturer, and a paper mill. Founded in 1895, DRUMET is now one of Europe's leading manufacturers of high-quality steel cables. When the socialist regime fell in 1989, DRUMET was among the healthiest of all Poland's state-owned enterprises: It was well poised to compete in the emerging market economy. The company was privatized in 1994; 80 percent of its stock is owned by a Polish investment firm and 20 percent by DRUMET employees. DRUMET is a modern enterprise with a complex management structure, a twenty-person environmental protection department, and a world-class approach to marketing and production.

The DRUMET factory abuts a densely populated residential area of 25,000 people. The proximity of the factory to employees' neighborhoods is a legacy of communist industrial and social policy. The major manufacturer provided neighborhood housing, schools, energy, health care, and recreational centers for its employees. DRUMET still maintains a vacation resort for its employees.

The steel cable manufacturing process involves treating high-temperature steel with hydrochloric acid (HCl) and molten zinc. After pretreatment on-site, wastewater from the facility is drained into the municipal sewage system. The contract between DRUMET and the Municipal Sewage Authority allows DRUMET to discharge water containing ten times more zinc than is permitted by national surface-water discharge standards. This is allowable because DRUMET is the only zinc source loading the Wloclawek sewer system, and its total zinc discharges do not threaten the city's compliance with national discharge standards for surface waters. But DRUMET's ability to negotiate a relaxed zinc standard in the absence of other zinc sources was balanced by the authorities' ability to impose an extraordinarily strict HCl standard in the presence of other significant HCl sources.

For decades, reducing airborne emissions of hydrochloride gas was the greatest environmental challenge at DRUMET. The facility uses approximately 80,000 pounds of HCl per week (2,000 tons per year), and much of it was lost to the atmosphere from point sources or fugitive emissions. Nevertheless, by the late 1980s, as the result of many incremental improvements, ambient air standards for HCl in the neighborhoods around DRUMET were rarely exceeded. Measured HCl levels averaged out to only 11 percent of the twenty-four-hour standard and 1.5 percent of the annual standard.

Because of the other industrial enterprises in Wloclawek, however, public health officials judged that total HCl levels in the larger area were still too high. So in 1988, despite the fact that DRUMET was then in compliance with national HCl emission standards, WWOS (the Polish environmental regulatory agency) ordered DRUMET to reduce total HCl emissions by more than 85 percent. DRUMET complained but began to upgrade its thirteen cable treatment units with new, completely sealed equipment at a cost of more than $400,000 each. The new units release no HCl and are supported by an HCl treatment system that purifies, recycles, and reuses all captured HCl. In fact, by 1995, DRUMET was selling its HCl purification services to other enterprises.

Clearly, WWOS based its order on a line of reasoning very different from U.S. or EU regulatory practice. First, WWOS subtracted from a "healthy" HCl level all the background HCl emissions from other regional sources, such as the paint factory and paper mill. Since these background levels were quite high, only a very small increment was left for DRUMET. Then it ordered DRUMET, which was already in compliance with national standards, to lower its emissions to the calculated increment. But why not order the paint factory or paper mill to lower their (much higher) emissions? Because WWOS judged that, unlike DRUMET, they were neither technologically nor financially capable of further improvements and that to push them into bankruptcy would cause unacceptable social harm to the community.

The DRUMET case is an example of an environmental regulatory system in which local and regional authorities exercise vastly greater discretionary power than their U.S. or EU counterparts. In setting emission standards for individual enterprises, regulators consider not only national standards but also background pollution levels, the technological and financial capabilities of the firm, and the social and economic importance of the firm to its community. In general, WWOS will push a firm to make all the improvements that it judges to be technologically and financially feasible. In the DRUMET case, it is clear that WWOS had the information and expertise to gauge this feasibility quite accurately.

DRUMET's managers accept WWOS's approach as legitimate and fair. "After all," DRUMET's director of environmental protection commented, "I have twenty five thousand people in the neighborhood to answer to!"

DISCUSSION

The severe environmental degradation that occurred in central Europe under communist rule is now well-known: Dead lakes, suffocating air pollution, and toxic soil contamination are the grim legacy of a system that allowed industrial growth to trump every environmental value. With the arrival of democracy and a free-market economy in 1989, Polish authorities were therefore confronted with an extremely difficult task: how to achieve dramatic environmental gains without undercutting the rapid privatization of formerly state-owned enterprises. So far, their enterprise-specific, discretion-rich approach has produced remarkable environmental gains with minimal social and economic dislocation. Indeed, between 1990 and 2000, the general tenor of mainstream U.S. and EU scholarship on the subject has changed from "what Poland should do" to "what we can learn from Poland."

Few issues in environmental ethics or environmental policy are as bitterly debated as the relationship between economic growth and environmental degradation. In this connection, see the discussion of the Environmental Kuznet's Curve hypothesis in Case 41: Is the Lifeboat Full?

QUESTIONS

1. From the U.S. or EU perspective, it seems utterly unfair to compel a firm that is already a good environmental actor to reduce its profits in order to mitigate the environmental and public health effects of other

firms' poor environmental performance. From the perspective of WWOS and DRUMET, it seems a perfectly sensible way to protect public health. Who is right?

2. Obviously, the environmental protection system in Poland gives local and regional authorities far wider discretion (and ultimately much more power) than does the U.S. system (see Case 11: Mr. Cone's Woodpeckers). What are the strengths and weaknesses of such a "discretion-rich" approach to environmental protection? Would such a system work in the United States?

3. Compare the Polish regulatory system to the "cap-and-trade" program used in the United States to regulate sulfur dioxide emissions (see Case 43: Trading Pollutants). Neither is a classic "command-and-control" model, but while the Polish system gives additional freedom to regulators, the U.S. system gives additional freedom to polluters. Which approach seems more likely to produce a good balance between environmental protection and economic growth?

4. What is the relationship between prosperity and environmental protection? Must a population achieve a certain level of material security before it can be expected to care about the protection of its environment? Are economic development and environmental protection always conflicting values? (See the discussion of the Environmental Kuznet's Curve hypothesis in Case 41: Is the Lifeboat Full?)

SOURCE

Brown, Halina Szejnwald, David Angel, and Patrick G. Derr. *Effective Environmental Regulation: Learning from Poland's Experience.* Westport, Conn.: Praeger, 2000.

38

SCIENTIFIC
INTEGRITY AT EPA

National Treasury Employees Union Chapter 280 (NTEU 280) represents professional scientists who work at the national headquarters offices of the U.S. Environmental Protection Agency (EPA). In March 2000, NTEU 280's "Principles of Scientific Integrity" were accepted by EPA's National Partnership Council and officially promulgated by EPA Administrator Carol Browner. Here are the principles:

PRINCIPLES OF SCIENTIFIC INTEGRITY

It is essential that EPA's scientific and technical activities be of the highest quality and credibility if EPA is to carry out its responsibilities to protect human health and the environment. Honesty and integrity in its activities and decision-making processes are vital if the American public is to have trust and confidence in EPA's decisions. EPA adheres to these Principles of Scientific Integrity.

EPA employees, whatever their grade, job or duties, must:

Ensure that their work is of the highest integrity—this means that the work must be performed objectively and without predetermined outcomes using the most appropriate techniques. Employees are responsible and accountable for the integrity and validity of their own work. Fabrication or falsification of work results are direct assaults on the integrity of EPA and will not be tolerated.

Represent their own work fairly and accurately. When representing the work of others, employees must seek to understand the results and the implications of this work and also represent it fairly and accurately.

Respect and acknowledge the intellectual contributions of others in representing their work to the public or in published writings such as journal articles or technical reports. To do otherwise is plagiarism. Employees should also refrain from taking credit for work with which they were not materially involved.

Avoid financial conflicts of interest and ensure impartiality in the performance of their duties by respecting and adhering to the principles of ethical conduct and implementing standards contained in Standards of Ethical Conduct for Employees of the Executive Branch and in supplemental agency regulations.

Be cognizant of and understand the specific, programmatic statutes that guide the employee's work.

Accept the affirmative responsibility to report any breach of these principles.

Welcome differing views and opinions on scientific and technical matters as a legitimate and necessary part of the process to provide the best possible information to regulatory and policy decision-makers.

Adherence by all EPA employees to these principles will assure the American people that they can have confidence and trust in EPA's work and in its decisions.

DISCUSSION

Many of the principles seem almost self-evident: Of course, scientists involved in setting national environmental standards should be honest, fair, and impartial. Nevertheless, it took fifteen years of union advocacy and congressional pressure to get EPA to accept them, and as of June 2002, EPA had neither developed any process to enforce the principles nor even agreed to meet with union leaders to begin discussing the development of such a process. Indeed, more than two years after their promulgation by EPA Administrator Carol Browner, the principles have yet to appear on any EPA website.[1]

Has the misuse of science or the misuse of managerial authority relative to science been a problem at EPA? Not according to Administrator Browner.

Testifying to Congress on October 4, 2000, Browner put the principles at center stage and stated flatly,

> Under the Clinton-Gore Administration, EPA has worked hard to ensure that every family in every neighborhood enjoys a healthy environment. . . . To this end, we have adopted as Agency policy the *Principles of Scientific Integrity*, proposed by our joint labor-management partnership council. It is essential that EPA's s scientific and technical activities be of the highest quality and credibility. Honesty and integrity, in all our activities, are vital if the public is to have trust and confidence in EPA's decisions. . . . The Agency has demonstrated a strong commitment to sound science as the basis for our decisions.[2]

But press reports and statements by senior EPA scientists suggest otherwise. EPA scientists have dissented publicly from the agency's official statement on the risks of malathion in food and drinking water.[3] Press reports from the late 1990s on have charged that EPA managers ignored or overruled the advice of their own scientists when making policy on a issues ranging from the use of methyl tertiary-butyl ether (MTBE) in gasoline to the use of municipal sewage as fertilizer.[4]

The issues of scientific integrity and retaliation at EPA continue to provoke controversy in the courts, in the streets, and in Congress. On August 18, 2001, Dr. Marsha Coleman-Adebayo won a $600,000 judgment against EPA and former Administrator Browner for discrimination and retaliation. On May 1, 2002, frustrated members of NTEU 280 picketed EPA's own International Science Forum, denouncing EPA management for refusing to implement the principles. On May 15, 2002, President Bush signed the Notification and Federal Anti-Discrimination and Retaliation Act (the "NO FEAR" Bill) into law: After congressional hearings that excoriated EPA managers, the bill passed both houses by unanimous votes of 420–0 and 99–0.[5] Nevertheless, the Bush administration's new EPA administrator, Governor Christine Whitman, seems no more eager to fully implement the principles than was her predecessor.

Dr. Dwight Welch, an EPA scientist and executive vice president of NTEU 280, argues for the need to implement the principles at EPA this way:

> Ask [EPA manager] Dr. William Sanders about assigning epidemiology work to political scientist Dr. Marsha Coleman-Adebayo. Is assigning a non-scientist scientific work an example of integrity? Dr. Coleman-Adebayo's assignment was to identify every pollutant which can be found in the human body. Is this something a political scientist normally does?

CASE 38

Dr. Brian Dementi is classified as a "scientific dissenter" here at EPA. However, in the real world of toxicology, such as the peer review panels on malathion or cholinesterase inhibitors, Dr. Dementi's views are supported as being correct. . . . In the EPA, the toxicology of these respective subjects are twisted to reflect something other than science.

Scientific fraud is almost a daily complaint here at NTEU 280. Indeed, I originally got involved when certain managers told me "Propane is not flammable." After they thought about it for a bit, they . . . backed off to the position, "Well, OK, propane is flammable but not as a propellant in pesticide aerosols." So when I gave them a physical demonstration, they again backed off with, "Well, OK, but accidents involving these products are not happening in the real world." When I supplied them with extensive documentation in the form of hundreds of CPSC [Consumer Products Safety Commission] accident reports, metropolitan fire investigator reports, etc., they assigned me to a discipline in which I was untrained to perform. . . .

How many examples do you need before you can see that scientific fraud is rampant within EPA?[6]

In late June 2002, Morris Winn, assistant administrator for administration and resources management at EPA, announced that EPA Administrator Governor Whitman intended to reissue the "Principles of Scientific Integrity" with a cover memo explaining her views on the principles.

On July 9, 2002, J. William Hirzy, Ph.D., senior vice president of NTEU 280 and a senior scientist in risk assessment at the EPA, summed up the then-current situation this way:

When I worked as a research and process development chemist in the private sector, I was almost always involved in research work that had a specific, management-directed goal in mind—[for example] make a plasticizer that won't mar polystyrene finishes on refrigerators. . . . Management never told me to lie about how well a plasticizer performed in an extraction test. . . . Management never told me to change the yield figures to make process economics look good. They never had to. . . . As Richard Feynmann put it when he investigated the *Challenger* disaster: "Mother Nature will not be fooled."

Those of us who work at EPA headquarters mostly don't have the pleasure of working at a research bench, asking Mother Nature questions, observing her answers and then deciding what next to do. The way we deal with science at headquarters is quite different. . . . There may be a court-ordered schedule of rule-making facing our Office management, and it

214

might involve setting what amounts to a "safe" exposure level for humans or other species. On occasion . . . the manager gets orders from up the line, perhaps even the White House or Capitol Hill, that the "safe" level is some particular value. . . . The manager then comes to a staff scientist and says, "This is the safe level that we are going to propose in the Federal Register. Write me a justification for it." What is sometimes stated openly, sometimes not, is, "I don't care what the literature says, my bosses have given me instructions on this, and if you want to stay on my good side and see some award money, you will craft for me an elegant justification of this 'safe' level."

This happens. And when the literature does *not* support what management wants to do, it is a moral problem for ethical scientists whose work involves reading the literature, making value judgments about the merits of the published work of other scientists, and writing technical support documents for Agency rule-making.

Some statutes permit management to set "safe" levels based on factors other than the physical and biological sciences. For example, Maximum Contaminant Levels (MCL) for drinking water are supposed to be set as close as possible to the Maximum Contaminant Level Goal (MCLG) . . . but the MCL can be set at a different level if economic, feasibility, or other factors so dictate. We have no problem with this situation: it is what the law passed by Congress and signed by the President and adjudicated by the Courts mandates. . . .

But we do have a problem when management orders up a phony MCLG so that a politically dictated MCL will have scientific "cover." We do have a problem when management prevents an EPA toxicologist from attending a pathology review at which malignant tumors are down-graded so that an economically important pesticide can achieve a lower cancer rating.

And when EPA management collects data on indoor air pollutants in its own buildings, conducts and publishes a major survey showing that EPA employees were sickened by the pollutants, admits that those pollutants made the employees sick, and then disavows its own results in order to protect an industry and "avoid lawsuits"—then we have a big problem. These are just a few high-profile, real-life examples of what scientific integrity means, or doesn't mean, at EPA headquarters. . . .

It took almost two decades of hard work to get EPA managers to accept a set of professional ethics for EPA scientists, now called the *Principles of Scientific Integrity*. But the job of establishing the *Principles* as a working policy is not complete, because there is still no agreed-upon method of resolving disputes that arise involving the principles. Under these conditions, the principles are not much more than pretty window dressing to which EPA management can point. . . .

On May 1, 2002, we began a new campaign to get the EPA to see the need to make the *Principles of Scientific Integrity* more than mere window dressing. This campaign was triggered by an incident in which a supervisor told a scientist who is a member of our bargaining unit, "It's your job to support me, even if I say 2 + 2 = 7!"

We . . . strive on a day-to-day basis to use the best scientific principles to honestly and ethically evaluate scientific research work done by other scientists so that work can be applied to the laws EPA administers. Our duty also requires us to be on guard to see that our work is not distorted or misused to subvert environmental laws. . . . Having the *Principles of Scientific Integrity* as a fully functioning internal EPA mechanism to both resolve disputes and admonish employees and managers against less than faithful execution of the law will be a giant leap forward in improving the administration of the Nation's environmental laws.[7]

The following day, EPA Administrator Whitman transmitted the following memorandum to all EPA employees, with a copy of the principles attached.

MEMORANDUM
SUBJECT: Principles of Scientific Integrity
TO: All EPA Employees
DATE: July 10, 2002

I am transmitting to you the attached Principles of Scientific Integrity and reaffirming the importance of maintaining sound science as the keystone for our work.

These Principles, developed in 1999 by the management and union membership of the National Partnership Council, established clear ethical standards, consistent with those in other research environments, to help protect the quality of science in the Agency. Our credibility with the American public depends on their trust, and by adhering to these Principles, we all work together to promote public confidence in the integrity of EPA's scientific and technical activities.

Thank you for demonstrating your firm commitment to EPA's Principles of Scientific Integrity in all that you do each day to advance the Agency's pursuit of its vital mission.

Christine Todd Whitman, Administrator[8]

Director Whitman has certainly reaffirmed the principles, but her memo does not concede what NTEU still seeks: that the principles can be used as grounds for a grievance under EPA's labor agreement. This means that professional scientists at EPA still cannot invoke the principles as legal grounds for refusing to comply with management directives.

QUESTIONS

1. The principles are a set of ethical claims, not a set of empirical claims. If you agree with them, what justifies your opinion that they are morally correct?

2. Do professional scientists, as such, have any special competence on questions of ethics? If not, what qualified the members of NTEU 280 to promulgate the principles?

3. Is scientific integrity more important in a regulatory context, such as at EPA, than in an advocacy or for-profit context? Would it be less wrong for a scientist working with Monsanto or the Sierra Club to "fudge" data than it would be for a scientist working at EPA?

4. Suppose that a professor of microbiology is found to have engaged in management-directed "fudging" while working as a paid consultant to an advocacy group or a for-profit corporation. Would this be grounds for her colleagues or her university to censure her?

5. The fourth paragraph of the principles asserts that EPA professionals should "Avoid financial conflicts of interest." Not surprisingly, EPA hires many of its best-trained and most experienced scientists away from private corporations. (Recall Dr. Hirzy's work in research and development for Monsanto.) Some of these scientists may arrive at EPA with private retirement plans heavily invested in the stock of their former employer. Should these scientists be required to divest themselves of such holdings? Should they not be allowed to participate in EPA assessments of their former employers' products? And what about products produced by competitors? What would a realistic set of guidelines be for these situations?

6. The sixth paragraph of the principles asserts that EPA professionals should "Accept the affirmative responsibility to report any breach of these principles." This is a very strong claim indeed, for, among other things, it obliges EPA scientists to police each others' compliance with the principles and report suspected breaches. In medical contexts, such requirements have often been labeled "squeal rules." If you were a scientist at EPA, would you be willing to accept this rule? Would you be

willing to act on it? Would you be worried about unfounded accusations made by rivals, disgruntled subordinates, or vindictive superiors? What sorts of guidelines might be needed to both protect reporting scientists from retaliation and protect reported scientists from false charges? The NO FEAR Bill was designed to provide these protections. Does it?

NOTES

1. The authors last checked the EPA website for the principles on July 25, 2003.

2. Carol Browner, *Statement of the Environmental Protection Agency before the Committee on Science, House of Representatives*, October 4, 2000, available at www.house.gov/science/browner_100400.htm.

3. The EPA policy documents and reports, including the dissenting views, are available on the EPA website at www.epa.gov/oppsrrd1/op/malathion.htm. For one of the dissenting views, see particularly www.epa.gov/oppsrrd1/op/malathion/dementi_1100.pdf.

4. For example, see (from very different perspectives) these: E. S. R. Gopal, "EPA Error Risked Halving India's Rice Harvest," *Nature* 403, no. 6766 (January 13, 2000): 130; Colin Macilwain, "EPA Science Overburdened by Congress," *Nature* 400, no. 6746 (August 19, 1999): 700; and Bonner Cohen, "Blinded by Science: Will Whitman Rein in the EPA?" *Washington Times*, January 26, 2001, available at http://c3.org/news_center/third_party/01-26-01.html, and *Under the Guise of Environmental Protection: EPA Revealed* (Washington, D.C.: National Wilderness Institute, August 2000), available at www.nwi.org/SpecialStudies/UnderGuiseReport/UnderGuise.html.

5. For a brief history and synopsis of the bill, see "President Bush Signs 'NO FEAR' Bill into Law," NTEU 280, *FISHBOWL* 18, no. 3 (May 2002) (NTEU Chapter 280, P.O. Box 76082, Washington, D.C. 20013). The newsletter is available at www.nteu280.org/Fishbowl/MAY%20FISHBOWL%202002.htm.

6. Dwight Welch, "Memo to Morris X. Winn, Assistant Administrator, EPA Office of Administration and Resources Management," reprinted in NTEU 280, *FISHBOWL* 18, no. 4 (June 2002), available at www.nteu280.org/Fishbowl/JUNE%20FISHBOWL%202002.htm.

7. This narrative is an abridged version of J. William Hirzy, "Scientific Integrity in a Regulatory Context—An Elusive Ideal at EPA," July 9, 2002. The full text is available at http://slweb.org/hirzy-commentary1.html. Doctor Hirzy is senior vice president of NTEU 280 and has been employed as a senior scientist in risk assessment at EPA since 1981. Before that, he was employed by Monsanto Company in research-and-development and environmental management positions. His article is used with permission.

8. "Subject: EPA Principles of Scientific Integrity," e-mail from Mike Moore (Moore.Mike@epamail.epa.gov), External Relations, Immediate Office of the Assistant Administrator (8101R), Office of Research and Development, U.S. Environmental Protection Agency, October 18, 2002, 12:34 P.M.

SOURCES

Browner, Carol. *Statement of the Environmental Protection Agency before the Committee on Science, House of Representatives.* October 4, 2000. Available at www.house.gov/science/browner_100400.htm.

Cohen, Bonner. "Blinded by Science: Will Whitman Rein in the EPA?" *Washington Times,* January 26, 2001. Available at http://c3.org/news_center/third_party/01-26-01.html.

———. *Under the Guise of Environmental Protection: EPA Revealed.* Washington, D.C.: National Wilderness Institute, August 2000. Available at: www.nwi.org/SpecialStudies/UnderGuiseReport/UnderGuise.html.

Gopal, E. S. R. "EPA Error Risked Halving India's Rice Harvest." *Nature* 403, no. 6766 (January 13, 2000): 130.

Hearing before the Committee of the Judiciary, House of Representatives, One Hundred Seventh Congress, First Session, on H.R. 169, Notification and Federal Employee Anti-Discrimination and Retaliation Act of 2001, May 9, 2001. Washington, D.C.: U.S. Government Printing Office, 2001. Complete transcript available at www.house.gov/judiciary/72302.pdf.

Hirzy, J. William. "Scientific Integrity in a Regulatory Context—An Elusive Ideal at EPA." July 9, 2002. Available at http://slweb.org/hirzy-commentary1.html.

Macilwain, Colin. "EPA Science Overburdened by Congress." *Nature* 400, no. 6746 (August 19, 1999): 700.

NTEU 280. *FISHBOWL* 18, no. 3 (May 2002). Available at www.nteu280.org/Fishbowl/MAY%20FISHBOWL%202002.htm.

———. *FISHBOWL* 18, no. 4 (June 2002). Available at www.nteu280.org/Fishbowl/JUNE%20FISHBOWL%202002.htm.

39

PEACE WITH
ALL OF CREATION

Lynn White's "The Historical Roots of Our Ecological Crisis" is one of the best-known and most widely reprinted essays in the history of environmental writing.[1] No doubt, White's thesis—that the Judeo-Christian tradition is ultimately to blame for the world's current ecological crisis—is controversial. And no doubt, White's prescription sounds radical. Speaking specifically to "Christians and neo-Christians," White declares,

> To a Christian a tree can be no more than a physical fact. The whole concept of the sacred grove is alien to Christianity and to the ethos of the West. . . . More science and more technology are not going to get us out of the present ecological crisis until we find a new religion, or rethink our old one.

Since it seemed unlikely that the world's two billion Christians would collectively "find a new religion," White concluded his essay by recommending St. Francis of Assisi as a model to those who wanted to "rethink the old one."

As a case study of such rethinking, we here excerpt the speech on ecology given by His Holiness, Pope John Paul II, on World Peace Day, January 1, 1990. Like White, the pope began his analysis with a reflection on the creation account in Genesis. And like White, he ended by invoking St. Francis:

The Ecological Crisis: A Common Responsibility

PEACE WITH GOD THE CREATOR, PEACE WITH ALL OF CREATION.

1. In our day, there is a growing awareness that world peace is threatened not only by the arms race, regional conflicts and continued injustices among peoples and nations, but also by a lack of *due respect for nature*, by the plundering of natural resources and by a progressive decline in the quality of life. . . . Faced with the widespread destruction of the environment, people everywhere are coming to understand that we cannot continue to use the goods of the earth as we have in the past.

2. Many ethical values, fundamental to the development of a peaceful society, are particularly relevant to the ecological question. . . . For Christians, such values are grounded in religious convictions drawn from Revelation . . . .

3. In the Book of Genesis . . . there is a recurring refrain: *"and God saw it was good."* After creating the heavens, the sea, the earth and all it contains, God created man and woman. At this point the refrain changes markedly: "And God saw everything he had made, and behold, *it was very good"* (Gen. 1:31). . . .

Adam and Eve's call to share in the unfolding of God's plan of creation brought into play those abilities and gifts which distinguish the human being from all other creatures. At the same time, their call established a fixed relationship between mankind and the rest of creation. Made in the image and likeness of God, Adam and Eve were to have exercised their dominion over the earth (Gen. 1:28) *with wisdom and love.* Instead, they destroyed the existing harmony . . . by choosing to sin. This resulted not only in man's alienation from himself . . . but also in the earth's "rebellion" against him (cf. Gen. 3:17–19; 4:12). . . .

5. The increasing devastation of the world of nature is apparent to all. It results from the behavior of people who show a callous disregard for the hidden, yet perceivable requirements of the order and harmony which govern nature itself. . . .

Clearly, an adequate solution cannot be found merely in a better management or a more rational use of the earth's resources, as important as these may be. Rather, we must go to the source of the problem and face in its entirety that profound moral crisis of which the destruction of the environment is only one troubling aspect.

6. Certain elements of today's ecological crisis reveal its moral character. First among these is the indiscriminate application of advances in science and technology. Many recent discoveries have brought undeniable benefits to humanity. [But] . . . it is now clear that the application of these discoveries in the fields of industry and agriculture have produced harmful long-term effects. . . . *We cannot interfere in one area of the ecosystem without paying due attention both to the consequences of such interference in other areas and to the well-being of future generations.*

The gradual depletion of the ozone layer and the related "greenhouse effect" has now reached crisis proportions as a consequence of industrial growth, massive urban concentrations and vastly increased energy needs. Industrial waste, the burning of fossil fuels, unrestricted deforestation, the use of certain types of herbicides, coolants and propellants: all of these are known to harm the atmosphere and environment. . . .

7. [A] lack of respect for life [is] evident in many patterns of environmental pollution. Often, the interests of production prevail over concern for the dignity of workers, while economic interests take priority over the good of individuals and even entire peoples. . . . On another level, delicate ecological balances are upset by the uncontrolled destruction of animal and plant life or by a reckless exploitation of natural resources. . . .

We are not yet in a position to assess the biological disturbance that could result from indiscriminate genetic manipulation and from the unscrupulous development of new forms of plant and animal life. . . . It is evident to all that in any area as delicate as this, indifference to fundamental ethical norms, or their rejection, would lead mankind to the very threshold of self-destruction.

Respect for life, and above all for the dignity of the human person, is the ultimate guiding norm for any sound economic, industrial or scientific progress. . . . No peaceful society can afford to neglect either respect for life or the fact that there is an integrity to creation.

8. Theology, philosophy and science all speak of a harmonious universe, of a "cosmos" endowed with its own integrity, its own internal, dynamic balance. *This order must be respected.* The human race is called to explore this order, to examine it with due care and to make use of it while safeguarding its integrity.

On the other hand, the earth is ultimately *a common heritage, the fruits of which are for the benefit of all. . . .* It is manifestly unjust that a privileged few should continue to accumulate excess goods, squandering available resources, while masses of people are living in conditions of misery at the very lowest level of subsistence. . . .

9. In many cases the effects of ecological problems transcend the borders of individual States; hence their solution cannot be found solely on the national level. Recently there have been some promising steps towards such international action, yet the existing mechanisms and bodies are clearly not adequate. . . . Political obstacles, forms of exaggerated nationalism and economic interests—to mention only a few factors—impede international cooperation and long-term effective action.

The need for joint action on the international level *does not lessen the responsibility of each individual state* . . . [to] facilitate necessary socioeconomic adjustments within its own borders, giving special attention to the most vulnerable sectors of society. The State should also actively endeavor within its own territory to prevent destruction of the atmosphere and biosphere, [and] . . . ensure that its citizens are not exposed to dangerous pollutants or toxic wastes. *The right to a safe environment* . . . must be included in an updated Charter of Human Rights.

10. The ecological crisis reveals the *urgent moral need for a new solidarity*, especially in relations between the developing nations and those that are highly industrialized. . . . The newly industrialized States cannot, for example, be asked to apply restrictive environmental standards to their emerging industries unless the industrialized States first apply them within their own boundaries. At the same time, countries in the process of industrialization are not morally free to repeat the errors made in the past by others. . . .

11. [A] proper ecological balance will not be found without *directly addressing the structural forms of poverty* that exist throughout the world. Rural poverty and unjust land distribution in many countries, for example, have led to subsistence farming and to the exhaustion of the soil. Once their land yields no more, many farmers move on to clear new land, thus accelerating uncontrolled deforestation, or they settle in urban centres which lack the infrastructure to receive them. Likewise, some heavily indebted countries are destroying their natural heritage, at the price of irreparable ecological imbalances, in order to develop new products for export. . . . The poor, *to whom the earth is entrusted no less than to others*, must be enabled to find a way out of their poverty. This will require a courageous reform of structures. . . .

12. Today, any form of war on a global scale would lead to incalculable ecological damage. But even local or regional wars,

however limited . . . damage the land, ruining crops and vegetation as well as poisoning soil and water, [and] . . . create situations of extreme social unrest, with further negative consequences for the environment.

13. Modern society will find no solution to the ecological problem unless it *takes a serious look at its lifestyle*. In many parts of the world society is given to instant gratification and consumerism while remaining indifferent to the damage which these cause. . . . Simplicity, moderation and discipline, as well as a spirit of sacrifice, must become a part of everyday life, lest all suffer the negative consequences of the careless habits of a few. An *education in ecological responsibility* . . . entails a genuine conversion in ways of thought and behavior. . . .

14. Finally, the *aesthetic value* of creation cannot be overlooked. Our very contact with nature has a deep restorative power; contemplation of its magnificence imparts peace and serenity. . . .

15. Today the ecological crisis has assumed such proportions as to be *the responsibility of everyone*. . . . The earth and its atmosphere are telling us *that there is an order in the universe which must be respected*, and that the human person, endowed with the capability of choosing freely, has a grave responsibility to preserve this order for the well-being of future generations.

Even men and women without any particular religious conviction . . . recognize their obligation to contribute to the restoration of a healthy environment. All the more should men and women who believe in God the Creator . . . feel called to address the problem. . . .

16. In 1979, I proclaimed Saint Francis of Assisi as the heavenly patron of those who promote ecology (cf. *Apostolic Letter Inter Sanctos: AAS* 71 [1979], 1509f). He offers Christians an example of genuine and deep respect for the integrity of creation. . . . Peace with all creation is inseparable from peace among all peoples. . . .

From the Vatican, 8 December 1989.
Joannes Paulus II

DISCUSSION

It is interesting and perhaps ironic to compare John Paul II's *The Ecological Crisis* to Murray Bookchin's "Social Ecology versus Deep Ecology."[2] Both essays were written in the last year of the Cold War—a forty-year-long political and military standoff that cost the world untold social and ecological damage. At first glance, the two authors seem to have as little in common as any two men on the planet: on the one hand, a former Polish philosophy professor who was elected to head the largest religious body on Earth, and, on the other, an American author and social critic who is regarded as a leading anarchist and utopian political theorist. But both men refer to their views as humanistic in a traditional sense, and clearly, both regard the world's "ecological crisis" as a fundamentally moral, social, and political problem. Neither believes that the environment can be protected or restored unless humankind attends simultaneously to the complexly interconnected issues of poverty, excessive consumption, political and personal violence, and unjust international relations. Each has been a persistent critic of both state socialism and laissez-faire capitalism.

Although it is the world's largest Christian denomination, the Catholic Church is certainly not the only Christian (or indeed religious) body to raise its voice regarding ecological issues. Neither was it the first to do so.[3] Lutheran, Methodist, Evangelical, Baptist, Episcopalian, Orthodox, Presbyterian,[4] and other bodies have all taken public positions on environmental issues. In most cases, the statements share certain general themes. The statement of the Evangelical Lutheran Church, for example, includes these points:

> All creation, not just humankind, is viewed as "very good" in God's eyes (Gen. 1:31). . . . We are called to care for the earth as God cares for the earth. God's command to have dominion and subdue the earth is not a license to dominate and exploit. . . .
> Twin problems—excessive consumption by industrialized nations, and relentless growth of human population worldwide—jeopardize efforts to achieve a sustainable future. These problems spring from and intensify social injustices. . . . In a world of finite resources, for all to have enough means that those with more than enough will have to change their patterns of acquisition and consumption. . . . Neither economic growth that ignores environmental cost nor conservation of nature that ignores human cost is sustainable. Both will result in injustice and, eventually, environmental degradation.

In the United States, major Christian and Jewish groups came together in 1993 to coordinate their environmental activities through the National Religious Partnership for the Environment.[5]

QUESTIONS

1. It is undoubtedly true that, to many Christians, a tree *is* nothing more than a physical fact. But is it also true, as Lynn White charges, that to a Christian a tree *can be* no more than a physical fact? How might John Paul II answer the question, What is a tree? How would you answer it?

2. Like most papal documents, *The Ecological Crisis* is addressed not only to Catholics and other Christians but also "to all persons of goodwill." How much of the pope's analysis depends specifically on Catholic or Christian beliefs about God? How much of it could be seriously engaged and debated on purely scientific and philosophical grounds?

3. The overwhelming majority of North Americans, even of those who do not "attend church," regard themselves as affiliated with some faith tradition. As a personal exercise, if you are such a person, how does the ecological teaching of your own tradition compare and contrast with that espoused by the pope?

4. Among its other diverse recommendations, the American Baptist Church's *Resolution on Individual Lifestyle for Ecological Responsibility* includes this item: "We should take responsibility for growing as much of our own food as we can. As we do so we should discover how to compost garbage and how to garden and farm organically." A backyard vegetable garden is an almost paradigmatic "local action." How would the widespread implementation of this recommendation effect regional or global change?

5. If you have access to sources that discuss Muslim, Hindu, and Buddhist views of environmental ethics, compare them with the pope's. How much common ground do the world's four largest religions— including, collectively, nearly two-thirds of the world's population— share on ecological issues? On what issues do they differ?

6. For his part, the pope takes an optimistic view of the possible role of international organizations in solving the ecological crisis. The International Whaling Commission might be an example of an international organization that has addressed a global ecological problem with significant success. Multinational negotiations to reduce the use of ozone-depleting chemicals were also successful. But World Bank programs to reduce world poverty and international negotiations to reduce carbon emissions seem, so far, to have failed.[6] In your view, how

should international organizations or initiatives be structured to improve their chances of success?

7. White writes, "More science and more technology are not going to get us out of the present ecological crisis." The pope writes, "Clearly, an adequate solution cannot be found merely in a better management or a more rational use of the earth's resources." They seem to be agreeing on something. What is it? Are they right?

NOTES

1. Lynn White, "The Historical Roots of Our Ecological Crisis," *Science* 155 (March 10, 1967): 1206.

2. Murray Bookchin, "Social Ecology versus Deep Ecology," *Socialist Review* 88, no. 3 (1988): 11–29.

3. In fairness, it should be pointed out that, from the pope's perspective, the liberation of Eastern Europe and, above all, the ending of the U.S.–Soviet nuclear standoff were the most urgent human and environmental issues confronting humankind until 1990.

4. For the respective denominations, see Evangelical Lutheran Church, *Caring for Creation: Vision, Hope and Justice*, adopted by the Third Churchwide Assembly, Kansas City, Missouri, August 28, 1993, available at www.acton.org/ppolicy/environment/theology/evang_luth.html; Methodist Church, U.K., *Methodist Church Reports: Environmental Policy for the Methodist Church*, 1999, available at www.methodist.org.uk/information/green.htm; Evangelical Environmental Network at www.creationcare.org; General Board of the American Baptist Churches, *Resolution on Individual Lifestyle for Ecological Responsibility*, adopted June 1990, amended March 1996, available at www.abc-usa.org/resources/resol/indvlife.htm; Episcopal Ecological Network of the Episcopal Church, USA, at http://eenonline. org; His All Holiness Ecumenical Patriarch Bartholomew, "Address at the Environmental Symposium, Saint Barbara Greek Orthodox Church, Santa Barbara, California, November 8, 1997," available at www.goarch.org/patriarchate/us-visit/speeches/Address_at_Environmental.htm; and Presbyterian Church, USA, *Restoring Creation for Ecology and Justice*, adopted by the General Council, 1990, available through the PC(USA) Environmental Justice Office at www.pcusa.org/environment/resources.htm.

5. National Religious Partnership for the Environment, www.nrpe.org.

6. For the Vatican's very polite but scathing critique of current World Trade Organization policies, see *Trade, Development and the Fight against Poverty: Some Reflections on the Occasion of the World Trade Organization "Millennium Round,"* Pontifical Council for Justice and Peace, Vatican City, November 18, 1999, available from the

Vatican online archives at www.vatican.va/roman_curia/pontifical_councils/justpeace/
documents/rc_pc_justpeace_doc_19991118_trade-devel_en.html.

SOURCES

A useful collection of online resources and links dealing with environmental issues from many different religious perspectives, including
Catholic, Protestant, Jewish, Evangelical, and Eastern, is available at www.
shc.edu/theolibrary/environ.htm.

Pope John Paul II. *The Ecological Crisis: A Common Responsibility.* January 1, 1990.
Available at www.vatican.va/holy_father/john_paul_ii/messages/peace/documents/
hf_jp-ii_mes_19891208_xxiii-world-day-for-peace_en.html.
White, Lynn. "The Historical Roots of Our Ecological Crisis." *Science* 155 (March
10, 1967): 1203–7.

40

PLUMBING MATTERS

The average toilet installed in the United States before 1994 consumes between 3.5 and 8 gallons of water per flush, and the flushes add up: More than a third of all the water used by U.S. households literally goes down the toilet. In fact, the average American uses 9,000 gallons of water a year to flush away his or her sanitary waste. For the entire United States, that amounts to 2.5 trillion gallons (or 320 million cubic feet) of water per year.

As a result of the Comprehensive Energy Policy Act of 1992, new toilets installed in American homes since 1994 have all been "water-wise"—that is, they have been designed to use no more than 1.6 gallons per flush. But this national law, like nearly all local, state, and national building codes, only applies to new toilets and does not mandate replacing old toilets.

DISCUSSION

Complete replacement of all older toilets with water-wise models would reduce U.S. household water use by roughly 200 million cubic feet per year. Savings would be even greater if the law were tightened to require the most efficient designs, which use only one gallon per flush, but these designs often rely on an air-assist system and are much more expensive. Calculations by *Consumer Reports* and various municipal water and sewer authorities estimate that the "payback" period for consumers (the time it would take for the reduced water use to compensate a home owner for the purchase cost) would could be less than two years in some areas and as long as seventeen years in other areas, depending on local water and sewer rates.

The potential payback to the environment, however, is large and permanent. Obviously, water-wise toilets conserve water, but they also improve sewage treatment: Denser sewage is more efficiently processed by treatment plants, and reduced sewage volume means that sewage has a slower flow rate so that it spends more time in the treatment tanks. For the environment and for water and sewer authorities, it is a win at both ends, as less water goes into the system, and cleaner water comes back out of the system.

Some older toilets can be retrofitted with smaller tanks hidden inside the existing tank. Indeed, even a brick or weighted bottle can be used to reduce tank capacity and hence water usage. But many older toilets cannot be retrofitted: Unless the bowl is designed to clear with the reduced water volume, it may require multiple flushes.

Total costs for even the most basic new fixture, with professional installation, begin at about $200 per unit. So the question of whether to mandate the replacement of otherwise functional older toilets is politically complicated. It is one thing for Ketchum, Idaho, to mandate that businesses and home owners replace noncompliant outdoor lighting fixtures with new fixtures; outdoor home lighting is not generally regarded as a necessity (see Case 31: The Dark Skies Ordinance). It is another thing to require that home owners install new toilets; in most people's view, "the throne" counts as a daily necessity.

Western U.S. water authorities have been more aggressive on this issue than authorities in regions not yet accustomed to water shortages. Some have mandated the replacement of toilets in public facilities, such as restaurants and bars. Some have offered subsidies to home owners who replace older toilets.[1]

QUESTIONS

1. Should the government, either directly or through water and sewer authorities, offer tax credits or other incentives to encourage consumers to retrofit older dwellings with water-wise toilets?
2. Should the government mandate the replacement of inefficient toilets, perhaps allowing a two-year window for compliance (see Case 31: The Dark Skies Ordinance)?

3. More generally, how aggressive should government authorities be when rewriting building, lighting, plumbing, heating, and electrical codes to achieve better environmental performance?

4. Should environment-related regulatory priorities be tailored to specific regional needs? For example, should water-wise toilets be mandated in areas of chronic drought but not in areas with abundant water resources? Local authorities may have better knowledge of local problems, but they may also be less willing to assume the costs and burdens of solving those problems. In what circumstances is it appropriate for the federal government to involve itself in local issues such as plumbing and building codes?

5. This case is an interesting "reverse image" of Case 32: The Answer Is Blowing in the Wind. That case asked when it was legitimate to *prohibit* environmentally beneficial home-owner practices; this case asks (among other things) when it is legitimate to *require* them.

NOTE

1. For examples of two interestingly different incentive programs, both in California, see www.ci.mtnview.ca.us/living/water_conservation.htm and www.slowtheflow.com/ulfts.htm.

SOURCES

City of Mountain View, California. *Water Conservation Programs: ULFT Toilet Replacement Programs.* 2003. Available at www.ci.mtnview.ca.us/living/water_conservation.htm.

Environmental Services Department, City of San Jose, California. *Ultra-Low Flush Toilet Programs.* 2001. Available at www.slowtheflow.com/ulfts.htm.

Kourik, Robert. "Building a Better Toilet." *Garbage* 6, no. 2 (summer 1994): 52–57.

"Low Flow Toilets." *Consumer Reports* 60, no. 2 (February 1995): 121–24.

U.S. Environmental Protection Agency. *Wastewater Technology Fact Sheet: High-Efficiency Toilets.* September 2000. Available at www.epa.gov/owm/mtb/hi-eff_toilet.pdf.

41

IS THE LIFEBOAT FULL?

Population growth has been a common concern for environmentalists since the 1968 publication of Paul Ehrlich's *The Population Bomb*. Typically, however, the focus of this concern was population growth in developing countries. Recent estimates by the U.S. Bureau of the Census predict that the U.S. population will nearly double—to about 571 million—over the next 100 years. Almost all this growth will be the result of immigration or of the higher fertility rates typical of first- and second-generation immigrants.

Population growth within the United States has received little attention from mainstream environmental groups despite its potential environmental ramifications. One recently organized group, Sierrans for U.S. Population Stabilization, argues that the United States should immediately and drastically reduce its immigration quotas. Here is an excerpt from one of its first press releases:

Sierrans for U.S. Population Stabilization is deeply concerned about unending population growth in our nation. The Census Bureau says that U.S. population will double within the lifetimes of children born today. This population doubling will mean twice as much traffic, sprawl, and pollution. It will mean twice the demand for lumber from our depleted forests, twice the impact on declining coastal fisheries, and twice the demand for water which is being consumed from aquifers before our very eyes.

Fortunately, the projected doubling of U.S. population is not inevitable. In fact, 90% of our population growth over the next few decades will be due to the consequences of mass immigration, not birthrates. We can easily avoid this population growth. As a voice for our children, our environment, and species who can not speak for themselves, we urge Congress to return immigration to traditional replacement levels, in order to protect what is left of America.[1]

DISCUSSION

Most scholars trace Western concern with population pressure to the 1798 publication of *An Essay on the Principle of Population* by Thomas Malthus. Malthus predicted that population, growing geometrically, would inevitably outstrip the means of subsistence, which increase only arithmetically. Neo-Malthusians such as Paul Ehrlich have taken up Malthus's ideas and applied them to the contemporary world. *The Population Bomb* predicted that there would be widespread famine throughout the world, including the United States, before 1980.

Undoubtedly, the most famous effort to analyze population and immigration issues in terms of the lifeboat metaphor is Garrett Hardin's "Living on a Lifeboat."[2] Specifically comparing the United States to a well-stocked lifeboat with excess capacity, Hardin asks whether we should take in any of the unfortunates who are swimming in the water around us. His advice, "Option Three," is simple: "Admit no more to the boat." And to those Americans who think this is abhorrent or who feel guilty about their good luck, the reply is equally simple: "Get out and yield your place to others." Whether nations may be usefully compared to lifeboats is, of course, quite controversial.[3]

Other neo-Malthusians argue that population growth must inevitably produce environmental degradation. John Holdren, for example, has argued that the environmental impact of population growth on the environment can be represented by the equation

$$I = (P \times A \times T)$$

where I = environmental impact, P = population, A = affluence, and T = technology.

According to Holdren, any increase in a society's population, affluence, or technology must result in an increased adverse impact on the environment. If this is true, then a society can reduce its environmental impact only by shrinking its population, reducing its affluence, or giving up some of its technology. According to Holdren's theory, the United States, which has very high affluence and technology scores, should expect population growth to have very adverse environmental impacts.

According to proponents of the Environmental Kuznet's Curve (EKC) hypothesis, Holdren's theory is wrong and has been refuted by economic and environmental history. These scholars claim that the relationship between economic growth and environmental degradation is not simple and not necessarily negative. On the contrary, they argue that economic growth (if accompanied by a reduction in income disparities) promotes environmental protection and leads to restoration rather than degradation. There is an enormous amount of literature on the EKC controversy.[4]

Economist Julian Simon, a "cornucopian" (one who holds the idea that people are the ultimate resource and that population growth is good), epitomized the belief that increases in intellectual resources (such as knowledge and technology) would always enable human beings to overcome limitations in physical resources (such as oil and water).

QUESTIONS

1. The majority of immigrants to the United States are Asian, African, or Latino. Would strict immigration limits therefore be racist?
2. From the perspective of those concerned about population growth, does it matter whether immigrants to the United States are highly skilled workers or political and economic refugees?
3. Some writers use the notion of "carrying capacity" to determine the ability of an ecosystem to support a given population. This concept examines the amount of food, water, and shelter available to a population. To what extent should other factors, such as open space, wilderness, and quality of life, be considered in determining the carrying capacity for the United States? To what extent should we consider the habitat needs of nonhumans? How would a cornucopian such as Simon respond to efforts to calculate such a carrying capacity? How would you go about determining the size of an "ideal" or "appropriate" population for the United States?
4. Many people believe that adverse environmental impacts have multiple causes. Within the United States, which of the factors cited by the

previously mentioned authors are really most important? Consumption patterns? Technological choices? Population growth? Research and education? Immigration quotas? Affluence? Income disparities?

5. Some optimists believe that science and technology will solve all our environmental problems: Water shortages will be solved by better desalinization methods, famine will be eliminated by new food production methods, global warming will be stopped by green energy technology, and so on. Are the optimists right? To what extent should we rely on technology to solve environmental problems?

6. Is the lifeboat analogy a useful tool for solving problems about immigration policy?

7. Sierrans for U.S. Population Stabilization was formed after the Sierra Club narrowly voted against a policy statement that would have had the Sierra Club support immigration reduction. Can you think of reasons why a prominent environmental group such as the Sierra Club would reject such a policy?

NOTES

1. Sierrans for U.S. Population Stabilization, press statement, August 8, 2001, presented with Colorado Congressman Tom Tancredo and former Colorado Governor Richard Lamm in support of H.R. 2712, the Mass Immigration Reduction Act of 2001, available at www.susps.org/info/press_statement_20010808.html.

2. Garrett Hardin, "Living on a Lifeboat," *Bioscience* 24 (1974): 561–68.

3. See William W. Murdoch and Allan Oaten, "Population and Food: Metaphors and the Reality," *Bioscience* 25 (1975): 561–67.

4. For an introduction to the EKC controversy, see K. Arrow, et al., "Economic Growth, Carrying Capacity and the Environment," *Science* 268 (1995): 520–21, and Theodore Panayotou, "Economic Growth and the Environment," CID Working Paper no. 56/Environment and Development Paper no. 4 (Cambridge, Mass.: Center for International Development, Harvard University, July 2000), available at www2.cid.harvard.edu/cidwp/056.pdf.

SOURCES

Arrow, K., et al. "Economic Growth, Carrying Capacity and the Environment." *Science* 268 (1995): 520–21.

Ehrlich, Paul R. *The Population Bomb*. New York: Ballantine, 1968.

Ehrlich, Paul R., and John P. Holdren. "Impact of Population Growth." *Science* 171 (1971): 1212–17.

Hardin, Garrett. "Living on a Lifeboat." *Bioscience* 24 (1974): 561–68.

Kolankiewicz, Leon, and Roy Beck. "Forsaking Fundamentals: The Environmental Establishment Abandons U.S. Population Stabilization." Center for Immigration Studies Paper no. 18. Washington, D.C.: Center for Immigration Studies, March 2001.

Murdoch, William W., and Allan Oaten. "Population and Food: Metaphors and the Reality." *Bioscience* 25 (1975): 561–67.

Panayotou, Theodore. "Economic Growth and the Environment." CID Working Paper no. 56/Environment and Development Paper no. 4. Cambridge, Mass.: Center for International Development, Harvard University, July 2000. Available at www2.cid.harvard.edu/cidwp/056.pdf.

Sierrans for U.S. Population Stabilization. Press statement. August 8, 2001. Available at www.susps.org/info/press_statement_20010808.html.

Simon, Julian L. *The Ultimate Resource.* Princeton, N.J.: Princeton University Press, 1981.

U.S. Bureau of the Census. *Annual Projections of the Total Resident Population as of July 1: Middle, Lowest, Highest, and Zero International Migration Series, 1999 to 2100.* Available at www.census.gov/population/projections/nation/summary/np-t1.txt.

Zuckerman, Ben. "Immigration and the Sierra Club: Did the Fuss Matter?" *Immigration Review* 33 (fall 1998): 11–13.

42

DEMOGRAPHY
AS DESTINY

A t the beginning of the twentieth century, the industrialized nations of the
Northern Hemisphere—the "West"—accounted for about a third of the
world's population. At the end of the century, the population of these countries accounted for only about 10 percent of the world's population and included only about 5 percent of its children under the age of eighteen. The
wealthy, developed nations of the north have very low fertility rates: with a
total fertility rate of about 2.1 needed just to maintain zero population
growth, fertility rates in the wealthy democracies range from about 1.7 (in
the United States) to barely 1.1 in some European countries. In fact, the total native population of the ten largest European states, which amounted to
about 9 percent of the world population in 1950, will amount to only about
2.3 percent of the world's population in 2025.

Most westerners view population growth *in* developing countries as a
problem *for* developing countries. Hence, they view U.S. and European aid
to population control programs in those countries as a well-intentioned, gen-
erous effort to help the world's poor. But that is not how U.S. and European
aid is viewed by many of its recipients. We excerpt here a few passages from
a speech delivered at Howard University by Gbenga Adewusi, Esq., a Nigerian attorney, author, and political activist:

> There is a basic axiom about demographics and political change. As the
> "haves" become fewer and the "have-nots" grow more numerous, a momentum

for redistribution of power and wealth is generated. This situation is described as "population pressure." . . . At this point, the "have-nots" enjoy a numerical advantage. . . . They have the military manpower to dominate the so-called "low-intensity conflict" situations, where systematic intervention by outside powers is especially difficult. Their sheer demographic weight gives them a voice in world affairs.

This means that those in power will have to exercise greater vigilance and higher levels of force to remain in power. And as the majority grows in size relative to the dominant minority, a point of "critical mass" will eventually be reached, at which time the ruling minority no longer can sustain its grasp over world power. This is the situation we saw emerge in South Africa between the 1940s and the 1980s. When the formal apartheid structure was put in force, the ratio of whites to blacks was about one-to-four. . . . But as the balance changed to one-in-eight or even one-in-nine, it became immensely costly and difficult to preserve the power structure. . . . White South Africa compromised because it was losing the numbers battle.

South Africa can be seen as an illustration of the larger issue of north–south relations. The objective of the industrialized nations will be to contain the rise of the south by limiting births. In fact, population control has become the primary objective of all so-called "foreign aid" given to the countries of the Southern Hemisphere. . . . The goal is to reduce drastically the population of people of color in the next generations, while at the same time trying to boost births among Europeans and persons of European descent.

Population growth will benefit Africa, Asia, the Middle East, and Latin America . . . during the process of industrialization . . . population growth has never been faster anywhere than in the United States between the early 18th century and the start of the 20th. And that . . . unprecedented growth rate does not even take into account some 100 million human captives tortured and taken here as part of Africa's involuntary "development aid" to the West. . . .

[T]he European world, including the United States and the international agencies under its control, spend some five billion dollars every single year to prevent births among people of color. . . . If a country needs capital for infrastructure, services, or even debt repayment, [the West will] . . . withhold money until certain demands have been met—like the establishment of an aggressive family planning policy. This opens the door to all of those so-called "non-governmental organizations" or NGOs, which are really just fronts for the governments that fund them. Now . . . desired fertility among Nigerian women was much higher—between eight and nine children. . . . So most of the population budget goes to trying to make them use these things against their will. There are threats and there are bribes. And above all, there is propaganda. In fact, a woman from Kenya complained to the press at the UN population conference in Cairo two years ago that "You wake up in the morning and you hear you're having too many babies. You go to bed at night, and you hear you're having too many babies. . . . Isn't it genocide, really?" . . .

American leaders and other Western nations are in there pushing birth control but they don't want people to know who is pushing it. That's why they hired all those NGOs. They . . . compel African leaders to adopt population policies so that they can say it is the Nigerian government's policy, or Kenya's, or Zimbabwe's. This is all about deception and coercion . . . the population program is a means to keep the developing world subjected to Western domination, a tactic to make sure that rich countries can continue to exploit the raw materials of the Southern Hemisphere. . . .

Almost seventy years ago, the British philosopher Bertrand Russell wrote: "It cannot be expected that the most powerful military nations will sit still while other nations reverse the balance of power by the mere process of breeding." They are not sitting still. Not at all. They are desperately trying to hang on to power. And they are doing it by intervening to prevent the birth of children to people of color all over the world—in Africa, Asia, Latin America, and the Arab world.[1]

DISCUSSION

Many Western readers will probably be surprised and perhaps even offended by Mr. Adewusi's perspective. A few may even dismiss his views as ignorant or paranoid. But it is not difficult, if one endeavors to look at things from the standpoint of the developing world, to pile up a mass of factoids that seem to justify his view. Consider these:

1. In 1992, the U.S. Agency for International Development was instructed to make population control, not HIV/AIDS prevention, its top priority for Africa. Despite an exploding HIV epidemic that has reduced life expectancy in many sub-Saharan countries from more than sixty to less than forty, that priority remained in place until 2001.[2]
2. In the West, the popular media and even some scholars discuss population issues in terms like these: "Poor countries have populations; rich ones have people. The poor breed; the rich have children. India and China have masses; the U.S. and EU have individuals."[3]
3. A resident of the United States in 2000 consumed twenty-five times more energy and nonrenewable resources than a resident of India. If India had

a population of four billion, it would still consume fewer resources than the United States.[4] Yet while the United States subsidizes population control activities in developing countries, it refuses to commit itself to reduce fossil fuel use.

4. In 1960, the richest 20 percent of the world's population had thirty times more wealth than the poorest 20 percent. In 2000, they had sixty times more wealth.[5] The gap is widening, not shrinking.

5. A recently declassified U.S. National Security Council report stated that population growth in Africa and South America threatened U.S. national security and that aggressive measures, including propaganda and covert funding, should be taken to halt it.[6]

6. The population densities of the Netherlands, Japan, Belgium, Germany, the United Kingdom, Italy, and France are, respectively, 390, 344, 337, 234, 244, 192, and 109. The population densities of Tanzania, Zimbabwe, Liberia, Mozambique, Zambia, the Republic of the Congo, and the Central African Republic are, respectively, 39.4, 28.6, 28, 22, 13.2, 9.8, and 6.3.[7] The latter countries have land and mineral resources at least equal to the former, yet it is the former countries that fund population control programs in the latter.

To oversimplify somewhat, Western scholars generally adopt one (or more) of four different perspectives on population growth in the developing world. The "environmental crisis" perspective is that additional population growth in developing countries would be an ecological disaster and should be strenuously discouraged. The "family planning" perspective is that additional population growth in developing countries would be bad only if it is the result of *unwanted* fertility—that is, only if poor women and couples are having babies they do not want to have—and therefore that foreign assistance should aim to empower poor women and couples to make and implement their own freely chosen reproductive decisions. The "developmental distributivist" perspective is that population is not the problem; rather, unjust patterns of resource consumption and distribution are the problem. Less common is the "cornucopian" perspective: People are the ultimate resource, and population growth is good. Of course, these perspectives are not all incompatible: One can adopt both the cornucopian and the family planning perspective, for example.

Advocates of the environmental crisis perspective doubt that the Earth can support even its present human population. Many cornucopians believe that the Earth could support a human population of 40 or even 50 billion in comfort. It seems fair to say that no one knows whether the Earth can support a human population of 10, 15, or 20 billion people living and consuming at the level of the United States, Europe, and Japan. It also seems fair to say that most of the world's citizens do aspire to that level of material prosperity.

QUESTIONS

1. Do you believe that the United States and the European democracies and Japan are secretly conspiring to reduce population growth in the developing world in order to maintain their military, economic, and political hegemony?
2. If you were an educated Nigerian, might you find Mr. Adewusi's analysis persuasive?
3. Is population growth necessarily a bad thing for developing countries?
4. Should the U.S. government withhold development assistance from developing countries that choose not to implement aggressive population control programs?
5. Of the four perspectives on population growth described in this case, which one (or two or three) are correct?

NOTES

1. Gbenga Adewusi, Esq., "Speech at Howard University," December 10, 1996, available at www.africa2000.com/indx/adewusi.htm.
2. These priorities are confirmed by the annual budgets of the U.S. Agency for International Development.
3. Jeremy Seabrook, "Consumption vs. Population," Third World Network Features, 1999, available at www.twnside.org.sg/title/1965.htm.
4. Seabrook, "Consumption vs. Population."
5. Seabrook, "Consumption vs. Population."
6. "NSSM 200: Implications of Worldwide Population Growth for U.S. Security and Overseas Interests," December 10, 1974, available at www.africa2000.com/sndx/nssm200all.html.
7. Densities calculated using the population and area statistics from the *CIA World Factbook 2002*, available at www.cia.gov/cia/publications/factbook/docs/gallery.html.

SOURCES

Adewusi, Gbenga, Esq. "Speech at Howard University." December 10, 1996. Available at www.africa2000.com/indx/adewusi.htm.

Africa 2000 Media Group. www.africa2000.com.

CIA World Factbook 2002. Available at www.cia.gov/cia/publications/factbook/docs/gallery.html.

"NSSM 200: Implications of Worldwide Population Growth for U.S. Security and Overseas Interests." December 10, 1974. Available at www.africa2000.com/sndx/nssm200all.html.

Seabrook, Jeremy. "Consumption vs. Population." Third World Network Features, 1999. Available at www.twnside.org.sg/title/1965.htm.

43

TRADING POLLUTANTS

In 1990, the Clean Air Act was amended to include a controversial initiative to use market forces to reduce sulfur dioxide (SO_2) emissions in the United States. The initiative created a "cap-and-trade" program that imposed phased reductions of total SO_2 emissions over several decades (the cap) while at the same time allowing individual emission sources to buy or sell allowances for the amount of SO_2 emitted (the trade).

The program requires that facilities burning fossil fuels have an allowance for each ton of SO_2 they emit. When the program was implemented, each electric generating plant using fossil fuel was allocated a quota of allowances. In order to meet increasingly stringent SO_2 emission limits, the plants would have two options: They could reduce SO_2 emissions by using scrubbers or switching to more expensive low-sulfur coal or improving their generation efficiency, or they could purchase emission allowances from plants that had achieved the necessary emissions reductions.

Not all the allowances were allocated to existing facilities. Each year, a significant fraction of the allowances are sold by auction. Since the number of allowances sold at auction decreases each year, total SO_2 emissions must decrease as well. Moreover, the auction is not limited to regulated facilities: Environmental groups can and have bid for and bought allowances in order to retire them, driving SO_2 emissions even lower.[1]

Despite some initial fears, the SO_2 allowance trading program has been a resounding success. In 2000, total SO_2 emissions were actually 10 percent below the allowable level, and so far the cost of compliance has been extremely low, with little or no impact on electricity prices.

The success of the program has spawned legislation aimed at expanding the trading program to other pollutants. For example, the Bush administration has filed bills extending the trading program to nitrogen oxides and mercury. A bipartisan bill proposes the trading of nitrogen oxides and carbon dioxide (CO_2). In principle, the approach could be applicable to any pollutant with significant and known point sources.

DISCUSSION

Traditional environmental protection programs relied almost exclusively on so-called command-and-control methodologies. In these programs, government regulators prescribed exactly how much of a given pollutant a facility (such as a power plant or factory) could emit.[2] Permissible emission levels were generally set by the Environmental Protection Agency at a level that would reduce significant environmental degradation and limit adverse health effects to those exposed to the pollutant. This command-and-control methodology was written into every major environmental law dealing with pollutants, including the Clean Air Act and the Clean Water Act. It has clearly been effective in reducing the quantity of key pollutants released into the environment each year in the United States.

Nevertheless, the command-and-control approach has come under increasingly strident criticism in recent years for its lack of flexibility. The major alternatives to command-and-control regulation are based on different kinds of market-based regulation. These approaches, like the SO_2 emission allowance trading program, all incorporate free-market elements that, while still requiring improved environmental performance from an entire class of polluters (such as the electrical generation industry), allow individual polluters a degree of flexibility. The SO_2 trading program is often cited by advocates of market-based approaches as an example of how such approaches can succeed. It is important to remember, however, that while the SO_2 program gives individual polluters a certain degree of flexibility, it imposes strict requirements on total SO_2 emissions and backs its requirements with stiff penalties.

Another proposed application of market-based approaches to environmental protection is a carbon tax. Buyers of fossil fuels would be charged a tax based on the amount of carbon in the fuel that they purchased. Purchasers of coal, gasoline, heating oil, natural gas, and so forth would pay the tax directly; purchasers of electricity would pay it indirectly as an added part of their electricity bills. In effect, the carbon tax would bill consumers for the amount of CO_2 they release to the atmosphere. The idea behind the carbon tax is that it brings market forces to bear on individual consumer decisions affecting CO_2 emissions and increases consumer awareness of how their consumption patterns impact the environment. Clearly, total CO_2 emissions in the United States are largely a function of consumer choices, such as how much electricity, gasoline, and heating fuel each of us uses. Electric generating plants are the largest point sources for CO_2 emissions, but their CO_2 emissions are not the result of any nefarious scheme to accelerate global warming. So much electricity requires so much fuel, and burning a ton of carbon generates 3.7 tons of CO_2 regardless of corporate intent or government regulation—the laws of chemistry are immune to both.

QUESTIONS

1. When environmental groups purchase and retire SO_2 emission allowances at auction, they help reduce total U.S. SO_2 emissions. They also make the allowances more expensive and indirectly raise the cost of generating electricity. Advocates of market-based approaches to environmental protection would say that this is entirely fair and that the additional freedom enjoyed by generators under the system more than compensates for the impact of retired allowances. Still, some argue that environmental groups should not be allowed to purchase emission allowances. Who is right? Would you donate to an environmental fund devoted to purchasing such allowances?

2. Emissions of CO_2 in the United States have many sources. If emissions from power plants should be regulated, why should not emissions from cars, clothes dryers, or woodstoves?

3. Would a carbon tax be useful in reducing the consumption of fossil fuels? If the tax were set at a high enough level to change your use of (for example) gasoline and electricity, would it unfairly burden the poor?

4. So far, all market-based environmental regulations in the United States have been "backed up" by a command-and-control system with heavy penalties. Is this necessary? Can companies or individuals be trusted to reduce polluting behaviors without the threat of penalties?

5. In the United States (as in the European Union and Japan), there are currently no environmental laws governing or limiting CO_2 emissions. The Bush administration has proposed a set of voluntary measures to reduce CO_2 emissions. Is this a reasonable first step to limit the production of greenhouse gases? What would you need to know to make a good guess about whether it will have a significant impact on CO_2 emissions?

6. In the discussion of Case 14: Not on Cape Cod, we considered "externalities" and the role they play in decisions about energy sources. One effect of the SO_2 emission trading system is to gradually internalize some of the costs of acid rain. One effect of a carbon tax would be to internalize some of the costs of producing greenhouse gases. In general, should such costs be internalized?

7. Individual nations that internalize the cost of contributing to *transnational* environmental problems (such as acid rain or global warming) may put their domestic industries at a serious competitive disadvantage, with the result that jobs move from countries that *do* internalize such costs to countries that do *not* internalize such costs. This is one reason why multinational agreements are often required to address problems such as the release of ozone-depleting chemicals, such as chlorofluorocarbons. If you represented the United States at international negotiations to reduce CO_2 emissions, what kind of agreement would you seek to balance U.S. economic interests against global environmental concerns?

8. Reexamine the menu of corporate choices presented in note 1. Would the CERES principles (see Case 36: CERES and Corporate Responsibility) provide any guidance as to which of these choices was socially and environmentally preferable?

NOTES

1. In general, a coal-burning utility has these options: 1) to burn high-sulfur coal without scrubbers and buy many allowances, 2) to burn high-sulfur coal with scrubbers and sell allowances, 3) to burn low-sulfur coal without scrubbers and buy few allowances, or 4) to burn low-sulfur coal with scrubbers and sell many allowances. For a clear discussion of how one utility went about weighing the costs and benefits of these options under the program, see Forest Reinhardt, "Acid Rain: The Southern Company," chapter 25 in *Environmental Management: Readings and Cases*, ed. Michael Russo (Boston: Houghton Mifflin, 1999), 312–17.

2. For a more detailed explanation of command-and-control standards, organized by industry, see Celia Campbell-Mohn, ed., *Environmental Law: From Resources to Recovery* (St. Paul, Minn.: West, 1993).

SOURCES

Campbell-Mohn, Celia, ed. *Environmental Law: From Resources to Recovery.* St. Paul, Minn.: West, 1993.

Environmental Law Institute. *Implementing and Emissions Cap and Allowance Trading System for Greenhouse Gases: Lessons from the Acid Rain Program.* St. Paul, Minn.: West, September 1997.

U.S. General Accounting Office. *Acid Rain: Emissions Trends and Effects in the Eastern United States.* RCED-00-47. Washington, D.C.: U.S. General Accounting Office, March 2000. Available at www.gao.gov/archive/2000/rc00047.pdf.

Wooley, David, and Elizabeth Morse. *Clean Air Act Handbook.* St. Paul, Minn.: West, 2002.

INTERNET
RESEARCH GUIDE

For scholars and students doing research on environmental topics, the Internet is both a blessing and a curse—a curse because of all the trash (deceptive, dishonest, devious, and downright dumb documents abound) and a blessing because of all the riches (nearly every government agency and nearly all important environmental organizations now make their materials available over the Internet). Particularly in the case of government agencies, but for many international environmental organizations as well, many important reports and databases are now published only in electronic format.

This is not a comprehensive list of Internet resources dealing with environmental issues. It is intended only to help you get started by pointing you at some of the "doorway" sites that will quickly link you to whole universes of information and opinion.

ENVIRONMENTAL ETHICS

The Center for Environmental Philosophy at the University of North Texas maintains a superb environmental ethics website (www.cep.unt.edu). Among other things, it offers extensive bibliographical resources (covering most articles and books published in the field) and an extensive set of links to other environmental websites. It is a probably the best place to start your browsing.

GOVERNMENT AGENCIES

Bureau of Land Management: www.blm.gov
Energy Information Administration: www.eia.doe.gov
National Marine Fisheries Service: www.nmfs.noaa.gov
National Park Service: www.nps.gov
U.S. Department of Energy: www.doe.gov
U.S. Department of the Interior: www.doi.gov
U.S. Environmental Protection Agency: www.epa.gov
U.S. Fish and Wildlife Service: www.fws.gov
U.S. Forest Service: www.fed.fs.us
U.S. Geological Survey: www.usgs.gov

STATE ENVIRONMENTAL AGENCIES

Links to all state environmental agencies can be found at www.clay.net/
stateg.html.

NONGOVERNMENTAL ORGANIZATIONS

Links to many prominent environmental groups can be found on the Natural Resources Defense Council website at www.nrdc.org/references/
environGroups.asp.

ENVIRONMENTAL REPORTS

Environmental reports can be found at the following sites:
  National Library for the Environment: www.ncseonline.org/NLE
  U.S. General Accounting Office: www.gao.gov

ENVIRONMENTAL LAW

Links to environmental statutes, regulatory documents, and judicial decisions can be found at www.environmentallawnet.com.

INTERNATIONAL RESOURCES

Foreign environmental agencies: www.unep.org/unep/ministry.htm
United Nations Environment Program: www.unep.org
World Health Organization: www.who.int
World Resources Institute: www.wri.org

INDEX OF CASES

Case 25: Hawaiian Feral Pigs
Case 26: Tasmanian Tigers

ENERGY ISSUES

Case 14: Not on Cape Cod
Case 15: Oil and ANWR
Case 16: The Grand Staircase
Case 32: The Answer Is Blowing in the Wind
Case 43: Trading Pollutants

ENVIRONMENTAL RACISM ISSUES

Case 4: Tigers and Tourists
Case 27: Golden Rice
Case 29: Mosquitoes, Disease, and DDT
Case 30: A Breath of Fresh Air
Case 33: The Tooele Chemical Weapons Incinerator
Case 35: Bhopal

EXOTIC SPECIES ISSUES

Case 22: Saving Mink, Killing Voles
Case 23: Have You Seen This Fish?
Case 24: Australian Cats
Case 25: Hawaiian Feral Pigs
Case 26: Tasmanian Tigers

FOREST ISSUES

Case 9: Taking Lake Tahoe
Case 11: Mr. Cone's Woodpeckers
Case 17: The Maine Woods National Park
Case 18: Old Growth on Mount Wachusett
Case 21: Monkey-Wrenching

INDEX OF SUBJECTS

ABOUT THE AUTHORS

Patrick G. Derr has a Ph.D. in philosophy from the University of Notre Dame. He is professor of philosophy and director of the Environment and Society Program at Clark University in Worcester, Massachusetts. He is also research professor at the Marsh Institute (Center for Technology, Environment and Development) at Clark University. He teaches courses in environmental ethics, medical ethics, and philosophy of science. He is the author or coauthor of numerous scholarly articles and books in medical ethics, environmental ethics, and environmental hazards management. His recent works on environmental issues (both cofunded by the National Science Foundation, the Environmental Protection Agency, and the National Institute for Occupational Safety and Health) involved substantial work on complex environmental case studies: *Effective Environmental Regulation* (by Halina Szejnwald Brown, David Angel, and Patrick G. Derr [Praeger, 2000]) and *Corporate Environmentalism in a Global Economy* (by Halina Szejnwald Brown, Patrick G. Derr, Ortwin Renn, and Allen W. White [Quorum Books, 1993]).

Edward M. McNamara has an M.A. in environmental science and policy from Clark University and a J.D. from Vermont Law School. He is an attorney with the Vermont Public Service Board. He has taught courses on environmental studies, including environmental ethics, at the College of the Holy Cross and Clark University. He has worked on environmental issues in government, academic, and nonprofit settings.